Bulbs

Bulbs

by
JAMES UNDERWOOD CROCKETT
and
the Editors of TIME-LIFE BOOKS

Watercolor Illustrations by
Allianora Rosse

TIME-LIFE BOOKS, NEW YORK

THE AUTHOR: James Underwood Crockett is an eminent horticulturist and writer on gardening subjects. A graduate of the University of Massachusetts' Stockbridge School of Agriculture, he has lived in—and cultivated a wide variety of plants in—California, New York, Texas and New England and has served as a consultant to many nurseries and landscapers. His monthly bulletin, "Flowery Talks," is distributed to more than a million customers annually through florists' shops. Mr. Crockett lives in Massachusetts.

THE ILLUSTRATOR: Allianora Rosse, who provided the delicate, precise watercolors of bulbous plants beginning on page 88, is a specialist in flower painting. Trained at the Art Academy of The Hague in The Netherlands, Miss Rosse worked for 16 years as staff artist for *Flower Grower* magazine. Her paintings and drawings of shrubs, trees and flowers have appeared in many books on gardening. Miss Rosse lives in New Hampshire.

GENERAL CONSULTANTS: Herbert Fordham, Chief Horticulturist, Waltham Field Station, Waltham, Mass. George Goddard, University of Massachusetts, Amherst, Mass. Dr. August de Hertogh, Michigan State University, East Lansing, Mich. Staff of the Brooklyn Botanic Garden: Louis B. Martin, Director; Robert S. Tomson, Assistant Director; Thomas R. Hofmann, Plant Propagator; George A. Kalmbacher, Plant Taxonomist; Edmond O. Moulin, Horticulturist. Albert P. Nordheden, New York City. George H. Spalding, Botanical Information Consultant, Los Angeles State and County Arboretum, Los Angeles, Calif.

THE COVER: Dazzling red tulips with delicate yellow edges point toward the April sun, ready to unfold their tapered petals. A variety called Rockery Master, they belong to the increasingly popular Greigii hybrid class of tulips.

Portions of this book were written by Henry Moscow. Valuable assistance was provided by the following individuals and departments of Time Inc.: Editorial Production, Norman Airey, Nicholas Costino Jr.; Library, Benjamin Lightman; Picture Collection, Doris O'Neil; Photographic Laboratory, George Karas; TIME-LIFE News Service, Murray J. Gart; Correspondents Maria Vincenza Aloisi (Paris), Friso Endt and Piet Van Harn (Amsterdam), Margot Hapgood (London), Elisabeth Kraemer (Bonn), Ann Natanson (Rome), Sue Wymelenberg (Boston).

CONTENTS

Flowers for all climates, all seasons 1

My fondness for bulbs, those marvelous natural storehouses of plant food, goes back to childhood days. When I was a 10-year-old boy on a New England farm, my uncle gave me my first gladiolus bulbs. By chance I chose to plant them on the south side of the barn, a sunny spot where the soil was somewhat sandy and rain water quickly drained away. That summer I proudly showed off a mass of stately, colorful flowers almost as tall as I was. When frost finally withered their swordlike leaves, I dug for the bulbs from which the flowers had sprung, to save them for the following year. The originals had disappeared, but they had produced offspring, and I discovered to my delight that I owned many more bulbs than I had started with. In a few years, I was storing bushels of them in the cellar every winter.

I was no prodigy. Since then, as a judge of flowers at county fairs, I have often found myself awarding blue ribbons to youngsters who have raised extraordinarily beautiful gladioluses, dahlias and tuberous begonias—all of which grow from what gardeners, for convenience rather than botanical exactitude, call bulbs. So if you have never emulated those young winners, you may be excused for assuming that bulbs are so easy to grow that a child can do it. That is true, but it is only a half-truth. Bulbs are easy to grow. A child can do it. Anybody can do it. Once. But to bring them back year after year to enrich the garden with uncommon beauty requires knowledge and work. Not a lot of work, just enough to justify your pride in the results.

But the relative ease with which you can grow bulbs is the least of their merits. Bulbs are plants for all seasons. With careful selection you can have bulbs in bloom at any time of year. There are some that push up through the snows of late winter, dozens that fill the garden with color before the magnolias bloom, more that thrive in summer's sun and others that arrive and linger after the leaves have fallen. A number can even be induced to flower indoors, brightening the house while January storms roar outside.

Blue Bismarck hyacinths, set among yellow violas, welcome spring in a burst of color. After the hyacinths' blossoms fade, their leaves are left to mature and wither—masked by the violas, which bloom all summer.

Bulbs are also plants for all places. Wet or dry, sunny or shady, wooded or open, almost any spot will prove suitable for some kind of flowering bulb. They will grow in gritty rock gardens and grassy meadows, in borders along the front walk and in out-of-the-way corners, beside ponds and streams and at the foot of stone walls.

Bulbs are an extremely diverse group of plants. Everybody knows the showy tulips, daffodils, hyacinths, dahlias, gladioluses and crocuses, but there are scores of others, lovely and exotic, within easy reach of every gardener but largely ignored or unknown. They range from 2-inch-tall winter aconites to 8-foot gold-band lilies with great clusters of 10-inch blossoms, and they can be fitted into any gardening plan. Most important for the weekend gardener with limited time, many bulbs need be planted only once and with minimum care will come up and bloom year after year.

WHAT BULBS ARE   So perhaps you can understand why, though I grow everything from annuals to evergreens, I am a bulb enthusiast who believes that if your garden lacks bulbs, it is not a complete garden. The enthusiasm was born with those first gladioluses of my childhood and increased so rapidly that I was not yet a teenager when I wrote for a job to Carl Purdy, the great horticultural pioneer who had a bulb nursery in northern California. He replied kindly: "Go to school first and learn all that you can about flowers."

One fact I learned early is that the plants loosely called bulbs are actually divided into five broad categories: true bulbs, corms, tubers, tuberous roots and rhizomes. A true bulb, such as a tulip or daffodil, is a complete or almost complete embryo of the plant to come, packed inside a covering of fleshy scales or layers of tissue that store the plant's food. (If you are curious enough to sacrifice a tulip bulb that you have just purchased, you can slice it in half vertically and see the embryo.) A corm, such as a crocus or gladiolus, is a solid mass of storage tissue with a basal plate below and buds, or eyes, on top. A tuber, such as a fancy-leaved caladium or gloriosa lily, is also a solid mass of storage tissue with eyes but no base plate. A tuberous-rooted plant, such as a dahlia, has swollen, food-storing roots; the bud eyes are not on the roots but on the base of the plant's stem. A rhizome, such as a canna, is a thickened underground stem that grows horizontally, with bud eyes on top and roots below (drawings, pages 10-11).

Despite these differences, all bulbous plants share one characteristic that sets them apart from other plants: a self-contained, highly developed food-storage mechanism that has adapted itself, bud and all, to live underground. Other plants have evolved in strange habitats—epiphytic orchids thrive high in trees, seaweed flourishes in the ocean—but bulbs alone are able to provide nourishment for themselves in the most diverse kinds of soil. Even after lying dormant for months, enduring drought, frost or searing heat, bulbs can spring back to life and continue their species when conditions improve. Through the miracle of adaptation, they survive and revive in all manner of environments. The violet-blue blossoms of chionodoxa grow in the mountain snows of Asia Minor, calla lilies bloom in the marshlands of tropical Africa, and colocasia (elephant's-ear) burgeons on the islands of the South Pacific; all of these environments, and others less harsh, provide the necessary temperature and moisture for the particular bulbs they harbor.

While all plants manufacture and store food to some degree, true bulbs, corms, rhizomes, tubers and tuberous roots accumulate enough nutrients to give them a head start on next season's growth. Many true bulbs and corms, in fact, contain not only complete plants but enough food to nourish their blossoms and leaves through the blooming period. That is why some bulbs, such as the autumn crocus, will flower on a shelf if you have neglected to plant them in time, and why some hyacinths and paper-white narcissuses will bloom if simply set in a bowl of moist pebbles. That is why anybody can get these bulbs to bloom once, with little or no effort. The flower is already there and so is the food for it.

But bulbous plants will not flower again unless their leaves—which, as in all green plants, manufacture sugars and starches through the process of photosynthesis—have time to replenish the depleted food supply for the coming year. After the blooms have faded, the leaves must have a normal growing and ripening period in order to build up strength in the bulb for next year's flowers. For this reason the foliage must never be cut until it has yellowed—a mistake all too many beginning gardeners make in an effort to keep things neat. Even after the foliage has completely withered, the bulbs are at work belowground, and whether they are dug up and stored or left to winter in the cold, they continue to undergo internal chemical change essential to growth and flowering.

At this point most bulbs enter a period of semidormancy during which they have neither roots nor top growth. Unlike other plants, which must be transported while growing in soil to keep them alive, most bulbs can be packaged dry and shipped as horticultural "products," freeing them from regulations that require quarantine for soil- and plant-borne diseases. This, combined with ease of handling, has made bulbs an international item of trade and the Dutch bulb industry a sizable factor in its nation's economy.

When you shop for bulbs, the best advice I can give you is to deal with reputable firms. Wrapped in the tight brown packages of their own tissue, bulbs can hide, even from a practiced eye, internal dam-

HOW TO BUY BULBS

(continued on page 14)

The different kinds of bulbs

During millions of years of evolution, plants have found many ways to survive; the bulb's way has been to go underground during adverse seasons and store food against the day when conditions are favorable for it to grow again. Today there are about 3,000 species of bulbs; and after many years of careful crossbreeding, thousands of varieties have been developed that bloom in almost every climate around the world. Although all these plants are loosely called bulbs, only about half of them are true bulbs; the others are either corms, tubers, tuberous roots or rhizomes. Despite the differences in their structures, shapes and habits, they have one characteristic in common: all of them gather food from the leaves of the plants during the growth cycle and pack these nutrients into their own storage bins so that they can eventually provide food for future plants.

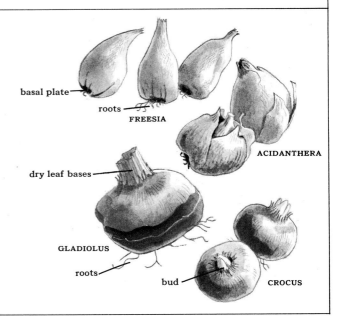

True bulbs

A true bulb is a complete or nearly complete miniature of a plant encased in fleshy modified leaves called scales, which contain stores of reserve food—starch, sugar and some proteins. These scales may be thin and tightly wrapped around the bud, as in a daffodil, tulip or onion, or they may be thicker and more loosely wrapped, as in a lily. Most bulbs have a covering of dry, papery leaves called a tunic. A disk of hardened stem tissue called a basal plate holds the food-storing scales together at the base of the bulb. When the bulb ends its annual period of inactivity and begins the growth cycle, new roots emerge from the outside edges of this basal plate.

Corms

The corm is the base of a stem that becomes swollen —and solid—with nutrients. It has no fleshy scales. The corm is covered by one or two dry leaf bases that are similar to the tunics that enclose true bulbs. And like the true bulb, the corm has a basal plate from which new roots grow. Corms may be rounded, like the crocus, or flattened at the top, like the gladiolus. The corm is completely expended during the growth cycle as its reserve of food is used up. The plant perpetuates itself, however, by simultaneously developing one or more new corms from the buds that appear either on top of or beside the old one.

Tubers

The tuber, which also stocks food in an underground stem, differs from the true bulb or corm in that it has no covering of dry leaves and no basal plate from which the roots grow. Instead, it has a tough skin that generates roots from many parts of its surface. Usually short, fat and rounded, it has a knobby surface with growth buds, or eyes, from which the shoots of the new plant emerge. Some tubers, like the begonia, grow larger as they store up food and produce growth buds. Others, like the caladium, produce new tubers that grow from the sides of the original one.

Tuberous roots

All bulbs grow underground, yet the tuberous root is the only one that is a real root; its food supply is kept in root tissue, not in stem or leaf tissue as in other bulbs. These bulbs are modified, fleshy roots that do not draw in water themselves; instead, they depend on a system of fibrous roots that take in moisture and nutrients from the ground. Like tubers, tuberous roots produce buds from which new plants grow. In the tuberous roots most commonly found in gardens, the buds are restricted to the neck of the root where they grow on the base of the old stem. This growing area is frequently called the crown.

Rhizomes

The rhizome (sometimes called a rootstock) is a thickened stem that grows horizontally, weaving its way along or below the surface of the soil, at intervals sending stems aboveground. The sources of these exposed stems are buds with small scalelike leaves that always appear on the top or sides of the underground rhizome. Some rhizomes, like the lily of the valley, send up small, upright detachable growths called pips, which have their own roots. The pips can be removed and stored for later planting.

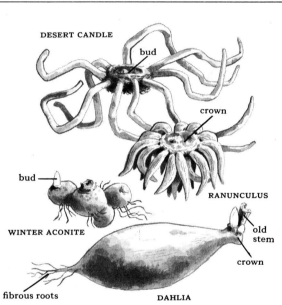

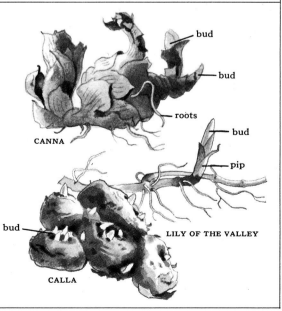

The growth cycle of bulbs

In the growth cycle of a bulbous plant, the underground bulb, nourished by its storehouse of food, goes through a number of distinct stages. The bulb sprouts roots, stems, leaves and flowers, simultaneously growing larger or producing new bulbs for the following growing season. After the leaves wither, it enters a period of dormancy. All bulbs progress through each of these stages, but the details of the cycle vary, as illustrated here, among the five major types of bulbous plants: true bulb, corm, tuber, tuberous root and rhizome.

The gardener with his spade or lifting fork plays a part in the growth cycle of many of these bulbs. Many of the true bulbs, such as the daffodils illustrated below, can be left in the ground through the winter in all parts of the country. Most other bulbous plants demand more care during winter dormancy. A corm like the gladiolus, a tuber like the tuberous begonia, and a tuberous root like the dahlia must be dug up in fall and stored in a dry place until spring in areas where the ground freezes. Even in the South such bulbs produce the biggest flowers if dug up, divided and stored until the spring planting season. The canna, a rhizome, may remain in the ground in mild areas but must be winter-stored north of Zone 7.

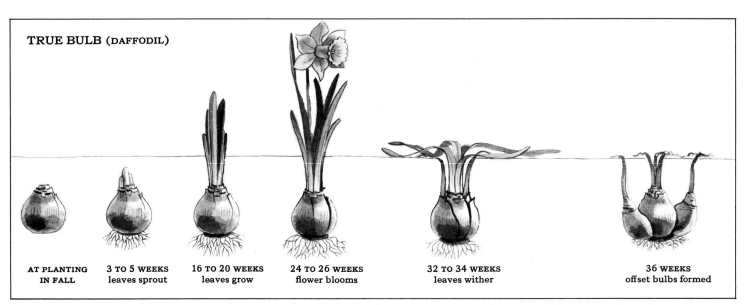

TRUE BULB (DAFFODIL)

| AT PLANTING IN FALL | 3 TO 5 WEEKS leaves sprout | 16 TO 20 WEEKS leaves grow | 24 TO 26 WEEKS flower blooms | 32 TO 34 WEEKS leaves wither | 36 WEEKS offset bulbs formed |

In the 6 to 8 weeks between the flowering and withering of a daffodil, the new growths called offset bulbs receive food from the leaves.

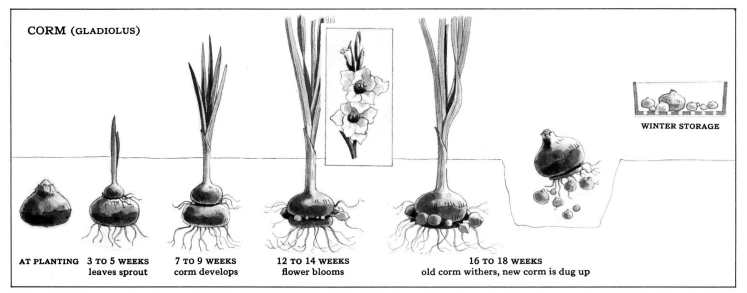

CORM (GLADIOLUS)

WINTER STORAGE

| AT PLANTING | 3 TO 5 WEEKS leaves sprout | 7 TO 9 WEEKS corm develops | 12 TO 14 WEEKS flower blooms | 16 TO 18 WEEKS old corm withers, new corm is dug up |

A new gladiolus corm forms on top of the old, which withers. The new corm also produces cormels, small corms that will someday flower.

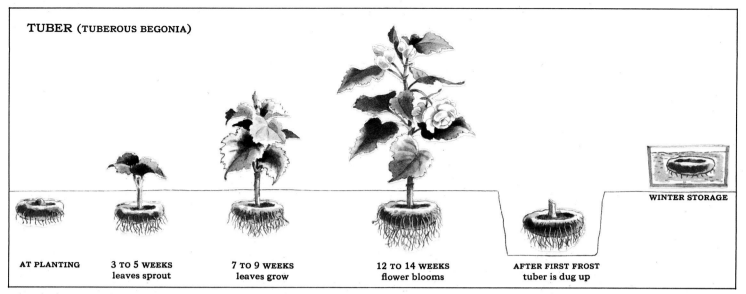

TUBER (TUBEROUS BEGONIA)

| AT PLANTING | 3 TO 5 WEEKS leaves sprout | 7 TO 9 WEEKS leaves grow | 12 TO 14 WEEKS flower blooms | AFTER FIRST FROST tuber is dug up | WINTER STORAGE |

After it flowers, the tuber of a tuberous begonia must be lifted and stored for the winter. New eyes will form for the next year's growth.

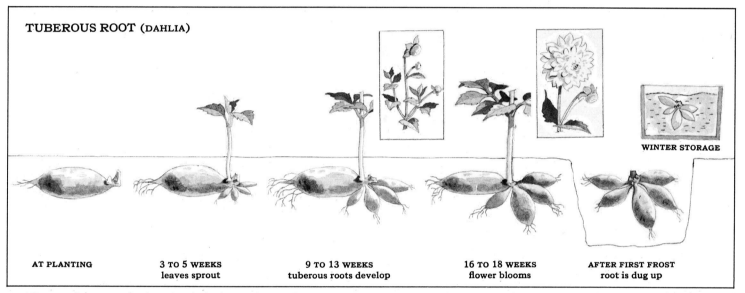

TUBEROUS ROOT (DAHLIA)

| AT PLANTING | 3 TO 5 WEEKS leaves sprout | 9 TO 13 WEEKS tuberous roots develop | 16 TO 18 WEEKS flower blooms | AFTER FIRST FROST root is dug up | WINTER STORAGE |

Dahlias send out new buds around the base of the old stem. From this area tuberous roots form; each grows fibrous roots for feeding.

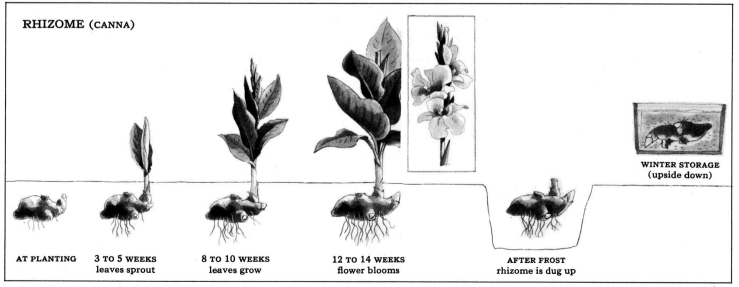

RHIZOME (CANNA)

| AT PLANTING | 3 TO 5 WEEKS leaves sprout | 8 TO 10 WEEKS leaves grow | 12 TO 14 WEEKS flower blooms | AFTER FROST rhizome is dug up | WINTER STORAGE (upside down) |

A rhizome, like the canna, becomes lumpy with new buds that push leaves and flower stalks up to the surface and send roots downward.

age they may have suffered since leaving the grower's fields. They may have been improperly dried, or cured, or they may have been overheated in shipment or storage, either of which can doom the embryonic flower inside. The terminology under which bulbs are sold is not much help: some are classified by their circumference in inches or centimeters; others are labeled "top size" or "exhibition," "medium" or "bedding," "small" or "miniature"; still others are called "jumbo," "first size," "second size" or "flowering size." If you buy from a top-grade nursery, garden center or mail-order house, however, you can depend on the fact that, despite the trade jargon, what you will get will be of a size and grade suitable for growing in your garden with satisfying results.

"Bargain" bulbs are rarely true bargains; it is far better to buy a few good bulbs than a number of inferior ones for the same price. The only true bargains in bulb buying come early in the season, when dealers offer preseason prices. In addition, you can almost always save money by buying bulbs in quantity, or by buying special collections, or package deals, of different kinds of bulbs offered by some dealers.

Bulb prices often are determined less by size and quality than by availability, with new, relatively scarce varieties of bulbs costing more than common types. In the case of daffodils, the number of noses on a bulb also figures in the cost. A daffodil bulb may have from one to three noses, or tips, from which individual flower stalks arise; the more noses, the more flowers the plant will bear, and accordingly, the higher the price of the bulb. Some daffodil bulbs, called splits, consist of a large main bulb and one or two small lateral bulbs that will eventually produce blooms. Splits also cost a little more than single bulbs.

Whenever you are buying bulbs in person, you can usually tell good ones from bad ones simply by picking them up: healthy bulbs are firm, not flabby; they have no soft spots, bruises or blemishes; and they are noticeably heavy in relation to their size.

WHERE TO PLANT BULBS When you are ready to plant your bulbs you should consider both their growing requirements and your own needs. Most bulbous plants, like my first gladioluses, do best in moderately sandy soil, but they can accommodate themselves to any soil in which other flowers will grow. With such exceptions as the calla lily, which will bloom with its roots submerged in water, they must have good drainage. So a sloping site is ideal: in their native habitats, where they grow wild, most of the bulbous plants are found on hillsides and mountainsides where drainage is naturally good. But most bulbs will do well on flat ground if the soil drains well.

The important thing is that they get moisture—not at all

times, but just during their natural growing season. Many of the popular spring bulbs—among them tulips, irises, crocuses and daffodils—originated in a zone that extends from Portugal eastward across southern Europe and North Africa to the Middle East and Asia Minor, and on to southwestern Russia, Afghanistan and Kashmir. In that zone, winters are mild around the Mediterranean and bitter cold on the grassy steppes and in the alpine regions where such plants as chionodoxa—glory-of-the-snow—thrive. Throughout the zone, however, whatever the variations are in winter temperatures, the bulbs' growing seasons are wet and the summers that follow are dry. Eons ago, these bulbs adapted their life cycles to the climates in which they lived, flourishing in spring and resting in hot, dry weather. Such bulbs do not do well when planted where the soil is wet in summer.

Most summer- and fall-flowering bulbs come from regions where rainfall is plentiful during their growing season—for example, gladioluses from Europe and South Africa, fancy-leaved caladiums from the jungles of South America. Autumn crocuses, native to the Caucasus Mountains, do best where the summer soil remains coolly moist; thus they will flourish among ground covers and in wooded areas. In similar fashion, most bulbs thrive in full sun, but a good many—such as grape hyacinths, caladiums, achimenes and tuberous begonias, to name a few—have adapted to shade and will do well in it provided they get direct sunlight or strong diffused or indirect light for a few hours each day.

With normal moisture and enough sun, the planting sites and arrangements for bulbs are almost unlimited. You can set spring-, summer- and autumn-flowering bulbs together, among perennials, in a wide border that will provide constant color for seven or eight months of the year—even longer in southern zones. Rock gardens are ideal for the small species tulips, winter aconites, grape hyacinths, daffodils, brodiaeas and calochortuses. Low-growing lilies and autumn crocuses can be planted in the midst of such ground covers as English ivy, creeping myrtle or ajuga, which will provide a dark background for the bright flowers, hide the withering leaves after the flowers have faded and conserve moisture around the plants. Lilies of the valley make a lovely ground cover in themselves, particularly under trees. Bulbs may be set in corners of the garden, in a patch of wood or on a sunny bank, where they will surprise strollers with their beauty. Such spots are perfect for what horticulturists call naturalizing, that is, planting clumps of bulbs where they have room to spread out and become part of the landscape, looking as though they had always been there. The tall, stately dahlias and gladioluses are better massed in beds of their own than naturalized (they must be dug up each year), and they look splendid

BULBS BY THE BILLION

Bulbs today are big business, accounting for some $300 million sales a year worldwide. Nearly 2 billion tulip bulbs are sold annually. West Germany, the most avid customer, buys 566 million of these; about half go to home gardeners, the rest to public parks and commercial growers of florists' plants and cut flowers. In the United States, the best-selling bulb is the gladiolus, with annual sales over 370 million corms, about 60 per cent of which are sold to commercial growers who raise them primarily for cut flowers. United States gardeners and florists purchase about 170 million tulip bulbs, 68 million bulbous iris bulbs, 67 million crocus bulbs and 35 million narcissus bulbs each year.

against a stone wall or fence. In my own garden, I grow at least a hundred dahlias every summer—and give away armfuls of flowers without ever seeming to diminish their number.

WHEN TO PLANT BULBS   The best time to plant bulbs varies somewhat with different kinds and in different parts of the country, but generally spring-flowering bulbs (and those summer-flowering bulbs that are winter hardy) are planted in the fall, and tender summer- and fall-flowering bulbs are planted in the spring. If you are going to set your bulbs in garden beds rather than naturalize them, dig up the chosen spot with a spading fork to a depth of at least 8 inches. Break up lumps of soil, remove large stones, weeds and old roots and rake the area smooth. Then spread peat moss 2 to 3 inches deep over the surface and work it in thoroughly with the spading fork. Peat moss provides organic matter that is essential for drainage control—it will hold moisture in a light sandy soil and help to eliminate an excess of it in heavy clay soil.

Bulbs, like other plants, need nitrogen for healthy foliage, phosphorus for a strong root system and potassium for firm growth and resistance to disease and cold. But in general their food requirements are less than those of most other garden flowers; the exceptions are such civilized plants as gladioluses and dahlias, which are far removed from the original wild species and have long been cultivated by man.

If I were to choose one fertilizer for bulbs, particularly for those left in the ground year round (which includes most spring-flowering bulbs and some summer-flowering ones) it would be bone meal, a slow-acting, long-lasting source of the phosphorus bulbs need to build good root systems. Apply it at a rate of 5 to 6 pounds per 100 square feet if you are planting bulbs in beds, or about a teaspoonful in each hole if you are naturalizing them, and scratch the same amount into the soil around the bulbs every fall thereafter. Dried cow manure, sold in bags at garden centers, is also an excellent fertilizer for bulbs. (If you have access to a source of fresh cow manure, by all means use that—but make sure it is not literally fresh or it can burn plants and roots and may contain harmful bacterial and fungus diseases. The manure should be well rotted before you use it.) The best inorganic fertilizer is a general-purpose one such as 5-10-5 (5 per cent nitrogen, 10 per cent phosphorus, 5 per cent potassium), which provides a balanced diet high in the phosphorus bulb plants especially need. That is what I use in my own garden for summer-flowering bulbs, at a rate of 1 pound per 100 square feet, dug into the soil at planting time and applied again every two or three weeks from the time the plant emerges from the ground until the buds take on color.

Most bulbs, whatever their blooming season, do best in a slightly acid soil that has a pH of 6.0 to 6.8. A soil-testing kit obtainable at garden centers will help you to determine whether your soil needs treatment and how much; many local agricultural extension services will also test soil samples for a small fee. To raise the pH of light or medium loam by ½ to 1 point, add 5 pounds of ground limestone to each 100 square feet of soil; if the soil is heavy, or abounds in organic matter, increase the dosage of limestone by one third. (There are two kinds of ground limestone, calcite and dolomite. I prefer the dolomite variety, which consists of calcium carbonate and magnesium carbonate, because the magnesium component aids in the process of photosynthesis.) Ground limestone acts slowly. Ideally, it should be dug into the soil many months before planting—in fall, for example, if you plan to plant summer-flowering bulbs the following spring. But not all gardeners are so foresighted. At the very least, it should be applied a week or two earlier than chemical fertilizers because when limestone and fertilizers are used together, the limestone acts to release the fertilizer's nitrogen, which is leached away before the plants can use it.

To lower the pH of an overly alkaline soil by ½ to 1 point, add ½ pound of ground sulfur or 3 pounds of iron sulfate per 100 square feet. Both of these substances have their advantages: iron

DIGGING AND DIVIDING BULBS

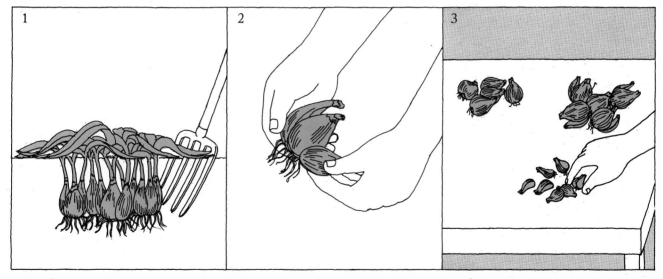

As daffodils and other bulbs multiply, they tend to become so crowded they produce smaller flowers. Every four to five years, lift out whole clumps with a spading fork after the foliage has withered.

After pulling the big clump of bulbs apart, break off any offsets, or smaller bulbs, that are not tightly fastened to the mother bulb. Work out of direct sunlight to avoid any danger of the bulbs drying out.

Replant all the bulbs immediately. Big ones (top), separated or in clusters, will produce flowers the next season. Small offsets (bottom) can be put in a nursery bed until ready to bloom in two or three years.

sulfate acts quickly, and its iron component fosters rich green foliage; ground sulfur, on the other hand, lasts for years. In heavy soils it is advisable to increase the amount of sulfur by one third.

HOW TO PLANT BULBS   True bulbs, such as tulips and lilies, and corms, such as crocuses and gladioluses, should be buried about three times as deep as their maximum diameter. (Measure from the soil's surface to the top of the bulb's shoulder, not its tip.) For a large daffodil bulb, this means about 7 inches and for a crocus about 3 to 4 inches. In stiff, heavy soil, they should go a little less deep; in light sandy soil, they may go a little deeper. As a rule, it is better to plant too deeply than too shallowly because deep-set bulbs multiply less rapidly than those at normal or shallower depths, delaying the day when they become overcrowded and must be dug up and transplanted. Deep planting also provides greater protection against frost and against mice and other rodents. But stay within the recommended range.

The proper depths for rhizomes, tubers and tuberous roots differ from those for bulbs and corms. Specific planting depths are discussed in detail in later chapters and in the encyclopedia section.

Some bulbs and corms possess the remarkable ability to adjust their depths to suit themselves, by means of roots that contract and elongate, as necessary. Crocuses and gladioluses, both of which

PROPAGATING LILIES FROM BULBILS

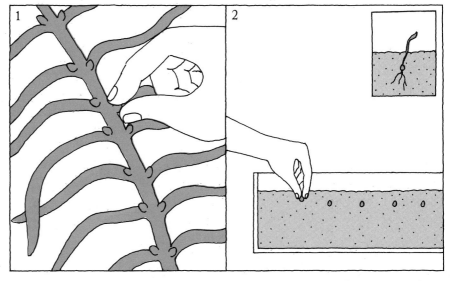

After such lilies as the tiger lily have flowered, the plants can be reproduced from the tiny bulbils that form where leaves join stems. Wait until the bulbils become ripe and can be broken off easily.

Plant the bulbils 1 inch deep in equal portions of loam, coarse sand and peat moss. Keep in a cold frame over winter. In spring, as they sprout (inset), shift them to the garden to bloom within two or three years.

grow from corms, actually develop two sets of roots, one to feed them and the other to position new corms properly by pulling them to the levels where they will be best protected against frost. It is for this reason that, although new corms form year after year atop their parents, no new corm ever finds itself at the surface of the soil; the roots always keep it in position.

The naturalizing of bulbous plants in rough grass or ground cover requires a different approach, since you do not want to dig up the whole area. With small bulbs or corms, work with a step-on bulb planter (*drawing, page 49*), removing a core or plug of soil up to 6 inches deep. Set the plug aside carefully, loosen the soil in the hole with a trowel and dig into it about a teaspoonful of bone meal. Set the bulb in the hole, firm the loose soil around it and replace the plug. Then step firmly on the plug with your heel.

To plant larger bulbs such as daffodils, or to plant several bulbs of any kind in one hole, cut a square by sinking a spade into the ground, once on each side. Lift out the square of soil and set it aside. Dig around in the hole until the soil is loosened to a depth of 4 or 5 inches beneath the proper planting depth for the particular type of bulb, and mix a couple of tablespoons of bone meal into the loosened soil. Then set the bulb or bulbs in the hole to the proper depth, cover with loose soil and replace the square of soil. I know of

PROPAGATING LILIES FROM SCALES

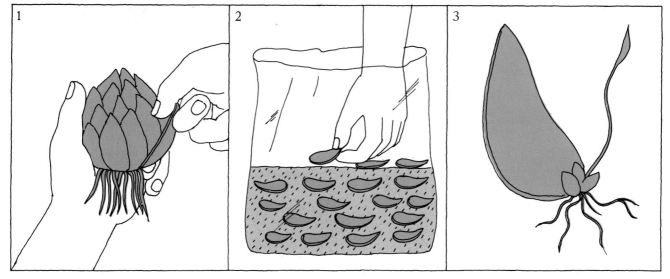

To propagate lilies from the scales that make up the bulbs, carefully break off healthy outer scales. You can safely remove as many as half the scales and still have enough of the bulb left intact for planting.

After dusting them with fungicide, space the scales well apart in slightly damp vermiculite or perlite in a plastic bag. Seal the bag and store it at a constant temperature of 68° to 72° for six to eight weeks.

After the bulblets develop on the scales, they need at least eight weeks of dormancy at 35° to 40°. Refrigerate the bag or pot the bulblets and store in a cold frame. Set them in the garden in spring.

fields of daffodils planted this way that have been untouched for 20 years and still greet each spring with a wealth of flowers.

Once you have your bulbs in the ground, you have little to worry about for a while—except field mice, chipmunks, rabbits, gophers, moles and a few other four-footed friends. They eat bulbs with gusto—except for daffodil bulbs, which contain a sticky, mildly poisonous sap. (If they are hungry enough they will eat the daffodils too, poison or no poison.) Methods of discouraging these animals range from the devious to the deadly. Some gardeners plant a few fritillarias among other bulbs because their musky smell is reputed to repel the trespassers. Other gardeners mix tobacco, red pepper, moth balls or naphthalene flakes in the soil. Gardeners sometimes resort in desperation to soaking bulbs in red lead before planting, or leaving poisoned grain on top of the soil. None of these methods is particularly effective and some actually pollute the soil or endanger children and pets, and that I certainly do not recommend. A more effective measure is enclosing bulbs, or entire groups of bulbs, in wire mesh, as shown in the drawings on page 47.

PROPAGATING BULBS Like virtually all other plants, bulbs can reproduce themselves from seed. (One of the largest plant nurseries in the country, in fact, was started by a young man who sowed great quantities of regal lily

MULTIPLYING DAHLIAS AND OTHER TUBEROUS-ROOTED PLANTS

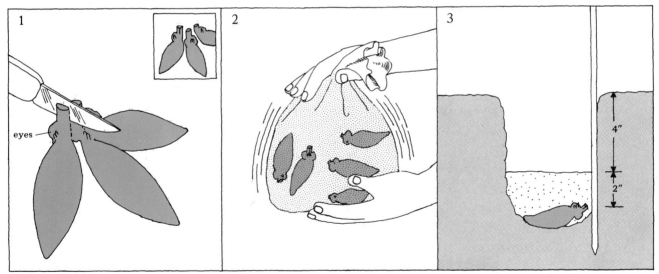

To propagate a bulb plant such as a dahlia, cut a clump of the tuberous roots into sections (inset), each with part of the old stem base and a bud, or eye. Cutting is easiest in spring when the eyes are most discernible.

To prevent infection on the cut surfaces, gently shake the roots in a plastic or paper bag with an all-purpose fungicide powder. Let the scars dry for two or three hours before setting out the root divisions.

Dig 7-inch-deep holes, driving in stake supports for tall varieties, and set one division in each hole with its eye upward, pointing at the stake. Cover with 2 inches of soil, adding more soil as the plant grows.

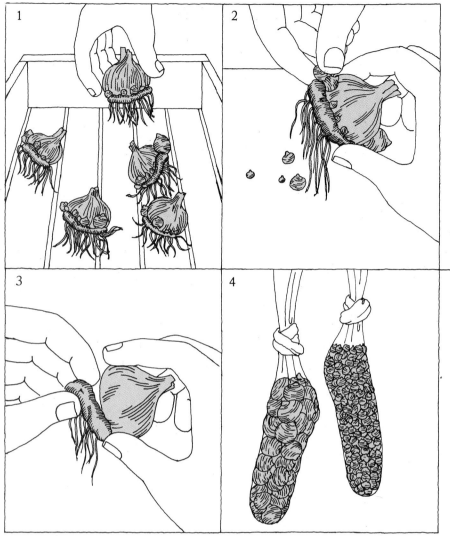

MULTIPLYING GLADIOLUSES FROM CORMS AND CORMELS

1. *When the gladiolus foliage has withered, dig up the corms, cut off the tops and spread the corms in a slatted box or over a wire-mesh screen. Let them dry for two to three weeks out of the sun before attempting to remove any soil that clings to the corms.*

2. *Pick the tiny dried cormels off the rim of the shriveled disk of old corm. Planted in spring in an out-of-the-way corner of the garden, and dug up each fall, the cormels will produce new flowering plants in two or three years.*

3. *As soon as the cormels have been picked off, the old corm should be carefully peeled off the base of the new corm and discarded. It has fulfilled its purpose and is exhausted; next year's flower stalk will come from its offspring.*

4. *After separating and cleaning the new corms and cormels, sort them by size, dust them with an insecticide-fungicide powder and hang them up in nylon stockings or open-mesh vegetable bags. The storage place should be cool— 50°, lower if possible—but not subject to freezing temperatures.*

seed, from which he raised 100,000 bulbs. Selling them at a dollar each, he raised enough capital to launch a full-scale nursery business.) But it may take three or more years for a bulb to grow from seed to a full-sized flowering plant. (Exceptions are dwarf dahlias and tuberous begonias, which will bloom their first year.) Also, hybrid bulbs may not, in horticultural jargon, "run true" when grown from seed; that is, the offspring may not resemble the parents.

In any case, nature has given bulbs speedier and more reliable ways to reproduce themselves, and gardeners can take advantage of these to propagate new plants. Most true bulbs grow larger each year until they reach a maximum size, at which point they form two or more smaller bulbs *(drawings, page 17)*. These natural divisions, or offsets, are the most common source of additional stock. Other bulbs produce many smaller bulbs beside the mother bulb; these bulblets also can be dug up, pulled off and replanted. Some bulbous plants produce tiny offspring, called bulbils, aboveground; in the case of lilies, these appear at the leaf axils where the leaves join the stems. Some members of the onion family, including many ornamental flowering alliums, produce bulbils instead of seeds at the tops of their flower stalks. Wherever they grow, bulblets and bulbils may be detached from their parents and planted *(drawings, page 18);* it usually takes two or three years for them to reach flowering size—a somewhat shorter time than the seed process. Some gardeners increase their scaly bulbs such as lilies by peeling off the scales and rooting them *(page 19)*.

Corms, unlike many true bulbs, do not grow larger each year. In fact, they shrivel and disappear by the end of the season, but they leave behind one or more new corms, and usually a number of tiny corms called cormels or cormlets, which may reach full size in two to four years. Cormels, like bulblets and bulbils, may be planted; that is how gladioluses and crocuses are multiplied *(page 21)*.

To multiply tubers, tuberous roots and rhizomes you have to use different methods. Just as the onion is a typical bulb, the potato is a typical tuber, and like other tubers it has eyes, which if planted will sprout new potato plants. The gloxinia, the gloriosa lily, the fancy-leaved caladium and the tuberous begonia are tu-

STARTING NEW PLANTS FROM TUBERS AND RHIZOMES

Propagate tubers, such as caladiums (inset), in spring. Cut them into sections, each with at least one large bud, or eye. Dust the cut surfaces with fungicide powder, let the pieces dry for two days, then plant them.

Cut up rhizomes, such as those of cannas (inset), into sections, with several eyes on each one. From Zone 6 north, start divisions indoors in damp peat moss or sand. Farther south, plant them outdoors.

bers too, and their eyes are incipient buds. Cut a tuber as you would cut a potato, making sure that each part has at least one eye, and you can have many more plants than you started with *(page 22)*.

What distinguishes the tuberous root from the tuber is that the tuberous-rooted plants, such as the dahlia, have their eyes all in one place, at the base of the original stem. There are no eyes in their swollen roots. So to multiply dahlias, you have to include a section of the original stem in every piece you cut *(page 20)*.

Rhizomes—from which cannas, callas and lilies of the valley rise—are thickened stems that grow horizontally, half submerged in the soil or slightly beneath it, with roots that spread down deep and eyes that are on or near the top. Rhizomes can be divided easily with a knife, but each segment must contain at least one eye. Usually the segments will produce flowering plants in their first season of independence *(page 22)*.

Horticulturists call all of these methods of propagation vegetative, or asexual, as opposed to sexual reproduction by means of seeds. Bulbs are among the plants that can propagate themselves both ways, and commercial growers make use of both. To develop new varieties, they crossbreed different varieties to combine different qualities of flower form, color, plant height and blooming time, then plant the seeds of the new hybrids. When the seedlings reach flowering size, they crossbreed them with other strains to gain qualities they have not been able to achieve the first time. But when the desired plant is finally created, the growers switch to vegetative propagation. This is the only way they can be certain every offspring will be an exact duplicate of the mother plant. Seeds produced by the hybrid plant are unpredictable—some may produce plants that revert to an earlier evolutionary stage, others may produce something totally new, still others may be sterile. But by vegetative propagation they can be sure of what will happen. All told, establishing a new variety of bulb in sufficient numbers to market can take as long as 15 to 20 years.

Nor does the process stop there. Each hybridizer will continue to try to produce still newer strains that will somehow be superior. A new strain that is widely accepted by most gardeners can be like a pot of gold at the end of the rainbow.

The prodigality with which bulbs multiply vegetatively can make digging them up more like a treasure hunt than a chore. There is much satisfaction in discovering several bulbs where only one was planted a few months earlier, and there is even more satisfaction when you have splurged several dollars for a few bulbs of an irresistible new variety in the spring and reap a five-fold harvest in the fall. Such a reward can make a gardener smug—and even wistful—when he contemplates some of his other investments.

The flamboyant history of bulbs 2

For all the lovely innocence that bulbs display in bloom, they have been involved in some strange goings-on during the course of history. Undoubtedly the most bizarre of these was the "tulip mania," a tidal wave of speculation in which tulips were traded for profit in the manner of corporate stocks, commodity futures or real estate. Tulip mania engulfed Western Europe early in the 17th Century, peaked in Holland between 1634 and 1637 and had such a sorry outcome that thereafter a professor of botany at Leiden, one Evrard Forstius, used to beat tulips to death with his walking stick whenever he encountered any. Before the wave crested, an otherwise sensible brewer had swapped an entire brewery for one bulb, a miller his mill for another. At its height the frantic trading in tulips made the Florida land boom and Wall Street speculations of the 1920s look almost colorless by comparison.

In those days tulips were still novelties in Europe: nobody there had so much as seen one before the Austrian Emperor Ferdinand I sent a Fleming named Ogier Ghiselin de Busbecq to Constantinople in 1554 to talk peace with Sultan Suleiman the Magnificent, who had invaded Hungary and besieged Vienna. Ferdinand's previous emissary had died from mistreatment received in one of Suleiman's prisons, but de Busbecq did not permit such perils to endanger his mission (which was successful), or to interfere with his personal interest in botany. On his way from Adrianople to Constantinople, de Busbecq saw "an abundance of flowers everywhere—narcissus, hyacinths and those which the Turks call *tulipam*—much to our astonishment because it was almost midwinter, a season unfriendly to flowers." (De Busbecq got the name wrong. The Turks call the tulip *lalé* and de Busbecq's interpreter probably said the flower looked like a *thoulypen,* or turban, which de Busbecq heard as *tulipam*. In any case, what he heard was shortened to "tulip.") De Busbecq bought some tulip bulbs—"which cost me not a little," he reported, for the Turks themselves paid considerable amounts for rare varieties—and brought them back to

Satirizing Holland's mania for tulips, a 17th Century engraving portrays Flora, goddess of flowers, in a wheeled "ship of fools." In her left hand are three prized varieties whose bulbs brought astronomical prices.

Ferdinand's imperial gardens in Vienna. Their fame and their seed soon spread, notably to Holland, where they caused great excitement as a novelty among wealthy burghers.

When the Flemish botanist Carolus Clusius left his post as the imperial gardener in Vienna in 1593 to become a professor of botany in Leiden, he took a stock of tulip bulbs with him and planted them in his garden. Overwhelmed by the sudden demand for his exotic specimens, Clusius decided to ask "such an extortionate price," according to one account, "that no one could procure them." But one dark night, while Clusius slept, somebody stole into his garden and made off with most of his best flowers, bulbs and all. Whoever did the job, a contemporary document relates, "wasted no time in increasing them by sowing the seeds, and by this means the seventeen provinces were well stocked."

Thus began the Dutch bulb business, which, considering the legendary dedication of the Dutch to hard work, could soon have coped with any commercial demand for bulbs. Ordinary bulbs, that is. But tulips are a bit like postage stamps; you can get all the ordinary ones you want for pocket change at the post office, but a rarity can cost a collector a fortune at auction. Tulips produce their own rarities because cultivated varieties "break"—unpredictably develop new colors and patterns that are sometimes extraordinarily beautiful. Why and how tulips can break long remained a mystery, but modern plant scientists have determined that the changes are caused not only by natural mutations but by a virus that spreads from bulb to bulb, introducing its own genetic message into the cells that control the tulips' color inheritance.

BULBS WORTH FORTUNES   It was these broken-colored rarities that rich 17th Century Dutchmen, Frenchmen and Englishmen coveted. Before long, owning an unusual tulip became a status symbol throughout Europe (one young Frenchman was reported delighted to have received an especially prized bulb as his bride's entire dowry). Tulip connoisseurs began to bid against each other, raising prices. By 1624 a single bulb of a red-and-white tulip with a blue tint at its base, christened Semper Augustus, sold for the equivalent of $1,200, and the seller immediately regretted that he had not asked more because, he belatedly noticed, Semper Augustus had two little bumps on it that would soon become bulbs themselves. The next year, $3,000 was offered for two Semper Augustus bulbs and not long after, at the top of the market, three of them went for $30,000.

At those prices, bulb collecting seemed only a rich man's game. But then came the widespread realization that anybody's bulb, in anybody's garden, might suddenly change color and earn its owner a fortune. All one had to do was plant bulbs and wait, then if a beautiful new flower resulted, give it a properly impressive name and a little local promotion. "If a change in a tulip is effected," a 17th Century Dutch chronicler wrote, "one goes to a florist and tells him, and soon it gets talked about. Everyone is anxious to see it. If it is a new flower, each one gives his opinion. . . . If it looks like an 'Admiral' you call it a 'General' or any other name you fancy, and stand a bottle of wine to your friends that they may remember to talk about it."

As the mania for tulips grew, every back yard in Holland blazed with its flowers. But the real madness came when bulb growing gave way to bulb speculation, which was nothing more than gambling at high stakes. Beginning in 1634, rich men and poor men, servants and masters, butchers and bakers vied to buy bulbs of likely strains, even though they had not yet bloomed, confident that they could quickly sell the contractual right to them at a higher price. Since the contracts specified only a future delivery of real bulbs, traders could buy and sell furiously without ever having held any bulbs in their hands, or even having seen them. What were being traded were simply pieces of paper, just as in the modern market for wheat futures. But tulip futures soon ran wild.

To raise the money for their deals, men mortgaged their houses, pawned their wives' jewels, sold the tools of their trade. In virtually every village in Holland, one tavern became a bulb exchange, into which otherwise solid burghers crowded to spend their days, and frequently their nights, buying and selling promises, watching ever-rising prices being chalked on slates and carousing to pass the time. The tavernkeeper collected "wine money" on every transaction, and hospitality ran as high as hope. "I have often been to a tavern," a character in a contemporary tale relates, "and eaten baked and fried fish and meat; yes, chickens and rabbits and even fine pastry, and drunk wine and beer from morning to three or four o'clock at night, and then arrived home with more money than when I left." In the trading that accompanied the feasting, "Oft did a nobleman purchase of a chimney-sweep tulips to the amount of two thousand florins [about $2,000] and sell them at the same time to a farmer; and neither the nobleman, chimney-sweep or farmer had roots in their possession or wished to possess them. Before the tulip season was over, more roots were sold and purchased, bespoke and promised to be delivered, than in all probability were to be found in the gardens of Holland; and when roots of Semper Augustus were not to be had . . . they were still bought and sold more often than those of any other species."

In one such transaction, according to the record of sale, the rights to a bulb named Viceroy brought its seller the following bounty: two loads of wheat, four loads of rye, four fat oxen, eight fat

(continued on page 30)

BULB BOOMS AND BUSTS

The tulipomania that sent 17th Century Hollanders into frantic financial speculation was not the only boom based on bulbs. In the 18th Century a craze for hyacinths swept through Europe; in Holland one specimen of a variety named Admiral Liefken sold for the equivalent of $20,300 and in England a new double-flowered type called King of Great Britain brought $2,400. In the 19th Century, when dahlias were in vogue in France, a single prized plant was exchanged for a rare diamond. Even as late as the 1940s demand for Easter lilies set off a minor land rush in California, where an acre of the exceptionally well-drained, light soil best suited to growing the bulbs rose in price from $25 to $1,000.

The iris: flower of royalty

Of all the figures in medieval heraldry, none is more wide-spread than the three-pronged fleur-de-lis, a symbol of royal power and of divine protection. The symbol first appears in the art of the earliest civilizations of both India and Egypt as a sign of life and resurrection. Although it may have derived from a lily, or even from a spear or arrowhead, it was more likely inspired by wild irises, which grow throughout much of Europe, Africa and Asia.

What is certain is that the kings of France adopted the fleur-de-lis as their royal standard. It was used as early as the Fifth Century on the banners of Clovis, King of the pagan Franks. And as France became a nation, spreading her power far beyond her shores, her soldiers carried with them the King's azure flag with the three golden flowers.

France's fleur-de-lis flew over the Crusaders in the Holy Land and in subsequent sorties along the Barbary Coast. In the painting at far left, British and French knights are called to combat with horns bearing the ornamental flowers. When England's King Edward III laid claim to the French crown he added the fleur-de-lis to the British Royal Arms (lower left), where it remained from 1340 to 1801. The King's son, Edward, Black Prince of Wales, displayed the stylized emblem on his armor (left) during his invasion of France.

In a 15th Century painting that depicts the symbol's divine origin, God hands an angel a banner emblazoned with fleurs-de-lis; a hermit (lower left) gives it to Clothilde, the Christian wife of the pagan Frankish King Clovis, who had promised to join her faith if victorious in battle. He won and, after his baptism in 496, he made the device his royal emblem.

By the time of France's King Philip the Fair (1285-1314), the fleur-de-lis appeared on a wide variety of royal robes and furnishings. At right, Philip receives homage from England's Edward II, ruler of the French province of Aquitaine.

The French royal emblem took on a new form during the reign of King Charles V (1364-1380), who is shown at left as he receives his uncle, Emperor Charles IV. The King decreed that the royal banners should no longer contain a field of fleurs-de-lis but only three, to symbolize the Holy Trinity. And to separate this emblem (above, left) from all others, he ordered lesser nobles to vary the arrangement, as in the inversion at right.

Throughout the centuries, the monarchs of France used the fleur-de-lis to decorate their most luxurious royal costumes. At left, Marie de Médicis, the wife of Henry IV, appears in a dress that is adorned with the symbol and also has a bodice cut in the shape of an inverted fleur-de-lis. King Louis XVIII (1814-1824), shown at right, continues the tradition. At far right, Charles X, the last of the Bourbon line (1824-1830), carries the custom even further, with fleurs-de-lis from his crown to his slippers.

swine, 12 fat sheep, two hogsheads of wine, four barrels of beer, two barrels of butter, 1,000 pounds of cheese, one complete bed, one suit of clothes and one silver tankard. In another deal, ownership of a bulb was traded for 12 acres of land, in yet another for a carriage, a pair of horses and the equivalent of $4,600 in cash.

Eventually, of course, real bulbs and not paper contracts had to be delivered. So long as florists and growers were willing to pay ever higher sums for unusual bulbs, the traders in bulb rights earned their profits. Prices rarely went down and for a while everyone got rich: a pauper in spring might live in a new mansion and sport a coach-and-four in fall. Then, one day in the spring of 1637 after three years of boom, the market collapsed. Many traders, suspicious of ever-increasing prices and bored with the game, began to dump large numbers of bulbs on the exchange, with the result that prices plummeted. Suddenly everyone wanted to sell and nobody wanted to buy. Men committed to deals defaulted and disappeared. "When my buyer pays me, I will pay you, but he is nowhere to be found," was heard everywhere. Men who had become rich overnight became poor again overnight. Some committed suicide. Others settled for 5 or 10 per cent of what they owed, with creditors happy to accept. It is small wonder that the whole business created some confirmed tulip-haters, including violent ones like the cane-wielding professor Forstius. Finally the government forbade further speculation and the Dutch began growing bulbs as a solid business —which today produces nearly two billion bulbs a year.

THE SAFFRON TRADE   Other kinds of bulbs—the crocus, the iris and the lily among them —have their own tales, different from the tulip's but in many respects just as strange. The crocus, for example, provided the basis of a lucrative trade for the Minoans, who lived for several thousand years on Crete in the Mediterranean. They manufactured saffron by pressing the dried stigmas, the tops of the female reproductive organs, of one of the 70 or so kinds of crocus that grew in the region. By exporting the resulting orange-yellow powder all over the known world the Minoans earned a good part of the wealth that kept them in splendor. Saffron was a spice, a dye, a scent and, to the medical men of the time, a miracle drug. It was said to banish backache and even paralysis (though for some reason it was supposed to work only for paralysis on the right side of the body).

Long after the Minoans had gone out of business—their civilization had all but vanished by 1100 B.C.—saffron still was almost as good a currency as gold, and a man could get a loan if he had a few handfuls of saffron-yielding corms for security. Those who did guarded their corms closely; the crocus apparently did not reach northern Europe until the time of the Crusades. It finally arrived in England, according to one account, after a pilgrim in Algeria hollowed out his staff, hid some crocus corms in it illegally and smuggled them out at the risk of his life. Whatever the truth of the tale, English farmers in Essex profitably raised crocuses for saffron for hundreds of years thereafter. Today saffron is used mainly as a spice, and a very expensive one. If you are tempted to grumble at the price of saffron in a supermarket, consider the fact that it takes 4,000 crocuses to produce an ounce of powder. If you should ever want to try producing a pinch or two of your own saffron, for saffron rice or for that splendid Spanish dish called *arroz con pollo* —rice with chicken—be sure *not* to use the bulb known as autumn crocus *(Colchicum)*. It is not a crocus, but a lily, and is poisonous; Greek slaves, in fact, used to eat it to make themselves sick and even to commit suicide. The ancients extracted their saffron from an autumn-flowering crocus, *Crocus sativus*, which despite its similar English name is quite different. As for me, I prefer crocuses in the garden; the grocer can supply the saffron for the kitchen shelf.

Like the tiny crocus, the much larger and statelier iris was long prized for merits other than its beauty. The Egyptian Pharaoh Thutmose III (1501-1447 B.C.) was intrigued by irises he saw during his conquest of Syria, and brought plants home with him, turning them over to his magicians and doctors to determine whether they had any potential as a medicine or aphrodisiac. Precisely what Thutmose' experts found out we do not know, but for centuries Europeans consumed vast quantities of irisroot, not only as a cure-all but for masking bad breath and for keeping bed sheets smelling fresh. Infants teethed on chunks of it and grownups wore bits of it on strings around their necks, presumably to ward off ills. This latter custom became so popular that the two main centers of production, Paris and Livorno, together shipped 20 million irisroot "beads" for necklaces every year. "Orrisroot"—another name for irisroot, most commonly the violet-scented root of *Iris florentina* —is still used today in toiletries and dentifrices.

More romantically, the iris has been identified—after years of debate among historians—as the fleur-de-lis *(illustrations, pages 28-29)*, which for centuries was the symbol of the kings of France. The French ruler who first adopted the symbol did so as a result of what amounted to a bet. He was Clovis the Frank, who lived from about 465 to 511 A.D. and who, as a pagan, was constantly nagged by his Christian wife to become a convert. According to one story, Clovis kept refusing until one day he found himself about to do battle with an exceptionally fierce-looking Germanic tribe invading his kingdom. Seeing the odds against him, he told his wife that if he won he would become a Christian. He did win, and to commem-

(continued on page 34)

THE VERSATILE IRIS

The lily: symbol of purity

"The angel Gabriel was sent from God unto a city of Galilee, named Nazareth, to a virgin [whose] name was Mary. And the angel came in unto her, and said, 'Hail, thou that art highly favored, the Lord is with thee: blessed art thou among women. . . . thou shalt conceive in thy womb, and bring forth a son, and shalt call his name Jesus.'"

One of the most tender scenes in the New Testament, St. Luke's account of the Annunciation provided a favorite text for the painters of the Renaissance. The Holy Ghost customarily appears overhead in the form of a dove. The Blessed Virgin is already crowned with a halo, signifying her holiness. In the 15th and early 16th Century paintings shown here, the angel, who had traditionally borne a scepter to show that he was God's herald, now comes holding a white lily, a symbol both of the Virgin's purity and of her role as Queen of the Angels.

This imagery was not new; Greek mythology claimed that the lily had first sprung from the milk of Hera, the wife of Zeus. Christian legend adopted and embellished the symbolism of flowers and their sacred associations. St. Bernard of Clairvaux, a mystic of the 12th Century, declared ecstatically of Christ's birth that "The Flower wished to be born of a Flower, in a flower, at the time of flowers."

Benvenuto Tisi Garofalo: *Annunciation*, detail Girolamo Mazzola-Bedoli: *Annunciation*, detail

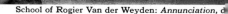

School of Rogier Van der Weyden: *Annunciation, d*

Sandro Botticelli: *Annunciation*, detail

Filippino Lippi: *Annunciation with Saint John the Baptist and Saint Andrew*, detail

Fra Filippo Lippi: *Annunciation*

Cima da Conegliano: *Annunciation*, detail

Fra Filippo Lippi: *Annunciation*, detail

Alesso Baldovinetti: *Annunciation*, detail

Bernardino di Betto Pinturicchio: *Madonna Enthroned with Saints*, detail

33

orate his change in spiritual allegiance, he replaced the three toads that he flaunted on his banners with a stylized version of the irises that his soldiers found growing near the field of battle. But the design did not get its name, fleur-de-lys, until Louis VII, in the Crusade of 1147 A.D., made it the symbol not only of France but of Christianity. Originally, it was "fleur-de-Louis"—flower of Louis—but the phrase was soon distorted into "fleur-de-luce"—flower of light—and eventually into "fleur-de-lys"—flower of the lily. But from all evidence the fleur-de-lys is an iris, not a lily.

THE ANCIENT LILY   The lily can spare the iris some honor; it has enough others of its own. One of the oldest plants known to man, it is mentioned in history for the first time on a tablet that was inscribed in Sumeria nearly 5,000 years ago. The tablet tells of a city in Persia that was surrounded by fields of lilies and in fact was named Susa, which means lily. Some scholars believe the lily spread from Persia in the caravans of nomads who took edible bulbs along as food for their long journeys; occasionally they would drop one, according to this theory, and it would take root and grow where it fell. In any case the lily traveled far, to Crete, Egypt, Greece, Rome and, probably in the baggage of homesick Roman soldiers, to northern Europe and England. Wherever it went, it took on an aura of sanctity. The Minoans associated it with their goddess Britomartis. The Greeks made it a symbol of their greatest goddess, Hera, and the Romans associated it with Juno, Hera's counterpart.

The lily is also closely intertwined with Christian history. Lilies grew in the Holy Land and carvings of them adorned the Temple in Jerusalem. (The "lilies of the field" that Christ described as surpassing Solomon in all his glory may have been lilies, but modern researchers believe it more likely that they were anemones.) For centuries the white lily was used by painters to symbolize the purity of the Virgin Mary *(pages 32-33)*. It was also used to make ointments and salves for medicinal and cosmetic purposes. As late as the 19th Century, fading European beauties were following a prescription of Dioscorides (41-68 A.D.), a Greek who served as a Roman army doctor and wrote a book about plants. Lilies, said Dioscorides, "being beaten small with honey . . . clear faces and make them without wrinkles." Another of his prescriptions, for a face oil, was more difficult to concoct: it required 3,000 lilies to prepare a single batch of the lotion, not to mention days of mincing, boiling and straining before the precious liquid was ready.

AN ADVENTURE IN CHINA   Any history of the lily would be incomplete without the story of one of the most beautiful lilies of all, the regal lily, which was unknown to most of the world until this century and which nearly cost its Western discoverer his life. An Englishman named Ernest Henry Wilson, a professional plant hunter, first came on the species in 1903 while traveling in the neighborhood of the remote Min River near the Chinese-Tibetan border, and later returned to collect plants on behalf of Harvard University's Arnold Arboretum. "In narrow, semi-arid valleys, down which torrents thunder and encompassed by mountains . . . whose peaks are clothed with snow eternal, the Regal Lily has her home," he wrote. "In late June and July it is possible to walk for days through a veritable wild garden dominated by these beautiful flowers." It was, as he implied, rough country, and on a return trip in 1910 to collect the lilies, he and his bearers—and Wilson's cocker spaniel—had to travel 22 days to cover 200 miles. One morning as they worked their way along a mountainside trail, the spaniel suddenly cringed, then leaped out of the way as a small rock hit the path and plunged down the precipice into the river far below. Wilson, riding in a sedan chair, shouted to his bearers to run, then scrambled out of the chair himself an instant before a giant boulder splintered it and carried the wreckage into the gorge. Wilson ran, seeking safety from the rockslide, as a stone sent his sun helmet flying. He had almost reached shelter in the lee of the cliff, where his bearers and the spaniel were cowering, when more rocks knocked him over. He tried to get up, but his right leg buckled underneath him. As he crawled along, stupefied by the piercing pain, the bearers reached out to pull him from the avalanche's path.

When the great rocks stopped thundering past, the party took stock: only Wilson had been seriously hurt, but his leg was broken in two places and the nearest help, a medical mission, was four days' journey away. Fighting to remain conscious, Wilson instructed his bearers to splint his leg with the tripod from the large, old-fashioned view camera that one of them carried for him. They were bandaging the leg when a train of pack-bearing mules suddenly appeared on the cliffside trail. The mules could not turn on the narrow path, and their drivers could not be asked to wait, for another avalanche might roar down the mountain at any instant. Wilson, the story goes, told his men to lay him across the path, and the mules stepped carefully over him, while the rest of his party flattened themselves against the rock wall to make room. Then, on an improvised stretcher, Wilson's bearers carried him to the mission on a forced march, making the four-day trip in three days. But the leg had become infected, and for a time amputation threatened. Wilson was still in the mission hospital when his regal lily bulbs were shipped to the United States, where they became a botanical sensation. For the rest of his life he walked with a limp, but he considered that a minor price to pay for so beautiful a find.

IN PRAISE OF HYACINTHS

Hyacinths, among the most lovely and sweetest-smelling flowers of spring, have inspired poems and legends for centuries. Greek mythology records two stories of their origin: in one version the hyacinth sprang up where the blood of Ajax, a hero of the Trojan War, soaked the ground; in another version it grew from the blood of the boy Hyacinthus, accidentally killed by a discus thrown by Apollo. Wild hyacinths abounded in ancient Greece, but it was in the Middle East that the flowers were first widely cultivated. The esteem in which they were held there is evidenced by these lines attributed to the 13th Century Persian poet, Saadi:

*If of thy mortal goods thou art bereft,
And from thy slender store two loaves
   alone to thee are left,
Sell one, and with the dole
Buy hyacinths to feed thy soul.*

Modern tulips and their glamorous past

Since they first spread from Turkey through Europe more than four centuries ago, tulips have been the best loved and most widely grown of all the bulbs. Along with roses and orchids, they have been the subject of the most intensive hybridizing efforts in the world of flowers; today there are more than 4,000 named varieties of tulips grouped into 15 different classes (*encyclopedia*).

Most modern tulips are descended from the oldest tulips in cultivation, the so-called lily-flowered type, which has pointed petals and was so admired by the Turks that it was one of the most popular decorative motifs during the 500 years of the Ottoman dynasty. As the early Dutch growers cultivated these bulbs, they developed tulips with rounded rather than pointed petals, double tulips with more than the normal six petals and the flamboyant multicolored types that set off Holland's ruinous tulip craze (*Chapter 2*). When these new European hybrids found their way back to Turkey, they in turn provoked a frenzy so ardent that the period from 1718 to 1730 is known as the "tulip epoch" of Turkish history. The multicolored Rembrandts in particular bewitched the Turks as they had the Dutch before them. Though no one knew at the time that most of the prized streaks and frills in these flowers were caused by a virus, professional Turkish gardeners dusted bulbs with "fertilizing powder," made by crushing infected bulbs, and thus unknowingly passed on the disease to achieve the exotic effects their masters demanded.

Tulips soon became a mainstay of gentlemen's gardens everywhere—in America, Washington and Jefferson were tulip fanciers. But tulips remained a cherished flower among simpler people, and as the Industrial Revolution swept families from country cottages to factory towns, the displaced rural folk took their tulips with them to cheer their dreary urban homes. These cottage tulips became popular among more affluent gardeners around 1880, and during the next decades the development of Darwins and Darwin hybrids, today's favorites, gave tulip growing a new impetus that has never abated.

At a 16th Century Turkish celebration, guests admire a huge artificial tulip as Sultan Murad III looks on from above.

Favorites of the sultans

In the days of the sultans, the graceful lily-flowered tulip became a widespread motif in Turkish design. Its presence in textiles like the one at far right is considered by museum experts to be almost a guarantee that the fabric is Turkish. After these tulips were imported into Europe in the late 16th Century, they were eventually eclipsed by newer breeds; but modern strains, like the Astor variety at right, have made the type popular once more.

ASTOR (MODERN LILY-FLOWERED TULIP)

16TH CENTURY TURKISH FABRIC

Modern and early species

ENGADIN (T. GREIGII SPECIES HYBRID TULIP)

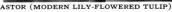

COPPERPLATE OF A TULIP BY GESNER, 1561

The first accurate European illustration and description of a tulip *(left)* appeared in a 1561 garden manual by the Swiss botanist Konrad Gesner, after whom plant classifier Linnaeus later named all garden tulips *Tulipa gesneriana.* In the last 100 years, plant explorers have found similar wild species in Central Asia. These tulips and hybrids of them, including the handsome Engadin at far left, are the basis of a whole new group, known as species tulips.

New beauty, by design or accident

As tulips took on the round-petaled shape of the familiar so-called single early class, mutations produced the brilliantly streaked or "flamed" flowers that delighted European tulip fanciers, as well as the parrots, whose slashed, feathery petals suggested the birds in fashion at the time. The multicolored tulips now called Rembrandts (because they were frequently seen in 16th and 17th Century Dutch paintings) gained their spectacular coloring from virus infections. By 1614, when the Dutch engraver Crispin de Passe published his illustrated book on garden flowers, striped tulips were well known *(top right)*. The frivolous French court was charmed by the bizarre parrots shown at bottom, left, in a late 17th Century engraving by the painter Jean-Baptiste Monnoyer. Modern striped and parrot types, such as Prince Carnival and Texas Gold shown here, still achieve the same colorful effects. One more 17th Century development was the double early tulip, like those shown opposite.

PRINCE CARNIVAL (MODERN STRIPED TULIP)

EARLY 17TH CENTURY STRIPED TULIPS

LATE 17TH CENTURY PARROT TULIPS

TEXAS GOLD (MODERN PARROT TULIP)

Many-petaled double early tulips, all colorful mutations of a variety called Murillo, flower among a mass of grape hyacinths.

By the late 17th Century, tulips were an honored part of every genteel garden, and wealthy aristocrats were so proud of their floral displays they would show them off as backgrounds in family portraits. In this depiction of Spring, painted in Germany in 1663, Count Johann von Nassau-Idstein, his wife and his daughter receive homage from Flora, Roman goddess of flowers, on a terrace that is rimmed with an array of potted ornamental plants. In the background, a many-colored collection of tulips blossoms among other flowers in beds laid out in a multitude of naturalistic and highly fanciful shapes.

Pride of a yeoman's front yard

The term "cottage tulip" celebrates the lasting love for large egg-shaped tulips among plain Englishmen, who prized them after the gentry turned up their noses at these flowers. Today they are again popular, in varieties like Greenland at right. But in 1657 Roundhead General John Lambert was a satirical figure on a playing card (*far right*) labeled "Lambert, Knight of ye Golden Tulip." A tulip fancier, he had retired on a pension to raise the flowers.

GREENLAND (MODERN COTTAGE TULIP)

GENERAL LAMBERT, ADMIRING A TULIP

Darwin's foursquare namesake

PINK SUPREME (MODERN DARWIN TULIP)

BULB-GROWER KRELAGE'S 1892 CATALOGUE

One of today's most popular tulips, and the progenitor of many other modern types, is the Darwin, bred in the late 1880s in Haarlem by E. H. Krelage & Son from old Dutch tulip stock and French varieties. Named for selectivity's patron saint, it caused a furor; experts stated that it was not new at all. But the flower's strong stems and squared base (*far left*) proved original. By 1892 it had received an international gold medal (*left*).

Today's tailor-made tulips

The quartet of modern tulips at right represents the remarkable outgrowth of new varieties from the prolific Darwin described above. Dainty Maid, a Rembrandt tulip, is typical of the modern class that resulted largely from changes in Darwin tulips produced inadvertently by virus infection. Other Darwin descendants were more calculated. Orange Sun, in the so-called Darwin hybrid class, was bred to combine the height and strong stems of the late-blossoming Darwin tulip with the big flowers and early-blooming habit of the species tulip *T. fosteriana*, resulting in large midseason flowers. Triumph tulips such as Orange Wonder, also bred to fill the gap between the early and late tulips, are crosses between single early tulips and Darwins. Still another type bred for midseason bloom was named for the Austrian botanist Gregor Mendel. A cross between Darwins and the old, small, early-blooming Duc van Tols, the Mendels include such beauties as Athlete (*bottom right*).

DAINTY MAID (REMBRANDT TULIP)

ORANGE SUN (DARWIN HYBRID TULIP)

ORANGE WONDER (TRIUMPH TULIP)

ATHLETE (MENDEL TULIP)

A tulip field in Holland blazes with Gudoshnik Darwin hybrids. Such displays attract close to a million tourists each spring.

The bulbs that bloom in the spring 3

In some centuries of their colorful history, bulbs have been used for flavorings and medicines, traded for high prices and emblazoned on the banners of royalty, but for thousands of years they have been grown above all for their beauty in gardens. And of all bulbs the spring-flowering ones own a special place in the hearts of gardeners: they bring the first welcome burst of color that signals the end of winter's cold, wet months. Country newspapers still hail the appearance of the first crocus on their editorial pages; city dwellers see early snowdrops in the park and begin to think of picnics and vacations that lie ahead. A little later, the northward surge of spring can be measured by the bright tide of daffodils that sweeps across the land. By February, sometimes earlier, they have begun to blossom in the South and West; in March the white and yellow blooms have reached Virginia, Missouri and northern California; in April the Northeast and Northwest are greeting their trumpetlike blooms together with the return of songbirds. By early May the golden chain of daffodils stretches clear across the continent from Nova Scotia to British Columbia.

Spring-flowering bulbs are not only beautiful but tough, and this ruggedness is part of their special wonder. After all my years of gardening, I still marvel every time I discover delicate-looking winter aconites coming up through the melting snow. Most spring-flowering bulbs thrive in Canadian gardens just as well as, and frequently better than, they do in gardens in the United States; the cooler temperatures prolong the life not only of the flowers, but also of the leaves, making for larger, healthier bulbs. But spring bulbs will do well almost anywhere except in the Deep South and, when a number of different species and varieties are planted to bloom in their natural succession, they can brighten the garden for two or three months (*picture essay, page 52*).

To most beginning gardeners, spring bulbs mean crocuses, tulips and daffodils, and certainly no garden should be without them. But there are more than a dozen other kinds, each of which may in-

Yellow Sun daffodils, white Van Wereld's Favorite daffodils and red lily-flowered Aladdin tulips brighten a spring garden in Victoria, British Columbia. White Greek anemones, at center, divide the daffodil beds.

clude many species and varieties that are as charming as they are easy to grow—the tall, imposing fritillarias, the graceful, mottled trout lilies, the gay, free-flowering ranunculuses, to name a few. Moreover, most spring bulbs are inexpensive, multiply prodigiously and put on a splendid show of color in the garden.

A BULB'S LIFE CYCLE But to prepare the show, they need time. Spring bulbs must be planted in the fall, when they look about as lively as split peas in a jar. They are not, however, going to sleep the whole winter away. Most true bulbs or corms are ready to release their stored-up energy and develop their embryonic leaves and flowers as soon as they are set in the ground. They quickly push out roots from their bottoms and, a little later, stems from their tops. The stems probe upward, sometimes to within a hair's breadth of the soil's surface. Then they halt, even if frost has not set in, guided against danger by their own internal biological clocks, which stop growth when the temperature falls below a certain point. Sometimes the bulbs are tricked by a late-winter thaw and pop the tips of their stems up barely above the surface of the soil, but they quickly put on the brakes when the cold returns and suffer no appreciable harm. Afterward, when the increasing warmth of the spring sun finally signals all clear, they start growing again.

To support this growth the bulb itself supplies nourishment to the immature leaves, which, as they ripen, replenish the food supply, create embryos for the next year's flowers and, in the case of corms, produce new corms to replace the old ones. This process continues for weeks after the flowers die. By the time the leaves yellow and wither, some types of bulbs have fattened again, others have been replaced by new ones and new corms have reached full size. Only then is the life cycle complete for the year, and the bulbs and corms are ready for their brief period of rest. Then—and only then—may the unsightly withered leaves be trimmed off.

WHERE TO PLANT BULBS The ease of concealing unkempt bulbs as they mature is one consideration in choosing sites for them. But to my mind it is more important to place the flowers where they can most readily be enjoyed. Spring bulbs will bloom while the temperatures still range in the 30°s and 40°s—at a time when I, for one, am not yet ready to stroll in the yard. So I put mine where I can see the flowers easily from the windows of the house. Plants bearing relatively large flowers—tulips and daffodils—may be planted some distance away and still be enjoyed. So may the little snowdrops, snowflakes, striped and Siberian squills, grape hyacinths and white crocuses, if they are planted in sufficiently large quantities and massed dramatically against a contrasting dark background such as a group of evergreens. But these little plants, as well as such colorful jewels as dwarf irises, spring meadow saffron and winter aconites, are equally appropriate in beds or borders near the front door where you and arriving guests can enjoy them at close range.

All spring bulbs like sun—full sun and as much of it as they can get—during and after flowering. But that is no reason not to plant them among trees—at least among deciduous trees, whose leaves generally will not have grown enough to shade the ground until after the bulbs have bloomed. You can plant them near evergreens, too, if you put them on the south side, where the low-angled sun of early spring will reach the plants much of the day. Spring bulbs, like many other bulbous plants, will grow even in shaded places, such as the north side of a house, if they get plenty of indirect sunlight.

Almost any yard will offer a number of suitable sites, and from them you can probably choose several where the withering foliage will be inconspicuous after the blossoms have faded. Tulips, winter aconites, grape hyacinths, irises of the reticulata group, daffodils, brodiaeas and calochortuses thrive in rock gardens, where later-blooming plants will hide their lingering leaves. Snowdrops, squills, daffodils and many others may be set in the midst of such ground covers as periwinkle, bugle, pachysandra or ivy, whose fo-

PROTECTING BULBS FROM RODENTS

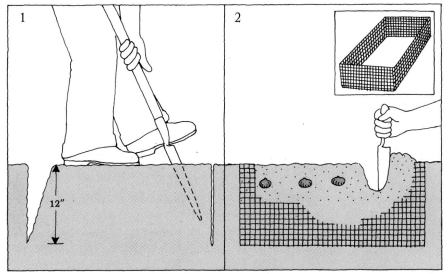

To fence a bed of bulbs against mice, chipmunks and gophers—which burrow underground for crocuses, tulips and lilies—dig a foot-deep trench around the bed before preparing the soil for planting.

Line the trench with ½-inch wire mesh (inset). Then prepare the soil and plant the bulbs at the proper depth. Prized bulbs can be placed in mesh baskets 2 inches deeper than the bulb's own planting depth.

liage will mask that of the bulbous plants after they have flowered. A perennial border wide enough to hold many kinds of bulbous plants is ideal: you can distribute your spring-blooming bulbs among those that flower in summer or autumn and thus provide constant color. Large formal beds or borders of bulbs all of one kind —tulips, for example—are extremely handsome. But the initial cost is likely to be greater because of the number of bulbs required; and when the flowers vanish, the gardener must cope with the problem of replacing them with other flowers.

A planting does not have to be big or expensive to be beautiful, just big enough for its setting. A clump of a dozen or two large-flowered tulips basking at the foot of a wall or backed by the rich, darker hues of evergreens is unforgettable. And I shall always remember a garden of spring bulbs surrounding a tiny cabin that sat near the base of a knoll covered with old birches and cedars— beneath the trees floated great drifts of daffodils that had undoubtedly been smaller clumps when they started.

Whatever bulbs you plant and wherever you plant them, do not set just a few here and a few there: the effect would prove spotty. For the same reason it is better not to mix two or more kinds of bulbs—for example, tulips and daffodils—in a single group. Set bulbs of a kind together in large enough numbers to dazzle the eye —and remember that the smaller the blossoms, the more you will need for a dramatic display. Where you want an informal look, plant to conform to the topography. Plantings look natural if they follow the land, flowing down the slopes of depressions.

EXTENDING THE BLOOM   The flower of a spring bulb seldom lasts more than about two weeks, but if you use a little ingenuity in planning the beds you can keep bright blooms coming week after week for a couple of months. The most obvious technique for extending bloom involves the use of several different varieties, some that bloom early, some that bloom in midseason and some that bloom late. Among tulips, for example, the species tulips and early tulips will blossom in mid- to late April in Zone 5 *(map, page 148)*, the triumph and Mendel varieties in late April and early May, cottage and Darwin tulips in mid- to late May. Daffodils are equally accommodating, offering a selection of varieties that will come up and flower in succession over a period of six weeks or more.

Even bulbs of a single variety can be made to provide flowers over a longer-than-usual period if you use a few tricks in planting. Location affects blossoming time. In light, sandy soil bulbs will come up sooner than in heavy clay. And the sunniest spots produce the earliest flowers, the shadiest places the latest ones. I have planted two beds of crocuses of the same kind, one in the sun and another

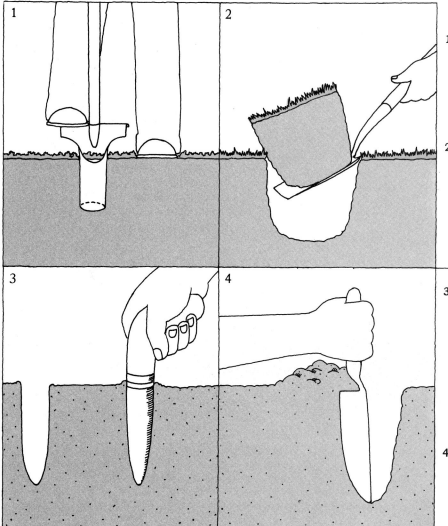

FOUR WAYS TO DIG HOLES FOR PLANTING BULBS

1. *To plant individual bulbs near other plants, or in a bed of ground cover such as ivy, use a step-on bulb planter that cuts cylinders of soil. It makes holes up to 6 inches deep and works most easily in damp, cohesive soil.*

2. *For deeper holes to accommodate clumps of bulbs, cut a square, straight-sided plug of sod with a spade and lift out the whole plug. Loosen the soil at the bottom of the hole with the spade and work in bone meal before the bulbs are planted and the plug replaced.*

3. *After a soil bed is prepared, a tool called a dibble or dibber quickly pokes holes of a uniform diameter and depth. Some of the more highly priced dibbles have depth markers on their sides, but it is easy to improvise a marker with tape. Drop a little loose soil or sand into the bottom of each hole to avoid leaving an air space in the tip of the pointed depression.*

4. *The garden tool most commonly used for digging holes in prepared soil is a trowel; to make holes rapidly, plunge the trowel into the ground and pull it toward you.*

on the north side of an evergreen hedge. The bulbs near the hedge produce blossoms just as large and lovely as their fellows, but they bloom three weeks later, which is what I intended.

PLANTING THE BULBS

For all spring-flowering bulbs, the sooner you plant in fall, the better. For one thing, the weather is more pleasant then; dedicated though I am to gardening, I would much rather work outdoors on a sunny September day than on a chilly November one. More important, the more time the bulbs have to put out their roots before the ground freezes, the stronger they will be. The only bulbs I would risk planting late in the fall are tulips, but even they benefit from being set in the ground as early in the fall as you can obtain them from your nurseryman or garden center. They will be much better off in the soil where they belong than lying on a shelf in a box. In

WIRING CUT FLOWERS

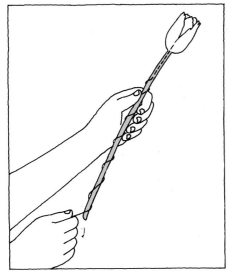

You can keep tulips and other tall cut flowers standing up straight and prevent them from bending toward the light by stiffening the stems with florists' wire. Insert the wire into the stem below each blossom and up into the flower's base, then gently wrap the wire down around the length of the stem. In the case of hollow-stemmed flowers such as anemones, the wire can be inserted up through the bottom of the stem until its tip reaches the head of the flower; the stems then can be shaped into graceful curves if desired.

CUTTING FOR FLOWERS

warm climates tulips, except for the species tulips in the West and Southwest, should be treated as one-season bulbs to be planted late in the fall and discarded after the spring blossoms have appeared. In Zones 8-10 bulbs of large-flowered garden varieties should be refrigerated at 40° to 45° until late November or December, simulating the rest period that prepares them for bloom, then planted 6 to 8 inches deep so the bulbs can be as cool as possible.

Preparation of the soil for spring-flowering bulbs follows the same steps as those described for all bulbous plants in Chapter 1. But where the earth is heavy and largely clay, an inch or two of coarse sand dropped into the bottom of each bulb hole will assure the fast growth of a good root system. Most bulbs also benefit from having a teaspoon of bone meal mixed thoroughly into the sand or soil at the bottom of the hole.

After you have planted your bulbs, be sure to soak the soil thoroughly. The water will wash the soil in around the bulbs, eliminating air spaces, and will start the bulbs rooting.

Because of their hardiness, none of the spring bulbs needs protection against cold after planting if set at the proper depth. But they do need protection then and in later years against unseasonable warmth: wherever alternate freezing and thawing occur, the soil will heave, and this movement can damage roots by shifting the bulbs. An aboveground layer of mulch, applied *after* the soil has frozen at least 2 inches deep, will usually keep the ground hard and eliminate this danger. The best mulches for this purpose are 5 or 6 inches of salt hay, 2 to 3 inches of pine needles, 2 inches of buckwheat hulls, sawdust, wood shavings or bark, or a thatching of evergreen boughs 6 to 12 inches deep. If you use salt hay or evergreen mulch, be sure to lift away the mulch before the bulbs' stems peep aboveground the following spring; if you wait too long, you may damage the tender shoots. If by chance they have sprouted, lift the mulch with a tined fork, not a rake.

Bulbs naturalized in grassy areas generally do not need an applied mulch because nature provides one, consisting of the grass's dead leaves. Low-growing bulbs such as crocuses will get ample protection if set among living mulches of ivy or other low ground covers, which insulate the ground against unseasonable thawing.

When spring-flowering bulbs blossom, many gardeners are content to enjoy them where they are planted. But when cut and brought indoors, they make fine arrangements. Cutting the flower stems does not harm the plants; in fact, the bulbs become stronger because no energy is wasted in allowing the flowers to mature and produce seeds. Do not, however, cut leaves, which must remain to build up the bulbs for the next year. The favorites for cutting are the large-flowered anemones, tulips and daffodils, but squills, grape hyacinths and snowdrops make interesting miniature arrangements.

Flowers cut from bulbs are unusually easy to care for. Unlike annuals and most other perennials, they do not need deep water, nor do they seem to benefit from the addition of cut-flower preservatives. Even a shallow dish can be used for arrangements so long as the end of each stem is submerged in clean water.

Anemones, tulips and ranunculuses can frustrate flower arrangers because the flowers and their stems bend toward the light no matter what position they are arranged in. The bending seems attractive to me, for a few gracefully curved stems add rhythm and charm to a flower arrangement. If you want the stems to stay in a certain position, you can wire them as florists do *(drawing, opposite)*. Flowers cut from spring bulbs do not last long, chiefly because indoor temperatures are so much warmer than those outdoors. However, if you set the flowers each night on a porch or some other spot that is as cool as possible (so long as it is above freezing), you can add several days to the life of the arrangements.

After your spring bulbs have finished flowering in the garden, leave them to build up energy for the next year's cycle; when the leaves have yellowed and withered, you can snip them off if you like. In the case of most spring bulbs, this is the last gardening chore of the year. However, to guarantee a good show for next year, certain bulbs should be dug up and replanted. The very large-flowered tulip bulbs produce their biggest flowers the first spring after planting, then the bulbs multiply into more but smaller bulbs. As a result, smaller flowers will appear in following years. The best way to guarantee large blossoms is to dig the bulbs up, sort them into various sizes and replant immediately, setting each size in separate groups. (Keep them out of direct sun while sorting, or they may dry out.) Eventually the small bulbs become larger, but if they are not dug up and replanted in enriched soil each year, they soon exhaust themselves and the soil around them through overcrowding. The same technique is used for hyacinths. On the other hand, daffodils, crocuses, fritillarias and most of the other spring bulbs will multiply and become more beautiful each year without being dug up and replanted. Only when they become so crowded that they produce fewer or smaller blossoms do they need to be lifted out and divided; the excess bulbs can be used to increase the size of the present bed or to start new beds elsewhere. When you replant, set the bigger bulbs where they will be conspicuous when they flower. The smaller ones can be planted in an out-of-the-way corner in the garden, a sort of nursery bed. When they have grown up they can be set in a place of honor to give you pleasure for years to come.

DIGGING UP BULBS

A timetable for year-round bloom

Wherever you live and however you garden, bulbs are a unique family of plants that can furnish flowers around the calendar, indoors and out. In hot parts of Florida, California and the Gulf Coast, tropical bulbs like cannas and white calla lilies blossom much of the year. In cooler climates, you can get almost the same result by plotting a series of bulbs to bloom one after another from spring through fall in the garden, and supplementing them with potted bulbs indoors in winter.

Most bulbs have such predictable habits that their flowering season, and their order of bloom within that season, can be charted on timetables like the ones below and on the following pages. When each season begins and how long it lasts vary with the climate zone (*map and table, page 148*), but the bulbs' order of blossoming remains the same. A single bulb may bloom only a week or two, but many genera include species and varieties that blossom at slightly different times; by planting a combination you can double or triple the period of bloom for each kind. You can also capitalize on the fact that some bulbs, such as squills, bloom earlier in full sun than in partial shade, and others, such as gladioluses, can be planted in batches to sprout serially over a period of months.

Early spring bulbs, like the crocuses at right, are best adapted to cool climates, although they may be planted as far south as Atlanta to begin flowering in mid-February. In the North, the earliest kinds blossom despite cold and ice, then multiply spontaneously to increase in beauty over the years.

EARLY SPRING BULBS IN ORDER OF BLOSSOMING*	LENGTH OF BLOOM
SNOWDROPS	2-3 weeks
WINTER ACONITES	1-2 weeks (2-3 weeks if several varieties are planted)
SNOWFLAKES	1-2 weeks
DWARF IRISES	1 week (4-6 weeks if several varieties are planted)
CROCUSES	2 weeks (4-5 weeks if several varieties are planted)
CHIONODOXAS	3-4 weeks
SQUILLS	1-2 weeks (2-3 weeks if several varieties are planted)
EARLY DAFFODILS	2 weeks (3-4 weeks if several varieties are planted)
EARLY TULIPS	1-2 weeks (2-3 weeks if several varieties are planted)
GRAPE HYACINTHS	2-3 weeks (4-5 weeks if several varieties are planted)

*For dates of blossoming season in your zone, see map and table on page 148.

In a Delaware garden, clumps of Yellow Mammoth crocuses push toward the March sun through lingering patches of snow.

Spring's gleaming jewels

Not only are spring bulbs extraordinarily colorful, but the choices are legion. Daffodils alone provide 11 broad classes of flowers in shades of pink as well as yellow and white, sizes from 1 to 5 inches, and blooming periods that cover a two-month span. For example, in Zone 5 miniature daffodils blossom in early March, jonquilla hybrids in mid- to late March, and trumpet varieties in April. One bulb, ranunculus, blooms beyond spring, over a period of three to four months. Individual blossoms, as a rule, last longer in cool weather than in warm, and the double, or many-petaled, varieties of plants like anemones usually remain beautiful longer than single-flowered ones.

When planted in pots, King Alfred daffodils can be replaced by later-blooming bulbs.   *A bed of poppy-flowered anemones makes*

SPRING BULBS IN ORDER OF BLOSSOMING*	LENGTH OF BLOOM
ANEMONES	2-4 weeks (8 weeks if several varieties are planted)
DAFFODILS	1-2 weeks (4-5 weeks if several varieties are planted)
HYACINTHS	2-3 weeks (4-5 weeks if several varieties are planted)
FRITILLARIAS	1 week (2 weeks if several varieties are planted)
TULIPS	1-2 weeks (4-6 weeks if several varieties are planted)
LATE SQUILLS	2-3 weeks (4 weeks if several varieties are planted)
RANUNCULUSES	3-4 months
IXIAS	2-3 weeks (4-5 weeks if several varieties are planted)
STARS-OF-BETHLEHEM	1-2 weeks (6-8 weeks if several varieties are planted)
ERYTHRONIUMS	1-2 weeks (3 weeks if several varieties are planted)

* For dates of blossoming season in your zone, see map and table on page 148.

a long spectacle of color for the garden.   *These crown imperial fritillarias rise regally to tower above flower beds and borders.*

Summer's varied splendors

The range of early summer bulbs is great, and can be made even greater by simple planting techniques. Such bulbs as tuberous begonias (*pages 58-59*) and cannas, which cannot stand freezing temperatures, can be started indoors in northern areas and moved out to the patio when the weather becomes warm. Gladioluses can go right into the garden after the last spring frost and will bloom from midsummer until fall if groups are set out every 7 to 10 days during spring and early summer. For less ambitious gardeners, the summer bulb stand-bys are the hardy lilies and ornamental alliums, which can be planted once and virtually forgotten about.

Fancy-leaved caladiums, lending a welcome note of coolness on hot days, flourish on patios as well as in garden beds and tolerate

EARLY SUMMER BULBS IN ORDER OF BLOSSOMING*	LENGTH OF BLOOM
ALLIUMS	2-3 weeks (all summer if several varieties are planted)
CALADIUMS	colorful foliage, early summer to frost
TUBEROUS BEGONIAS	early summer to frost
LILIES	3-4 weeks (all summer if several varieties are planted)
CANNAS	10-12 weeks
GLADIOLUSES	2-3 weeks (10-12 weeks with successive plantings)
CALLAS	10-12 weeks
TIGRIDIAS	6-8 weeks
TUBEROSES	2-3 weeks (6-8 weeks with successive plantings)
AGAPANTHUSES	6-8 weeks

*For dates of blossoming season in your zone, see map and table on page 148.

any light from brilliant sunshine to deep shade.   *Giant alliums rise up on leafless 3-foot stalks above perennial yellow coreopsis.*

Tuberous begonias provide a colorful display all summer and into fall. Upright kinds thrive in pots or garden beds; trailing types

suit window boxes or hanging baskets. The porch above is built of wood slats to give the plants partial shade and good ventilation.

Fall's bright surprises

Just when the garden seems spent, the late bulbs bring it back to life with a burst of fresh color. Some of them, like lycorises, produce only flowers in the fall, then foliage appears the next spring to replenish the bulbs. Sternbergias provide a sunny note for a week or more in September; colchicums and autumn-flowering crocuses *(below, right)* survive beyond the first frosts. But dahlias are the most long lasting—a single plant will blossom from midsummer until freezing weather, its blooms growing larger and brighter as the nights become cooler. Though dahlias must be dug up before the earth freezes, such late bloomers as autumn crocuses can stay in the ground year round.

Through their long blooming period, cactus dahlias may produce 50 flowers per plant.　　*Fragrant Neapolitan cyclamens are small,*

SUMMER AND FALL BULBS IN ORDER OF BLOSSOMING*	LENGTH OF BLOOM
DAHLIAS	midsummer to frost
ACIDANTHERAS	8-10 weeks
LYCORISES	2-3 weeks
HAEMANTHUSES	2-3 weeks (3-4 months if several varieties are planted)
FALL ZEPHYRANTHES	2-3 weeks (2-3 months if several varieties are planted)
NERINES	1-1½ weeks (3-4 weeks if several varieties are planted)
CYCLAMENS	4-6 weeks
STERNBERGIAS	1-2 weeks
AUTUMN-FLOWERING CROCUSES	2-3 weeks (6-8 weeks if several varieties are planted)
COLCHICUMS	2-3 weeks (6-8 weeks if several varieties are planted)

*For dates of blossoming season in your zone, see map and table on page 148.

yet tough enough to survive most winters.   *An autumn-flowering species, the showy crocus blooms for weeks after the leaves fall.*

Winter's flowers-to-order

When winter comes, flowering bulbs prove a boon to indoor gardeners. Tropical bulbs such as the large-flowered hippeastrums are familiar as house plants and easy to grow indoors. So are clivias *(below, right)* and cyclamens, though they demand night temperatures of 50° to 55°. With a little extra effort, you can induce many spring-flowering garden bulbs to bloom in winter *(Chapter 5)*. Most need a period of cold before they flower and are often started outdoors in cold frames. But by selecting varieties of bulbs with different blooming periods, such as tulips, hyacinths and daffodils, and by moving the plants into light and warmth a group at a time, you can enjoy a four-month show.

Although snow has stilled the gardens outside, this window is alive with yellow jonquils and freesias, white and yellow narcissuses,

WINTER BULBS IN ORDER OF BLOSSOMING*	LENGTH OF BLOOM	PLANTING TIME
FLORISTS' CYCLAMENS	4-6 months (with 50°-55° night temperatures)	(buy plant in fall)
TAZETTA NARCISSUSES	1-2 weeks (3½ months if forcing of bulbs is started at intervals)	4-6 weeks before bloom
HIPPEASTRUMS	1-2 weeks (3-4 months if forcing of bulbs is started at intervals)	2-4 weeks before bloom
CROCUSES	1 week (2 months if forcing of bulbs is started at intervals)	fall
DAFFODILS	1½ weeks (4 months if forcing of bulbs is started at intervals)	fall
TULIPS	1½ weeks (4 months if forcing of bulbs is started at intervals)	fall
HYACINTHS	2 weeks (4 months if forcing of bulbs is started at intervals)	fall
LILIES OF THE VALLEY	1½ weeks (5 months if forcing of pips is started at intervals)	fall
CLIVIAS	3-4 weeks	any time
GLOXINIAS	2 weeks (all winter with successive plantings)	12 weeks before bloom

For techniques of forcing bulbs to winter bloom, see Chapter 5.

scarlet tulips, and salmon and purple hyacinths.　　A Kafir lily *(Clivia miniata)* glows like a flame, warming the gray winter days.

Summer's grand parade of color 4

When the first three dahlia plants ever seen outside Mexico arrived in Madrid in 1789, the royal gardener to King Charles IV of Spain had them guarded as though they were crown jewels and forbade his assistants to share them with anybody. No wonder. Of all the myriad kinds of bulbs that flower in summer, the dahlia most flatters the gardener's ego. It begins blooming in midsummer and continues tirelessly until frost cuts it down. Depending on the variety, dahlias produce blossoms as small as a quarter or as big as a dinner plate, in every color but blue. (Horticulturists have been trying for years to breed a blue dahlia but have not yet succeeded.) The more the blooms are cut, the more the plant bears—up to 50 or even 100 blooms per plant in a season. It is not so hard to understand why dahlia fanciers sometimes verge on fanaticism about their hobby and grow nothing else.

Much as I admire dahlias, though, summer is too rich in blooming bulbs to permit one favorite to monopolize the season. Half a hundred genera of bulbous plants flower in summer, although the most popular—in addition to dahlias—are lilies, gladioluses and tuberous begonias. Among lilies alone there are hundreds of varieties, with flowers held upright like cups, horizontally like trumpets or hanging like bells, on stems that range in height from less than a foot to 8 feet. The spectrum of colors that has been brought about through modern hybridizing methods is astonishing. Beginning gardeners tend to think of lilies as white, and indeed the familiar Easter lily, *Lilium longiflorum,* and many others are. But in the genus *Lilium*—which includes all the true lilies, as opposed to day lilies, *Hemerocallis,* and the many other plants that have the word "lily" in their common names—hues range from yellow to orange to red to purple, with many varieties spotted and striped.

In addition to the incomparable flower shapes and colors of the lilies, two other qualities have made them favorites among summer-flowering bulbs. One is the long period of time during which their flowers will blossom. Although the blooming period of any

Enchantment lilies are Asiatic hybrids that blaze with blossoms in early summer. Vigorous 3-foot-tall specimens, they multiply prolifically and quickly establish colonies in any location where the soil is well drained.

one variety is shorter than that of dahlias, modern hybridizers—working sometimes with the help of computers—have been able to offer a broad choice of types and colors to provide bloom in any part of the summer. If you make a selection of early, midseason and late-flowering varieties you can have lilies in your garden for four or five months. The other quality contributing to lilies' popularity, particularly for gardeners who like a minimum of work, is the plants' hardiness. All the modern hybrid lilies will survive cold winters outdoors in the garden anywhere in the United States and southern Canada; the bulbs, unlike those of most other summer-flowering bulbous plants, can be planted in either fall or early spring and do not have to be dug up and stored over winter.

In planting lilies, few home gardeners want—or can afford—to duplicate the vast displays seen in public arboretums and parks. This is just as well; lilies have often been called the aristocrats of the garden, and like aristocrats they are used to standing alone. They are striking in small groups, particularly if their statuesque stalks and bright, sculptured flowers are highlighted against a dark background of evergreens. But wherever a few lilies stand, they still draw the eye, and for this reason the taller varieties can be used with stunning effect to terminate a garden vista.

THE STATELY GLADIOLUSES   Although dahlias and lilies have been long-time favorites in gardens and as cut flowers, the all-round champion in the latter category is the gladiolus. It has been a mainstay of the florist trade for years; more land in the United States (some 20,000 acres) is devoted to the raising of gladioluses commercially than to any other bulb. The stately flower spikes, which range from 1 foot in height for the miniature strains to over 5 feet for the large-flowered types, come in every color of the rainbow, including blue. When considering gladioluses for the garden, you might bear in mind one small problem; the lower blossoms on each spike bloom and fade before the upper ones open, and unless you remove the blossoms as fast as they wither, gladioluses in a display bed or border tend to look unkempt. For this reason I grow mine in rows in a cutting garden near my vegetables, out of sight, and bring the flower spikes indoors just as the lower blossoms are beginning to open. Every few days I rearrange the flowers, pulling off the faded lower blooms as the upper ones open and shortening the stems until just the flowering tips are left to float in a shallow dish. Treated this way, gladioluses offer more color per stem than any other flower I know.

THE LUSH BEGONIAS   The fourth of the big four of summer-flowering bulbs is the tuberous begonia, widely popular like the other three but for different reasons. Tuberous begonias bear flowers more varied and colorful than most other summer-flowering bulbs. Some resemble roses, others camellias, others carnations; they come in flower sizes up to 10 inches across and in a brilliant sunset of colors from yellow and orange to pink and red, with pure white thrown in. And they can be kept in bloom even longer than lilies. They can be started indoors and brought outside to flower on a porch or patio from spring until frost. Moreover, since tuberous begonias are among the most colorful of shade-tolerant plants, they provide bright beauty for enjoyment at close range on a shady terrace or under trees, where most people like to sit on hot summer days. Among my favorites are hanging-basket begonias, *B. tuberhybrida pendula,* which can be hung from an eave or a low tree branch to provide a cascade of glowing hues in the shade of early evening. Tuberous begonias are virtually disease free, can be grown in pots or in wire or plastic containers *(drawings, page 68),* and produce an extraordinary harvest of blossoms that inevitably become a focal point, on a patio, next to a front door or wherever else they are placed.

But to limit your choices to even these four widely grown summer bulbs would be to miss some of the loveliest and most unusual flowers in the plant world. As you browse through the encyclopedia section, do not overlook the cannas, bold tropical plants with brilliant flowers and large leaves, or the lesser-known acidantheras, crocosmias, pineapple flowers and calla lilies, a quartet of handsome species native to Africa. Among other exceptional choices is the camassia, lovely but rugged and undemanding. A bulb that flowers in late spring and early summer, it is rarely seen in American gardens, although it was here to greet the first colonists and was prized by the Indians, who fried its bulbs, which are poisonous when raw, and ate them. (The name "camassia" derives from the Indian word "quamash," which is still used as one of its common names.) It grows everywhere from Pennsylvania to the Pacific Coast and from Minnesota to Texas; it produces starlike blue, purple or white blossoms atop stalks 1½ to 3 feet tall, and it enhances any border, rock garden, poolside or woodland where it is planted. Another interesting choice is the spider lily *(Hymenocallis),* which originated in the American tropics and will thrive in summer gardens, displaying clusters of long-stemmed white or yellow flowers and handsome foliage within a month after it has been planted. For cut flowers, there is the melodiously named chincherinchee *(Ornithogalum thyrsoides),* whose lovely cuplike blossoms, borne on stems that grow as long as 30 inches, will often last six weeks in a vase. At least 20 other summer-flowering bulbous plants from *Allium* (onion) to *Zantedeschia* (calla lily) also make good cut flowers, and some of them are almost as long lived as the chincherinchee. For

UNUSUAL SUMMER BULBS

shady spots, caladiums merit display in groupings of their own—not for their flowers, which are generally hidden, but for their huge variegated white, green and red leaves. Tuberoses, with their 3- to 4-foot-tall spikes of white flowers, are not only lovely but bring a gardenialike fragrance to the garden on summer evenings.

In choosing among the many summer bulbs, consider your own timetable as well as theirs. If you go away on a summer vacation at about the same time each year, pick bulbs of varieties that will bloom before you depart and others that will flower after you return. Whatever the dates, there are varieties that will fit your schedule—for example, in Zone 5 *(map, page 148)*, foxtail lilies *(Eremurus)* and some alliums will bloom in June, tigridias, tritonias and oxalises in July, acidantheras and tuberoses in August, zephyr lilies *(Zephyranthes)* in September. (For other choices, see the encyclopedia section and the timetables on pages 57 and 61. The encyclopedia does not list day lilies, peonies and the many irises that are not true bulbs; they occasionally appear in bulb catalogues but are generally treated as perennials.)

PLANTING SUMMER BULBS   Summer-flowering bulbs come from so many parts of the world and belong to so many genera that they have few things in common except that they bloom sometime between spring and fall.

PLANTING BULBS IN HANGING BASKETS

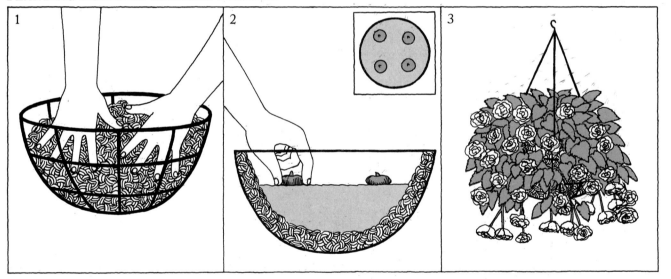

To display a trailing plant such as a tuberous begonia, line the inside of a wire or plastic plant basket with a 1- to 2-inch-thick layer of stringy sphagnum moss (not peat moss), and press the moss firmly into place.

Fill the lined basket two thirds full with a mixture of equal parts of potting soil, peat moss and sharp sand or perlite; then set three or four tubers on top as shown (inset) and cover them with ½ inch of mixture.

The bulb-filled basket will soon brim with flowers to make a beautiful show on a porch, on a partly shaded terrace or under trees. Water every day or two and feed monthly with liquid house-plant fertilizer.

Some, like most lilies and camassias, originated in cold climates and are hardy enough to survive winters outdoors anywhere in Zones 3-10. Others such as the caladium, which is native to the banks of jungle rivers in South America, are tender, or susceptible to cold; even their dormant tubers cannot stand temperatures that fall lower than 55°. In most of the United States such bulbs must be dug up in fall before the ground freezes if they are to be saved for flowering the next year. Resistance to cold—or the lack of it—determines not only how a bulb should be handled during winter but also when it should be set out to grow in the garden.

The encyclopedia specifies details for each bulb, but as a general rule, hardy summer bulbs should be planted at the same time as spring-flowering bulbs, that is, in the fall. All summer bulbs that in cold climates must be dug up and stored each fall—a category that includes gladioluses and dahlias as well as caladiums—must be planted in the spring, the precise time depending on the plant. Caladiums and tuberous begonias, for example, are so tender that they cannot safely be set out until night temperatures remain above 50°. Since this late planting time leaves far too short a summer for the plants to mature in the garden, they should be started indoors two months before dependably warm weather is due, then moved out in pots or planted in outdoor beds in the garden when the weather has become reliably mild.

Dahlias are generally planted outdoors as soon as the ground has warmed up and there is no further danger of frost. Gladioluses may be planted in series, a week to 10 days apart, continuing until mid-July—at least where I live in Massachusetts. As a more general rule, they may be planted until 60 days before the first expected frost—the gladiolus becomes virtually a year-round plant in frost-free areas. Successive plantings greatly extend the flowering season, since gladioluses of a single variety that are planted in series will bloom in the order in which they were planted. But some called "early blooming" take less time to flower than do those designated "midseason" or "late"—so three different varieties planted the same day may bloom weeks apart. By planting in sequence and using different varieties, the shrewd gardener can keep a supply of gladioluses available for cutting all summer long.

Like the spring bulbs, the summer bulbs adapt to almost any garden soil, as long as it is well drained. Work 2 to 3 inches of peat moss into the top 8 inches; in especially heavy clay soils, also dig in a 2-inch layer of coarse sand. Most lilies particularly abhor "wet feet" and will not tolerate standing water within their root zone, which in some varieties goes down as far as 2 feet below the surface. For this reason, many gardeners find it useful to set lilies in

WHERE TO PLANT

(continued on page 72)

Planting depths for summer bulbs

If you plant your bulbs too deep, they will exhaust themselves trying to reach the surface; if you plant them too shallow, they may dry out or be killed by frost. For a true bulb, such as a lily, or a corm, such as the gladiolus, the general rule of thumb is to plant so the bulb is covered with soil equal in depth to approximately three times the bulb's maximum diameter (measured from the surface of the soil to the shoulder, not the tip, of the bulb). But many summer bulbs are not true bulbs or corms, and exceptions to the rule exist even among those that are, so that proper planting depths vary considerably, as in-

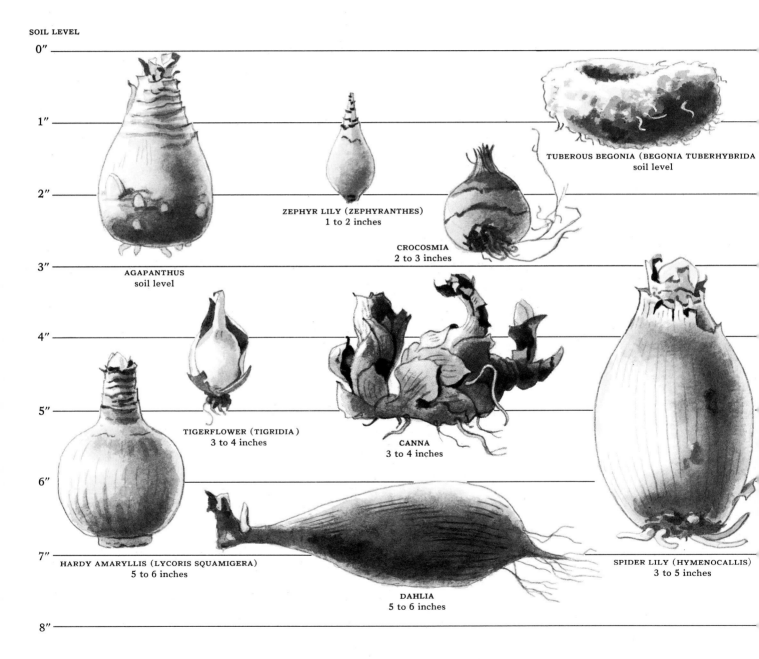

SOIL LEVEL

0"

1"

2"

3"

4"

5"

6"

7"

8"

9"

AGAPANTHUS
soil level

ZEPHYR LILY (ZEPHYRANTHES)
1 to 2 inches

CROCOSMIA
2 to 3 inches

TUBEROUS BEGONIA (BEGONIA TUBERHYBRIDA
soil level

TIGERFLOWER (TIGRIDIA)
3 to 4 inches

CANNA
3 to 4 inches

SPIDER LILY (HYMENOCALLIS)
3 to 5 inches

HARDY AMARYLLIS (LYCORIS SQUAMIGERA)
5 to 6 inches

DAHLIA
5 to 6 inches

70

dicated in the chart below of depths for 16 of the most common summer-flowering types. The fleshy rhizomes of the agapanthus, for instance, should be set upright just beneath the surface of the soil. The tubers of the glory lily, on the other hand, should lie horizontally and be covered with 4 to 5 inches of soil. Specific planting depths for other bulbs are listed in the encyclopedia section, Chapter 6. In very heavy clay soil plant the bulbs an inch or two shallower than specified, in very light sandy soil an inch or two deeper. But stay within this range or you will run a risk of getting no flower at all.

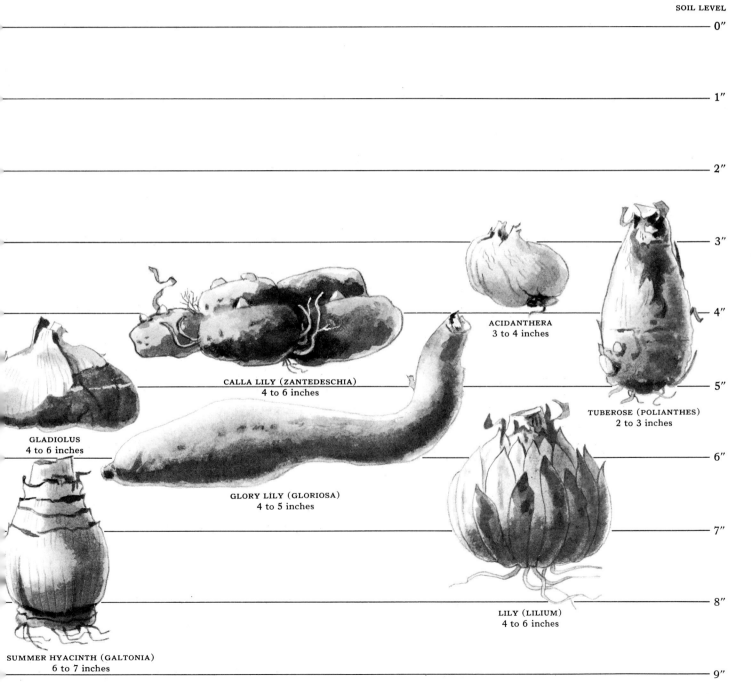

SOIL LEVEL

0"

1"

2"

3"

ACIDANTHERA
3 to 4 inches

4"

CALLA LILY (ZANTEDESCHIA)
4 to 6 inches

5"

TUBEROSE (POLIANTHES)
2 to 3 inches

GLADIOLUS
4 to 6 inches

6"

GLORY LILY (GLORIOSA)
4 to 5 inches

7"

8"

LILY (LILIUM)
4 to 6 inches

SUMMER HYACINTH (GALTONIA)
6 to 7 inches

9"

beds raised 8 to 12 inches higher than the surrounding soil and contained by sides of brick, stones or blocks. Most summer-flowering bulbs like sunshine, but some prefer partial shade, some thrive in cool, moist corners, and others grow in hot, dry beds. Even the part of the country in which you plant a bulb can affect its habits—the same bulb, for example, may demand shade in the heat of southern California or Texas but full sun in cooler Colorado. So it is wise to check the needs of each plant you choose in the encyclopedia section before locating it in the garden.

In locating your bulb beds, also bear in mind that strong winds present a danger to the taller bulbous plants, even if they are tied to stakes; a summer squall can ruin a beautiful stand of lilies or gladioluses, snapping them or knocking them over. Ideally such tall plants should be placed in the lee of a house, a garden wall or a clump of shrubs or trees that will provide protection from prevailing winds. Do not, however, put sun-loving plants too close to such shelter if it will put them into shade, for they should receive full sunshine for at least five or six hours a day.

CARE OF GROWING BULBS   Once the bulbs have been planted at their proper depth and spacing (chart, pages 70-71, and encyclopedia), they need only minimal care. During extended dry periods, when the foliage wilts and stays wilted for three days, the soil around the plants should be thoroughly watered. A mulch of 2 or 3 inches of wood chips, ground bark or other organic material should be applied to keep the soil cool and moist and to discourage weeds, particularly around lilies, dahlias, gladioluses, tigridias and cannas. Insects and diseases are not usually troublesome; the chart on pages 150 and 151 tells how to cope with them if they attack.

In windy places, stake plants that grow more than 3 feet tall by tying them to plant stakes made of bamboo, wood or heavy wire. I like wire stakes the best because they are more flexible than other kinds and bend a bit with the breeze, easing the strain on the stems of the plants; being thinner, they are also less conspicuous. Put the stakes in the ground while planting the bulbs; to wait until plants are well grown is to risk damaging bulbs or their root systems when you thrust the bottom tips of the stakes into the soil. When plants have reached about two thirds of their full height, use soft green garden twine or plastic-covered wire twists to tie them gently to the stakes, placing one tie a few inches above the halfway point on the stem, the other a few inches below the lowest blossom. Tie the twine tightly to the stake, then loop it loosely around the plant and tie it again; a tight binding around the stem itself would constrict the plant as it grows.

At least once a season I give my bulbous plants a feeding. Summer bulbs vary in their needs for nutrients—true bulbs such as lilies, which remain in the ground year after year taking their nourishment from the soil, require a slow-acting organic fertilizer such as bone meal that releases its nutrients over a long period of time. On the other hand, plants that are in the ground only half the year or less should be given a quicker-acting chemical fertilizer such as 5-10-5. Where plants grow in rows, as most of my dahlias and gladioluses do, scatter 5-10-5 in a 12- to 18-inch-wide strip on each side of each row, using ½ pound of fertilizer on each 100-foot-long strip, that is, 1 pound per 100-foot row of flowers. Repeat this feeding once a month until you can see the color of the flowers as the buds start to open. For smaller plantings, apply a dusting of 5-10-5 to the soil around each plant in a circular band, beginning about 6 inches from the stem and extending outward another 12 inches, up to 18 inches in the case of larger plants. In either case the fertilizer should be scratched into the soil with a hoe or spading fork and then watered, for it remains useless until dissolved. For plants that have been protected by a mulch, scatter the fertilizer on the mulch and water it into the soil.

In cases where plants have pale leaves or are not making the growth they should make, I give them a quick energy boost by applying a fertilizer to the leaves rather than the ground around the

MAKING A WALL PLANTER

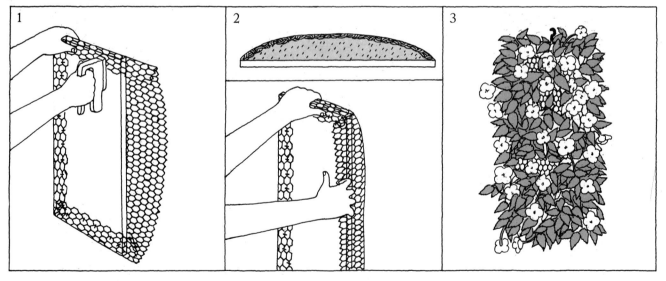

For a distinctive and decorative display of trailing achimenes, wrap 1-inch chicken wire over a 1-by-2-foot board, bowing the mesh out 4 inches, and staple it to the back at the top, bottom and one side.

Line the mesh with moist sphagnum moss; stuff equal parts of damp peat moss and perlite inside it (top drawing); then fold the open side of the mesh back over the board and staple to form a firm cushion.

To cover the planter with flowers, insert the rhizomes at 6-inch intervals through the mesh into the peat moss mixture. Keep moist and feed about twice a month with half-strength house-plant fertilizer.

plant. Mix this foliar fertilizer with water as the manufacturer directs and spray on the plants' foliage; the solution will drip off the leaves onto the ground to feed the roots as well.

CUTTING FLOWERS

When you want to cut flowers for the house, choose blooms that are neither full-blown nor tight buds; buds just opening are best because they will last longest. Cut the stems with a sharp knife, and leave as much of the foliage as possible on the plants; they will need it for further growth. Plants such as spider lilies that have bare, leafless stalks should be severed an inch or two above ground level; a flowerless, leafless half-stem is neither useful nor sightly.

Cut flowers early in the morning or, even better, late in the afternoon to prolong their lives indoors—flowers cut in the heat of the midday sun do not survive as well. After cutting, immerse the stems immediately in deep, warm water (about 100°) and place them in a cool location for a few hours—overnight is better. Keep the flowers upright in a vase if you want the stems to remain straight. The flowers should get fresh water once a day; at the same time a bit of the stems should be removed to expose fresh cells for water absorption. Cut flowers will last longer if they are kept out of direct sun in a relatively cool place.

As I suggested in Chapter 3, you do not have to be timid about cutting flowers. It is good for the bulbs, freeing them of the drain on their energies that the production of seed imposes, and it permits them to fatten themselves for the next year. For this reason, flowers that are not cut for indoor arrangement should be removed as soon as they fade so that they do not go to seed.

FLOWERS FOR EXHIBITION

Many an amateur gardener, while cutting dahlias, lilies or gladioluses in his garden, has been struck by the extraordinary beauty of a particular bloom as he severed it from the plant. The thought has entered his mind: I'll bet this one could win a prize. That is how many gardeners, as they become more proficient at growing bulbs, decide to try raising flowers expressly for exhibition. Despite the stories you may hear, it is not difficult, and a blue ribbon at a local flower show or county fair can be quite a thrill. And remember, just because a flower is not perfect does not mean it will not win a prize; it only has to be the best one exhibited at that particular show.

In raising flowers for competition, all you need do is follow a few guidelines.

First, buy absolutely top-grade bulbs, and carefully observe the requirements for planting depths, drainage needs, fertilizing and watering. You should guard particularly against the temptation to overfertilize, however; many an anxious or overeager amateur gives his plants an extra shot or two for good measure, only to find that this encourages coarse blooms or excessive foliage and few flowers.

Timing, of course, is important if you are to have blossoms at their best on the date of the show. In the case of gladioluses, many bulb catalogues give the average number of days to flowering for the particular variety you intend to exhibit. You can bracket your target date by counting back this number of days from the date of the show, then making three plantings, one on the indicated starting date, one five days before and one five days after; out of this coverage you are almost bound to get flowers at the peak of bloom on the day you want them. In the case of dahlias, the first few blossoms on a plant usually make the best ones for exhibition purposes; later ones are generally more profuse but of a smaller size. Plants set out between the middle of June and the first of July usually produce their biggest flowers during September, when many flower shows are held.

Stick a wooden or plastic plant label in the ground next to each plant with the planting date and the name of the variety on it; if you cannot remember the plant's exact varietal name you cannot enter it in most serious flower shows.

Plant each plant a little farther than normal from its neighbor so that it has extra room to grow in; plants set close together compete for nutrients in the soil and the lack of space and air circulation among them can encourage disease.

A mulch around the plants is desirable, particularly for dahlias, which like plenty of moisture constantly in the soil (the Aztec name for the dahlia in its native Mexico was *acocotli,* meaning "water pipe"). A 2- to 3-inch layer of peat moss, pine needles or wood chips will not only retain moisture for the shallow-growing roots but will also prevent the soil from being compacted as you walk around tending the plants.

Shield exhibition plants from wind and stake them securely. Shade at midday also helps; where summer sun is intense, show-winning gardeners often protect the emerging blossoms from wilting or bleaching and losing their delicate colors by erecting a light screening of lath strips or cheesecloth above the plants, high enough to permit good air circulation.

To get the largest and best-nourished dahlia blossoms, cut off all but the strongest and healthiest main stem if the tuber produces more than one; then, after two sets of leaves have developed on this stem, pinch off the growing tip between your thumb and forefinger. This will force the development of four lateral flower-bearing stems, each of which will produce a cluster of flowers unless they are disbudded. To disbud them, pinch off all but the center bud on each stem as the buds appear. The nourishment that would have gone to the other flowers will then be concentrated on the single

BULBS: EDIBLE AND TOXIC

Bulbous plants are among the most popular of foodstuffs. Onions, potatoes and radishes are staples of the modern kitchen. South American Indians eat starchy roots of a species of canna, and Pacific Islanders build their diet around the tubers of Colocasia esculenta, known as elephant's-ear or taro.

But many other bulbs are deadly poisons, among them autumn crocus (Colchicum) and lily of the valley (Convallaria). Others such as crinums, glory lilies (Gloriosa), ranunculuses and zephyr lilies (Zephyranthes) are toxic in varying degrees. And yet one poisonous bulb is an important foodstuff in South America. It is cassava (Manihot esculenta), a tuber that contains deadly amounts of prussic acid until cooked; after cooking it can be ground into a coarse meal or made into tapioca pudding, both of which are perfectly safe, nutritious foods.

show bloom on each stem. In midsummer, it usually takes about a month from the appearance of the original four laterals to the opening of the first flowers on the plant.

A couple of days before you intend to cut show blossoms, water the plants thoroughly to make sure they will be as healthy and full of moisture as possible. The evening of the day before the show, take your vase or a pail of water to the garden, cut the best flowers that are almost completely open, and plunge the stems immediately into the water. Take the flowers to a cool, dark place such as a basement, cut off the leaves that remain on the stems underwater and leave the flowers in the water overnight. The next day put the flowers in bright indirect sunlight, which will help them draw up as much water as possible, then cut the stems once more by a fraction of an inch, before taking the flowers, still in water, to the show.

STORING SUMMER BULBS   Once the flowering season is over, some attention must be given to winter care. In cooler climates, summer-flowering bulbs that do not qualify as winter hardy—and that means most summer bulbs—must be dug up and stored as frost approaches (unless, of course, you are willing to sacrifice the bulbs and buy new ones next year). The time to dig is when the foliage has thoroughly withered or has been browned by frost.

WINTER STORAGE FOR SUMMER BULBS

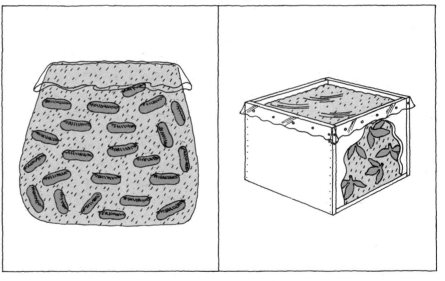

Summer-flowering bulbs are easily kept in plastic bags, with enough dry peat moss, vermiculite or perlite to separate them. Fold the top of the bag but do not seal; keep it in a cool, dry place (55° to 60°).

Bulbs such as dahlia roots must be kept at 40° to 45° to prevent sprouting. Store in the same material in a box lined and covered with plastic film, then tip the transparent top against a cool basement wall.

For gladioluses, tuberous begonias, acidantheras and other bulbs that become completely dormant in cool-climate winters, cold-weather care is relatively easy. When the bulbs have been dug up, allow them to dry for a week or two in a shaded, well-ventilated place such as a garage or tool shed. Then remove any clinging soil with your fingers. Place the bulbs in a paper bag with a small amount of fungicide powder and shake them; the thin coating of powder each gets will help prevent rot during storage. If you have a relatively small number of bulbs to store—a dozen large begonia tubers or as many as a hundred tiny achimenes rhizomes—place them in plastic or paper bags with enough dry peat moss, vermiculite or perlite to keep the bulbs from touching one another; separating them this way prevents the spread of decay if one bulb rots. Do not seal the bags; simply fold over the tops. Larger numbers of bulbs can be buried in open boxes or wooden flats filled with peat moss, vermiculite or perlite, with the bulbs spaced so that they do not touch. Cover the boxes or flats with insect screening; this will protect the bulbs from hungry mice while allowing them to get ample ventilation.

Storage temperatures for bulbs should range between 45° and 60°. Below 55° achimenes, for example, suffer fatal chills, and at much above 45° dahlias may sprout prematurely or rot. Now that root cellars and house cellars with earthen floors are rare, finding a good storage area for summer bulbs is not always easy. Most modern cellars are too warm and too dry. Unheated garages are too cold. Heated garages kept at 55° are ideal, but not every gardener has one. In your search for the right place, a minimum-maximum thermometer may prove helpful. This is a device with a U-shaped column of mercury that records the high and low temperatures reached in a given period and retains the record until the thermometer is reset. If you hang it in a few places in the cellar or the attic, moving it daily, you probably will find one or more that meet the temperature specifications. I discovered such a spot for my dahlia roots at the cool cellar wall farthest from the furnace. I line boxes with sheets of plastic, tack plastic instead of insect screening over the boxes to keep the material in, then tilt the tops of the boxes up tightly against the wall; the more or less stable temperature there, plus the insulation of the vermiculite or perlite in the boxes, keeps the dahlia roots at a perfect 40° to 45° through the winter and into spring. For my other bulbs, I partitioned off an area of the cellar and insulated it against the heat of the furnace. The plastic bags and covered boxes ensure that the mice will not beat me to them. After all, having gone to the trouble of planting my bulbs, taking care of them, and then packing them away to rest, I do look forward to enjoying them again next year!

Plants for fall and winter bloom 5

When early autumn's gusts begin to tumble the leaves from the trees and only a few of the late summer bulbs still flower in the waning sun, my garden suddenly becomes young again. White, lavender and rosy purple blossoms up to 8 inches across open on the leafless stems of the colchicum, which is confusingly called the autumn crocus though it is not a crocus. True crocuses of the autumn-flowering variety, rose tinted, white and pale lavender, pop up nearby, to the surprise of visitors who do not know there are crocuses that bloom in fall. Dainty yellow blossoms of sternbergias, surrounded by glossy leaves, glow in an ever-widening band around the base of an oak. Rose-lilac clusters of what look like lilies linger on the 3-foot stems of the lycoris, or hardy amaryllis.

All of these flowers are only part of the evidence that the blooming season of bulbs never ends. When they fade, I know that there will be others, alive and growing indoors, to grace the Christmas dinner table and brighten the windows on dark February days. And if I lived in a warmer climate than that of Massachusetts, almost anywhere in Zones 9-10, I could have such beauties as the gloriosa lily, the dahlia and the gladiolus growing outdoors in my garden almost the whole winter through.

Not counting these latter types of bulbs—which are covered in the preceding chapter because they are summer flowering in most parts of the country—there are four categories of fall- and winter-flowering bulbs. One group embraces those that, like the colchicum and the autumn-flowering crocus, grow and bloom naturally outdoors in September and October, even in the cooler climates of Zones 3-7. The second group consists of daffodils, hyacinths and other bulbs that normally are spring flowering in the garden but that can be induced to blossom in midwinter indoors. Once brought to bloom earlier than their normal season, bulbs of this type cannot be induced to flower again indoors the following year, for the procedure strains their resources to the utmost. But they do not have to be thrown away, for they can recover in the garden. The third

A Dutch hyacinth bulb, cut in half, reveals a perfectly formed embryonic flower surrounded by layers of nourishing tissue. The bulbs normally bloom in spring but can be induced to flower indoors in winter.

group includes plants such as the amaryllis of the *Hippeastrum* genus and the tazetta narcissus, which will blossom outdoors in fall and winter in very mild climates, like those of Zones 9-10, but must be grown indoors in pots wherever the ground freezes. The fourth group includes delicate bulbs of tropical origin such as gloxinias and smithianthas, which can stand no winter chill at all and must be treated as indoor house plants. Because their requirements differ, this chapter will deal with the various categories separately.

OUTDOOR AUTUMN BULBS   The bulbs that can be counted on to add color to a fall garden range from extremely hardy ones that defy sub-zero weather (they are the ones that can be left in the ground the year round, even in Zones 3-7) to tender ones that cannot stand even a touch of frost (after flowering, they must be dug up and stored indoors over winter in Zones 3-8). They differ in the times at which they can be purchased—crocosmias in spring, for example, lycoris in midsummer, colchicums and autumn-flowering crocuses in August, and some cyclamens virtually all year. (The cyclamens most suitable for outdoor culture are not the large-flowered tender variety that florists display but several small-flowered species—see the encyclopedia, page 109—that are winter hardy even in cold climates.) But two pieces of advice apply to them all: order your bulbs early, to ensure good quality and to avoid disappointment, because the demand may exceed the supply; and plant them as soon as possible after you receive them. Speedy planting helps bulbs do their best by giving them maximum time to establish themselves before blooming time arrives; because colchicums and autumn-flowering crocuses bloom so early in fall, they in particular must be put in the ground immediately. When dealers receive them in August, the bulbs already are on the verge of bursting into bloom, and if they lie around unplanted for a few days, they may start flowering wherever they are. Such prematurely blooming bulbs will not do well when you finally get them in the garden.

But if you purchase your fall bulbs as you do your spring and summer bulbs—choosing firm, heavy specimens devoid of soft spots and blemishes—and if you plant them promptly, you can hardly miss. After they have bloomed, dig up frost-susceptible bulbs and store them until the next planting time. Leave the hardy bulbs undisturbed in the soil to multiply and bloom year after year.

SPRING FLOWERS IN WINTER   Some varieties of virtually all the spring-flowering bulbs, including tulips, hyacinths, crocuses, daffodils and bulbous irises, can be persuaded to bloom indoors in winter as shown on page 85, bringing the garden into the house from early January through April. Commercial flower growers and a good many amateurs refer to the techniques as "forcing." Though I use the term myself, I rather dislike it, for no force is involved. The procedures consist, broadly, of manipulating temperatures and light conditions to simulate the period of cold needed by bulbs for their annual rest period, then awakening them earlier than they would wake by themselves if they were outdoors. The techniques for forcing should not be confused with the care of regular house plants that are allowed to bloom in their own good time indoors.

Purchase bulbs for indoor forcing as soon as they come on the market in late summer or early fall; bulbs ordered from a catalogue will be shipped at the correct time. Buy only varieties recommended for forcing, for not all kinds lend themselves to it. Unpack the bulbs as soon as you get them, and pot them as soon as possible. If you cannot pot them immediately, keep them in a cool, dark place (55° to 60°) until you can.

Many of the spring bulbs, including hyacinths and crocuses, can simply be grown in pebbles and water like the tazetta narcissuses (drawings, page 83) or even in water alone. A way that has been popular since Victorian times involves setting individual bulbs in a so-called hyacinth glass, a short vase shaped somewhat like an eggcup or hourglass; the upper cup of the glass keeps the bulb dry and free from rot while allowing the roots to grow into the water in the compartment below. Because the glass allows you to see the roots taking form, this method of forcing a bulb to flower makes an easy and instructive project for a child. However, once a bulb has been grown in plain water, without nutrients, it will have completely exhausted itself and must be discarded.

All bulbs do better when grown in soil, or a soil-based potting mixture. It need not be rich, but it should have an open structure to allow good drainage, as well as some organic matter to conserve moisture. You can use ordinary packaged potting soil bought at a garden center, or a mixture of 1 part packaged potting soil or ordinary garden loam, 1 part peat moss and 1 part perlite or vermiculite. Bulbs have sufficient reserve food to produce good flowers without fertilizer, but if you want to save your bulbs for planting in the garden later on, you should add a small amount of fertilizer to rebuild their strength after flowering. I generally use a level teaspoonful of 5-10-5 dry fertilizer to each quart of potting soil or mixture, stirring it in thoroughly before potting the bulbs.

Either clay or plastic pots serve for bulbs. Hyacinths are often planted individually in standard flower pots because a single plant makes a handsome display; most other bulbs, however, look better planted in groups in the broader, shallower pots called pans or bulb pans, which are half as high as they are wide. Pans not only provide more space with less height than standard pots but do not

SAFFRON COOKIES

Saffron, undoubtedly the world's most expensive spice ($20 or more an ounce), is made from the dried stigmas of the autumn-flowering crocus, Crocus sativus. Cooks value it both as a flavoring and as a yellow food coloring in recipes such as the following, which will make about six dozen saffron cookies. The cookies are not as costly as the price of saffron might suggest —the quantity required in the recipe, ¼ teaspoonful, costs less than 30 cents.

1 cup softened butter
¾ cup sugar
1 egg
¼ teaspoon ground saffron soaked in 1 tablespoon hot water
2½ cups flour
½ teaspoon baking powder
⅛ teaspoon salt

Cream the butter and sugar together until they are light and fluffy. Beat in the egg, then the saffron and water. Gradually sift in the flour, baking powder and salt. Refrigerate until firm. Shape small pieces of the dough into balls, place on baking sheet and flatten into round cookies with the back of a fork. Bake at 400° for 7 to 10 minutes.

tip over easily—a frequent problem with potted plants that grow tall. If you use clay pans or pots, soak them overnight before you begin planting, so that they will not absorb moisture from the growing medium and deprive the plants. Clay or plastic pots that have been used before should be washed thoroughly to remove vestiges of old soil that may carry disease agents.

Bulbs should not be buried deeply, but set so their tips just reach the surface of the soil, which should be ½ to 1 inch below the rim of the pot. Do not press the bulbs into the soil; fill the pot part way first, putting in only enough soil to hold the bulb at the proper level, and firm this soil down. Then set the bulbs on top and fill in more soil around them to cover them. Finally, water thoroughly. Some bulbs, notably tulips, have a flat side and a round side; the flat side should face outward toward the rim of the pot so that the largest leaf, which sprouts from the flat side, will grow gracefully over the edge of the pot.

Spring bulbs that are going to be forced should be potted in September or October and put in a place where their roots will grow and where they will have increasingly cool temperatures. If you live in a warm climate such as that of Zones 8-10, you will have to simulate the needed cold period by storing the bulbs for a month or two in a refrigerator before potting. If you live anywhere else you can simply bury the pots outdoors or put them in a cold frame, a low outdoor enclosure with a movable top designed to serve as a miniature unheated greenhouse. For ideal chilling, the bulbs should be kept at about 50° for three or four weeks in order to form a good root system, followed by temperatures that eventually drop close to freezing (about 33° to 35°). This entire

(continued on page 86)

Bulbs to grow indoors

Of all the bulbs that will flower out of season indoors, the easiest and most rewarding to grow are the three types shown on the following pages: tender tazetta narcissuses such as the paper-white type at right as well as the Grand Soleil d'Or and Chinese sacred lily, the amaryllises of the genus Hippeastrum and such hardy spring bulbs as crocuses, tulips, hyacinths, daffodils and squills. All can provide bright flowers during the dark months, from December or January to early spring. But each type has its own habits and needs. Tazetta narcissuses, for example, can be grown without soil, but these bulbs exhaust themselves and are not worth saving after they bloom. Amaryllises and spring bulbs, on the other hand, are best grown in an enriched potting mixture. The amaryllises may be kept as house plants for years; it is good practice to hose out some of the soil each spring and replace it without disturbing the roots. Hardy spring bulbs can be brought into flower indoors only once, but they may be knocked out of their pots when the leaves have matured and set in the garden the following fall to return to their normal outdoor blooming habits.

Paper-whites
for Christmas

These tazetta narcissuses (paper-whites) can be put into pots in September to blossom before Christmas. Bulbs started in midwinter are more developed and will bloom in six weeks. Plant at 10-day intervals through February, for three months of flowers.

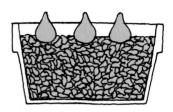

1. Fill a pot or bowl—one without a drainage hole—to within 2 inches of its rim with pebbles, pearl chips, coconut fiber, charcoal or coarse sand and saturate the potting material with water. Bury the bottom quarter of the narcissus bulb, keeping its base above the water line. Space the bulbs about 1 inch apart if you are planting them in groups.

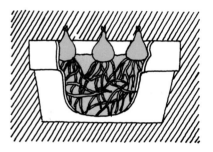

2. Set the container in a cool (about 50°), dark and well-ventilated location for several weeks. Check the water level occasionally with your finger tip; it should be just beneath the base of the bulb, but not touching it. Keep the roots in water as the bulbs begin to sprout; the roots will shrivel and die quickly if they are allowed to become dry.

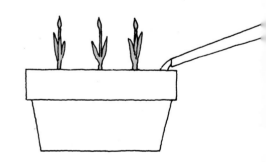

3. When pale green shoots become 3 or 4 inches tall, move the pot to the bright indirect light of a north window or curtain-shielded south window for three or four days. Then set the pot in sun, and move it back to indirect light when the flowers open. Keep the roots moist and rotate the pot occasionally. Discard after the flowers fade.

Amaryllises
all winter

1. *Cover the pot's drainage hole with a curved piece from a broken clay pot. Fill to within 1 inch of the rim with the enriched potting mixture recommended for Hippeastrum on page 119. Plant the bulb so that half of it is buried in the mix.*

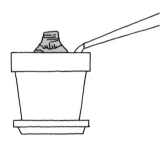

2. *Firm the soil and drench it. Do not water again until the bulb sprouts. Move it into the sun; begin regular watering.*

3. *When the plant flowers, move it out of direct sunlight to preserve the blossoms. Feed monthly with house-plant fertilizer as long as the foliage remains green.*

Amaryllises bloom year after year indoors, thriving best when the roots crowd the pots. They are large in size and require pots 2 to 4 inches wider than the bulbs. Their blossoms appear in about two to four weeks. Planted from October to March, they bloom from December to April.

4. *When flowers fade, cut the stems to 2 inches and set the pot in bright sunlight. Do not remove leaves until they wither.*

Spring bulbs
for the new year

Spring bulbs such as the crocuses, hyacinths and tulips above will flower indoors from January to April provided they are exposed to cold first (drawings, right). Groups look best in shallow bulb pans, but single hyacinths are often grown in standard 3- or 4-inch pots.

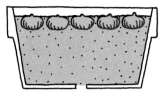

1. Using packaged potting soil enriched with 5-10-5 fertilizer at the rate of 1 level teaspoon to 1 quart of soil (enough for a 5-inch pot), fill the bulb pan or pot to within 1 to 3 inches of the rim—leave enough room for covering the bulbs—and add water. Firm the potting soil and rest the bulbs on top of it, spacing them about ½ inch apart. Then add more soil until only the tips of the bulbs show through the surface. Water the pot thoroughly.

2. Place the pans or pots in a cold frame. Cover them with 3 or 4 inches of perlite or shredded styrofoam, carefully filling all of the spaces between them. Keep the sash wide open for about a month after the first fall frost, then close it to prevent the bulbs from freezing. Leave the early-flowering bulb varieties outdoors for at least 12 weeks, late-flowering ones for 16 weeks, to allow their roots to develop. No further watering is necessary.

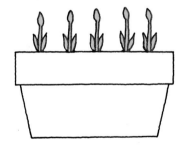

3. After the specified time, transfer the pans to a cool (50° to 55°), airy place indoors with indirect sunlight for a week or two. When the shoots are 4 to 6 inches tall, move the pans to a sunny window. When the buds take on color, move the plants back into indirect sunlight to make the blossoms last. Snip off flower stems when the flowers fade, but let the leaves grow to maturity if you plan to set the bulbs into the garden in fall.

preparation period should cover at least 12 weeks for bulbs such as hyacinths, crocuses and daffodils—which naturally bloom early in spring and for this reason are easier to force—and up to 15 or 16 weeks for later-flowering types such as tulips.

Bulbs set outdoors must be covered to keep them from freezing so that you will not have to pry them out of hard ground in mid-winter. If you bury your pots, embed them up to their rims in coarse sand and cover them with a 4- to 6-inch layer of soil plus a 4- to 6-inch blanket of an insulating mulch such as salt hay or wood chips. I prefer to use a cold frame, setting the pots in it and filling in around them and covering them 3 to 4 inches deep with perlite or shredded styrofoam; either material offers good insulation and can easily be removed. Pots should be thoroughly watered before being placed in the ground or cold frame; they will require no further moisture until they are brought indoors.

When the essential 12 to 16 weeks have passed, take indoors only as many pots as you wish to flower shortly; by bringing in successive groups of pots, you can space out the period of indoor bloom. As you remove the insulating material from the pots, be careful not to injure the new shoots, which may have pushed up an inch or two above the surface of the potting soil. Put the pots in a cool room—as close to 50° to 55° as possible—and in indirect light, not full sun. Keep the plants in these conditions for 10 days to two weeks. When the shoots are 4 to 6 inches tall, shift the pots to the coolest sunny window sill available and leave them there until the buds show color. At that point, put the plants back in indirect light and keep them as cool as possible, especially at night, to extend the life of the flowers. Throughout their indoor growth and bloom, keep the plants well watered. Each pot of bulbs thus treated will stay in flower for a week to 10 days. When the flowers disappear, snip off the stems but not the leaves, return the pots to the coolest sunny place in the house and water the bulbs less and less frequently—just enough to keep the leaves green until they wither. The bulbs can be left in the pots while dormant if the soil is kept dry, or removed from the pots and stored in a dry, well-ventilated place at 60° to 70° until the normal fall planting season. When you plant them, set them where they will be relatively inconspicuous, for they may not flower well, or at all, the following spring. After two or three seasons, however, they will have recovered their vigor and can be moved to a more prominent garden location.

THE INDOOR-OUTDOOR BULBS   In the third category of bulbs—the so-called tender ones that can be grown outdoors in winter in Zones 9-10 but cannot survive winters in the ground in northern regions—are many that will bloom indoors ahead of their normal season. Among the most cooperative are the tender tazetta narcissuses called paper-white, Soleil d'Or and Chinese sacred lily. The fact that such bulbs take to indoor growth readily is hardly surprising, since conditions in today's well-heated houses differ from the mild climates in which the plants normally grow outdoors; some tazettas, for example, are native to the south of France, where winters are not cold enough to freeze them, but sufficiently chilly to inhibit flowering before spring. If you plant the bulbs in groups at 10-day intervals beginning in September, you can enjoy their blooms indoors for three months. Since they are so easy to grow *(page 83),* I consider them excellent specimens for the beginner to experiment with. Inexpensive bulbs, they are generally grown in an inert, nonnutritive material such as pebbles or pearl chips, and are discarded after flowering.

Although I am fond of the tazettas, my favorite among the tender bulbs for indoor culture is the amaryllis (*Hippeastrum,* not other plants also called amaryllis); it produces huge, handsome flowers and in enriched potting soil will blossom year after year with only a modest amount of care. The growing technique, shown on page 84, applies to other tender bulbs such as sprekelias. Amaryllises are relatively expensive, as bulbs go, but I think it is worth buying the biggest and best bulbs I can find for the biggest and most spectacular blooms. I know I will get my money's worth.

In the fourth category are two of the most beautiful of the bulbous plants, the gloxinia and the smithiantha, or temple bells. Since these are of tropical origin, they are grown as house plants the year round everywhere in the United States. The gloxinia, happily, can be brought into bloom at virtually any time of the year and is ideal for winter culture. The process takes from two to four months from potting to flowering, since the period of dormancy of one bulb is not always the same as another. So, to be sure of having Christmas color, plant gloxinia bulbs in late summer. The smithiantha starts flowering in summer but continues to bloom well into winter. Growing instructions are simple and are given in the encyclopedia.

BULBOUS HOUSE PLANTS

Indoors or outdoors, even the most dedicated gardeners will have space for only a few of the many fall- and winter-flowering bulbs, or the other bulbs I have discussed in this book. But even a few can be a source of continuing delight. Before the last planting of paper-white narcissuses finishes blooming on my window sill, the outdoor bulbs of early spring—pristine snowdrops, golden winter aconites, clumps of sky-blue grape hyacinths and squills—are beginning to push their way through the lingering patches of snow in my garden. They are my guarantee that spring is here regardless of the weather, and that the bright circling year of bulb flowers has once again begun.

An illustrated encyclopedia of bulbs 6

Which bulbs are likely to thrive in your garden? Can they stay in the ground all year, or must they be dug up in fall? When should you plant them, and how? These are a few of the questions that are answered in the following encyclopedia, which lists the characteristics, uses and requirements of 85 genera of bulbous plants.

Each entry specifies the climate zones in which the bulb is hardy—that is, where it can withstand winter cold; these recommended growing areas are keyed to the zone map on page 148. Two additional maps on page 149 show the average dates of the last frost in spring and the first frost in fall, to guide you as to when to plant and dig up bulbs and when to move potted plants indoors and out. Unless otherwise stated in the entries, the plants described will grow in ordinary well-drained garden soil; to assure good drainage, dig 2 to 3 inches of peat moss into the top 8 to 10 inches of soil. Space the bulbs as specified in the entries, measuring from the center of one to the center of the next. Unless an entry states otherwise, the general rules for fertilizing bulbs apply: If the bulb is to be left in the ground over winter, mix bone meal into the soil at planting time at a rate of 5 to 6 pounds per 100 square feet; repeat each fall, scratching fertilizer into the soil. If the bulb must be dug up each fall, use 1 pound of high-phosphorus fertilizer such as 5-10-5 per 100 square feet at planting time; repeat this feeding every two or three weeks from the time the plant sprouts until buds take on color. Most bulbs do not require special watering but if foliage stays wilted for three days, give the plants a thorough soaking.

The plants are listed alphabetically by their internationally recognized Latin botanical names; for example, the white Chinese ground orchid, *Bletilla striata alba,* is listed under the genus name *Bletilla;* the species name *striata* is followed by the varietal name *alba,* meaning white. Common names, which often vary from region to region, are cross-referenced to their Latin equivalents. For quick reference, a chart of the characteristics and uses of the bulbs illustrated appears on pages 152-154.

The extraordinary range of floral colors and shapes offered by bulbs, both in gardens and indoors, is shown in this painting by Allianora Rosse, which groups 28 of the plants described in the following chapter.

MAGIC FLOWER
Achimenes 'Master Ingram'

ACIDANTHERA
Acidanthera bicolor murielae

A

ACHIMENES

A. heterophylla 'Yellow Mist,' *A.* hybrids.
(All called magic flower, nut orchid, widow's-tear)

From spring through fall, achimenes bear masses of colorful 1- to 2½-inch-wide blossoms, often with handsome veining in their throats. They are extremely delicate and are usually grown in containers because they require warm temperatures throughout their growing season. They are widely grown in greenhouses and as indoor pot plants and are also suited for outdoor pot culture on shaded porches or patios when night temperatures remain above 60°. Their slender stems, which may trail up to 18 inches, make them especially attractive in hanging baskets.

Among the many choices is an excellent yellow variety of the species *A. heterophylla* called Yellow Mist. Most of the plants cultivated today, however, are hybrids; the best include Adelaide (pastel blue); Charm (deep pink); Master Ingram, also called Cardinal Velvet (deep red with a yellow throat); Purple King (deep purple); and Sparkle (a bright rose-pink dwarf variety).

HOW TO GROW. Achimenes do best outdoors in light shade and indoors in bright indirect or curtain-filtered sunlight, and also thrive with 14 to 16 hours a day of artificial light from the special fluorescent lamps used for house plants. Night temperatures of 65° to 70° and day temperatures of 75° or higher are ideal. Pot in a mixture of 2 parts peat moss to 1 part packaged potting soil and 1 part sharp sand or perlite, with ground limestone added at a rate of 3 to 5 ounces per bushel. Plant the rhizomes in late winter or early spring, covering them with ½ to 1 inch of soil. Keep moist and feed monthly during the growing season with a standard house-plant fertilizer at half strength. After flowering, the plants should be allowed to die down to the soil. Leave the dormant rhizomes in the pot or sift them out and store in dry vermiculite, peat moss or perlite. Keep them at 60° from October through February.

Achimenes can be propagated during dormancy from tiny underground rhizomes or from those that occasionally appear at the leaf joints. Break these into ½-inch pieces and plant six to eight pieces in a 6- to 8-inch clay pot; each will produce a flowering-sized plant in about two months. New plants can also be propagated from seeds or stem cuttings in spring. Seedlings require about three months at 70° before they are large enough to blossom.

ACIDANTHERA

A. bicolor; A. bicolor murielae, also called *A. murielae; A. hybrida tubergenii*

Acidantheras, native to Ethiopia, are close relatives of gladioluses, and they look it. They grow from corms, sending up tall spikes that bear delightfully scented, creamy white flowers that open in sequence from the bottom of each spike, often blossoming from August until October. Plants are highly effective grouped in clusters of a dozen or so in borders, or close to the house where their fragrance is particularly welcome. They also make splendid cut flowers. *A. bicolor* grows 1½ to 2 feet tall and has especially fragrant 2-inch-wide flowers with chocolate-brown centers; *A. bicolor murielae,* the most common acidanthera in cultivation, grows 2½ to 3½ feet tall and has flowers up to 4 inches across, with red to purple center markings. A cross of these two plants, *A. hybrida tubergenii,* is similar to *A. bicolor,* except that its flowers open three weeks earlier and the central markings are reddish. Removing faded flowers encourages the spikes to branch, giving more blossoms and extending the flowering season.

HOW TO GROW. In Zones 7-10 acidantheras can be left in

the ground over winter or dug up and stored as they must be from Zone 6 north. Plant the corms in spring after all danger of frost has passed. Plants do best in full sun and should be grown in sheltered spots protected from high winds. Space the corms 6 to 9 inches apart and cover them with 3 to 4 inches of soil that has been enriched with compost or well-rotted cow manure. Apply a light dusting of 5-10-5 fertilizer when the plants emerge and again three to four weeks later.

Since they require a long growing season, it is advisable from Zone 6 north to plant the corms indoors in pots or in a cold frame about a month before the arrival of 50° to 60° nights. Transfer the plants to the garden without breaking the soil balls. Corms can also be planted in tubs so that the plants can be moved into a protected area at night if frost arrives before flowering stops.

When the leaves have turned brown in fall, dig up the corms, shake off the soil—being careful to save the cormels —and let them dry for a few days in an airy place out of the sun. Cut the tops back to 2 inches from the corms and pull off the dried remains of the previous season's corms. Store them over the winter at 55° to 60° in dry peat moss, perlite or vermiculite. If the corms are left in the ground in Zones 7-10, lift and separate the corms every three or four years in early spring.

Propagate from the small corms and cormels that develop at the base of the large corms. Plant the cormels separately in rich soil; they require at least two growing seasons to reach flowering size.

ACONITE, WINTER See *Eranthis*
ADDER'S-TONGUE See *Erythronium*

AGAPANTHUS

A. africanus, also called *A. umbellatus; A. campanulatus,* also called *A. africanus mooreanus; A.* hybrids; *A. praecox orientalis,* also called *A. orientalis.* (All called agapanthus, blue African lily, lily of the Nile)

Natives of South Africa—not the Nile as one common name suggests—agapanthuses grow from thick fleshy roots that send up mounds of straplike leaves. Their leafless flower stalks bear clusters of 1- to 4-inch blue or white flowers through much of the summer. *A. africanus,* an evergreen species, and *A. campanulatus,* which is deciduous, grow 18 to 24 inches tall and produce 12 to 30 flowers in a cluster. The evergreen *A. praecox orientalis* may become 5 feet tall and produce clusters of 100 or more flowers. Two attractive evergreen hybrids are Peter Pan, with dark blue flowers on 12- to 18-inch stems, and the 18- to 24-inch-tall Dwarf White. Excellent garden flowers in mild climates, agapanthuses can be grown anywhere in tubs or as house plants and are long lasting as cut flowers.

HOW TO GROW. Evergreen agapanthuses can be grown outdoors without winter protection in Zones 9-10; the foliage may be damaged if the temperature drops below 25° but the plants will recover. The deciduous *A. campanulatus* will survive as far north as Zone 7, but must be given a winter mulch such as salt hay or wood chips in Zones 7-8. Agapanthuses do best in gardens in full sun but will tolerate light shade; in very hot climates light shade is desirable. Plant them at any time, spacing them about 24 inches apart and setting them so that the tops of the roots are just below the surface of the soil. During the spring and summer growing season apply light feedings of any garden fertilizer every month or two; during the rest of the year no food should be given.

Because they blossom more freely when crowded and since their roots should be disturbed as little as possible,

AGAPANTHUS
Agapanthus africanus

For climate zones and frost dates, see maps, pages 148-149.

agapanthuses are often grown in containers even in mild climates. Use wooden tubs—the burgeoning roots can burst clay pots. Pot in 1 part packaged potting soil, 1 part coarse peat moss and 1 part sharp sand or perlite with ground limestone added at a rate of 3 to 5 ounces per bushel. During the growing season give the plants plenty of moisture and feed every month or two with a standard house-plant fertilizer; during the rest of the year keep the mix on the dry side and withhold fertilizer. In cold climates, bring the plants indoors before the first fall frost.

Propagate by dividing the fleshy roots of the evergreen species in spring, the deciduous plants in fall.

ALLIUM

A. albopilosum, also called *A. christophii* (giant allium, Persian onion, star of Persia); *A. caeruleum,* also called *A. azureum* (blue globe onion); *A. cyaneum* (bluebell garlic); *A. flavum* (golden onion); *A. giganteum* (giant onion); *A. karataviense* (Turkestan onion); *A. moly* (golden garlic, lily leek); *A. neapolitanum* (daffodil garlic, Naples onion); *A. rosenbachianum* (Rosenbach onion)

The *Allium* genus, best known for its edible members —onions, garlic, chives, shallots and leeks—also includes hundreds of unusual and even spectacular ornamental species that grow anywhere from 6 inches to 5 feet tall; their flower heads, varying in size from 2 to 10 inches across, consist of great numbers of blossoms that range in color from white through shades of yellow, pink and red to lavender, blue and deep purple. Few other plants grown from true bulbs will provide flowers over such a long period: a number of the allium species will bloom in spring, others in summer, still others in fall.

The common name of onion is shared by most, and indeed most give off an onionlike odor when cut or bruised, although the flowers of *A. neapolitanum* have a pleasant fragrance. The leaves, which lie close to the ground below the leafless flower stalks, are either round and hollow, like those of onions, or flat and straplike.

The tall-growing species, standing like sentries, are striking accents in perennial and shrub borders and can be grouped in beds by themselves as conversation pieces; the dwarf species are well suited to rock gardens.

All ornamental alliums make excellent cut flowers (the onion odor of the cut stems quickly disappears when they are placed in water). The flower heads of almost all species can be left in the garden and allowed to dry on the stalks, then cut for indoor arrangements.

Among the many species available, the following are recommended: *A. albopilosum,* which grows 2 to 3 feet tall and bears deep lilac flower heads 8 to 10 inches in diameter in early summer; *A. caeruleum,* which grows 18 to 24 inches high and produces sky-blue flower heads 2 inches across in midsummer; *A. cyaneum,* 8 to 10 inches high, whose dark blue nodding flowers appear in 2-inch clusters in early summer; *A. flavum,* 12 to 24 inches high, which has golden yellow flowers in loose 2-inch flower heads in midsummer; and *A. giganteum,* 3 to 5 feet high, which bears lilac flowers 4 inches across in midsummer.

Also recommended are: *A. karataviense,* which grows 6 to 8 inches high and produces silvery pink 4-inch flower heads in late spring; *A. moly,* 6 to 18 inches high, which has bright yellow flower heads 2 to 3 inches across in late spring; *A. neapolitanum,* 8 to 12 inches high, which bears 3-inch white flower heads in late spring; and *A. rosenbachianum,* 2 to 3 feet high, which produces purple 4- to 5-inch flower heads in midsummer.

HOW TO GROW. Most alliums can be grown throughout Zones 4-10 (exceptions are *A. giganteum* and *A. neapoli-*

TOP: GIANT ALLIUM
Allium albopilosum
BOTTOM: GOLDEN GARLIC
A. moly

tanum, which survive winters only from Zone 6 southward). All species do best in full sun.

Plant the bulbs in spring or fall in holes two to three times as deep as the diameters of the bulbs, spacing them 6 to 18 inches apart depending on the ultimate height of the species. Almost any type of garden fertilizer, scratched into the soil around the plants once in the spring shortly after the new growth has begun to emerge, will supply them with sufficient nutrients.

Clumps of plants may be left undisturbed for years and dug only when they become too crowded to blossom freely. In Zones 4-5, protect the bulbs from alternate periods of freezing and thawing by applying a winter mulch such as salt hay or wood chips.

Propagate after the foliage matures from the small bulbs that develop in the ground around the larger ones, or from the bulbs that appear at the tops of the faded flowers of some species. New plants may also be started from seeds, planted as soon as possible after they ripen, but they will take two to three years to reach flowering size.

ALSTROEMERIA
A. aurantiaca, A. caryophyllea, A. 'Ligtu Hybrids,'
A. pelegrina. (All called Peruvian lily, lily of the Incas)

Peruvian lilies, most of which are native to Chile or Brazil rather than Peru, bear massive clusters of as many as 50 orange, yellow, lilac, pink or red 1½- to 2-inch-wide lilylike blossoms atop 1- to 4-foot-tall stems from early summer until midsummer.

The petals of many flowers are streaked or marked with brown or green. Most types are not fragrant, but *A. caryophyllea,* a red-flowered species, is sweetly scented. The plants, crowded with narrow 3- to 4-inch leaves, grow from clumps of white rhizomelike roots that are brittle and must be handled carefully.

The most widely available types are *A. aurantiaca* (orange with red stripes) and its varieties, Dover Orange (orange red) and Lutea (bright yellow), all of which grow 2½ to 3 feet tall. The excellent Ligtu Hybrids bear flowers in many pastel blends and grow 2½ to 4 feet tall. *A. pelegrina* (lilac pink with purple spots) and *A. pelegrina alba* (white) grow 1 to 2 feet tall. Peruvian lilies are usually grown in flower and shrub borders, and they provide excellent cut flowers.

HOW TO GROW. *A. aurantiaca* and the Ligtu Hybrids can be left in the ground over winter in Zones 6-10, and even in Zone 5 if planted at the base of a sunny wall and given a winter mulch such as salt hay or wood chips. *A. caryophyllaea* and *A. pelegrina* are hardy only in Zones 8-10. Farther north, Peruvian lilies are generally grown in pots, for great care must be taken to avoid disturbing the roots if they are dug up for winter storage.

Peruvian lilies do best in full sun except in hot areas, where they should be given light shade. Since they require particularly good drainage, an ideal location is a slope, which also offers protection against late winter frosts because cold air cannot settle there. Enrich the soil with decayed cow manure or compost.

Plant dormant roots in early spring or early fall, spacing them 12 inches apart and setting them horizontally in holes 6 to 9 inches deep. On windy sites, use stakes for support as the flower stems grow.

Plants purchased in containers can be set into the garden at any time or transplanted into 8- to 12-inch pots or tubs. Pot the plants in a mixture of 1 part peat moss, 1 part packaged potting soil and 1 part sharp sand or perlite, with ground limestone added at a rate of 3 to 5 ounces per bushel. In cold climates bring the container-grown plants

PERUVIAN LILY
Alstroemeria aurantiaca

For climate zones and frost dates, see maps, pages 148-149.

into a cool, but above freezing, location during winter (below 40° is ideal).

Propagate in fall or early spring by dividing the root clumps, but only when slackening flower production makes division necessary.

AMARCRINUM See *Crinodonna*

AMARYLLIS
A. belladonna, also called *Brunsvigia rosea* and *Callicore rosea* (belladonna lily)

The belladonna lily—not to be confused with the large-flowered amaryllis *(Hippeastrum)* popular as a house plant, or the hardy amaryllises of the genus *Lycoris*—has a strange life cycle: its straplike leaves appear in spring and die away before a single flower blooms. By early summer they are gone and it is not until a month or more later that the leafless 2-foot flower stalks rise to be crowned in late summer with clusters of sweetly fragrant blossoms that bloom for six to eight weeks.

The flowers, six to 12 in a cluster, are about 3 inches in diameter and pink, rosy red, mauve or white in color, usually with contrasting yellow throats. Belladonna lilies are extremely handsome when planted amid low shrubs or grouped in perennial borders, especially if they are surrounded with an airy blanket of baby's breath or a ground-cover plant to cloak the withered leaves and act as a foil for the flowers. Belladonna lilies are also popular among gardeners as pot plants.

HOW TO GROW. Belladonna lilies grow with weedlike abandon in sunny parts of the West in Zones 9-10, and do reasonably well in the garden as far north as Zone 5. Plant the bulbs in late summer or early spring in well-drained soil enriched with compost or well-rotted cow manure, spacing them about a foot apart.

In Zones 9-10, cover them with 1 to 2 inches of soil. In Zones 5-8, give them the sunniest possible location and extremely well-drained soil and cover them with about 9 inches of soil. Feed once with a light dusting of 5-10-5 fertilizer when the foliage appears.

To grow belladonna lilies in pots, plant them in late summer, setting the bulbs so that the top half of each one is above the surface of the potting medium. Use a mixture of 1 part peat moss, 1 part packaged potting soil and 1 part sand or perlite; add ground limestone at a rate of 3 to 5 ounces per bushel. Keep the potting medium barely moist until the foliage begins to appear, then water more liberally and feed monthly with a standard house-plant fertilizer as long as the foliage is growing.

When the leaves wither and fade away, keep the potting medium dry until midsummer, then give it a thorough soaking. Thereafter keep the medium barely damp until flower stalks begin to appear. Potted plants must be moved indoors to a sunny place before the first fall frost so that the foliage can mature.

Propagate from the small bulbs that develop beside large ones. Do not dig up the lilies except to propagate them; they flower best when left undisturbed for several years either in the ground or pot bound in containers.

AMARYLLIS See *Hippeastrum*
AMARYLLIS, HARDY See *Lycoris*
AMARYLLIS AUREA See *Lycoris*
AMARYLLIS FORMOSISSIMA See *Sprekelia*
AMARYLLIS HALLII See *Lycoris*
AMARYLLIS LUTEA See *Sternbergia*
AMARYLLIS PURPUREA See *Vallota*
AMARYLLIS RADIATA See *Lycoris*

BELLADONNA LILY
Amaryllis belladonna

ANEMONE

A. apennina (Apennine anemone); *A. blanda* (Greek anemone); *A. coronaria* (poppy-flowered anemone); *A. fulgens* (flame anemone); *A. pavonina,* also called *A. fulgens annulata grandiflora* (peacock anemone)

When Jesus said (Luke 12:27), "Consider the lilies, how they grow: they neither toil nor spin; yet I tell you, even Solomon in all his glory was not arrayed like one of these," He apparently referred not to lilies but to the poppy-flowered anemones, which grow in greater abundance in the Holy Land and are still among the most colorful plants of spring everywhere.

Most species come in white and shades of pink, red, blue and purple; the blossoms open in sunlight and close at night and in cloudy weather.

Two species with daisylike blossoms about 2 inches in diameter are the Apennine anemone, which grows 6 to 9 inches tall and the 3- to 6-inch-high Greek anemone. Both species grow from tubers that look like small black twigs. The flowers, which often last a month, are effective in great drifts planted beneath flowering crab apples, dogwoods and spring-flowering shrubs.

The poppy-flowered anemone bears 3-inch blossoms and grows 12 to 18 inches tall; among its outstanding strains are Creagh Castle, de Caen (sometimes known as Great French) and the somewhat more lushly petaled St. Brigid. Both the flame anemone, which comes only in scarlet, and the peacock anemone, whose most famous strain, St. Bavo, comes in a complete range of anemone colors with brightly contrasting (usually yellow) centers, grow a foot or so tall and bear flowers around 2 inches across.

Poppy-flowered, flame and peacock anemones grow from claw-shaped tubers. The flowers make handsome groups in perennial borders or among ground covers, especially on banks where the sloping ground assures good drainage. They are also excellent and long lived as cut flowers. When picking anemones, always use a sharp knife or shears and cut off the stems close to the ground; if you pull or snap off the stems you may tear the crowns of the tubers.

HOW TO GROW. Apennine and Greek anemones do best in Zones 6-9, but can be grown farther north in protected parts of the garden if covered with a deep winter mulch such as salt hay or wood chips.

Poppy-flowered, flame and peacock anemones prefer long cool springs followed by dry summers, as in Zones 9-10 on the West Coast. These species may also be grown as permanent garden plants, set out in fall, as far north as Zone 7, but from Zone 6 north they should be planted in very early spring and dug in late summer and stored at 55° to 60° in dry peat moss, perlite or vermiculite until the following spring.

All anemones do well in full sun or light shade; protection from the sun during the hot part of the day is advisable in southern areas. The best soil is a well-drained one with a pH of 6.5 to 7.0. Enrich with well-rotted manure or compost. Except in moist climates such as that of the Pacific Northwest, tubers benefit by being soaked in tepid water for as much as 48 hours before planting.

Set the tubers of Greek and Apennine anemones 4 to 6 inches apart and cover with 2 inches of soil. Set the tubers of other species with the claws down about 8 inches apart and cover them with 2 to 3 inches of soil. Even small tubers often produce large plants.

Propagate by dividing tubers in late summer after the foliage has matured. Plants may also be grown from seeds, which require about 18 months to reach flowering size.

ANOMATHECA See *Lapeirousia*

TOP: GREEK ANEMONE
Anemone blanda

BOTTOM: POPPY-FLOWERED ANEMONE
A. coronaria 'St. Brigid'

For climate zones and frost dates, see maps, pages 148-149.

ST.-BERNARD'S-LILY
Anthericum liliago

BABOONROOT
Babiana stricta hybrid

ANTHERICUM
A. liliago (St.-Bernard's-lily)

Named for St. Bernard of Montjoux, the priest who founded a refuge for travelers in the Alps—and after whom the famous rescue dogs are also named—this alpine flower has been cultivated in gardens for centuries. Growing from clusters of fleshy tuberous roots, it sends up narrow grass-like leaves about a foot long that are followed by slender 18- to 24-inch flower stems. The snow-white blossoms, 1 to 1½ inches across, bloom in clusters for about eight weeks from spring to midsummer. The plants make attractive additions to perennial borders and rock gardens and can be naturalized in rough grass or in lightly shaded woodlands.

HOW TO GROW. St.-Bernard's-lilies do best in light shade in Zones 6-9, and may be grown in protected sites in Zone 5 (and in unprotected ones if covered with a winter mulch such as salt hay or wood chips). Plant in early spring or in fall, setting the tuberous roots 3 to 6 inches apart, covering them with 3 to 6 inches of soil and mulching with finely ground bark to keep the soil evenly cool and moist. Feed once with a light dusting of 5-10-5 fertilizer when the plant emerges. Plants resent root disturbance and often do not blossom the first year after planting. Allow colonies to grow for several years before dividing them. Propagate in the fall by carefully pulling the fleshy roots apart. Plants can be grown from seeds sown in a cold frame immediately after ripening in fall; they usually reach flowering size in two or three years. Spring-sown seeds may lie dormant an entire year before sprouting.

B

BABIANA
B. stricta hybrids, formerly known as Gladiolus plicatus (baboonroot)

Baboons are fond of eating the corms of *Babiana* in its native South Africa and Asia, hence the common name baboonroot. Closely related to gladioluses, these plants grow 6 to 12 inches tall and bear spikes of 10 to 20 sweetly scented blossoms. The flowers, about an inch across, come in blue, rose, crimson, yellow, violet or white. The leaves are sword-shaped, like those of gladioluses, but are deeply pleated and hairy rather than smooth. Plants blossom outdoors in late spring or early summer for three to five weeks and are particularly suited to rock gardens and flower borders.

HOW TO GROW. Baboonroots grow most successfully in those parts of the Southwest and West where summer rainfall is minimal. They can be grown outdoors in Zones 8-10 without winter protection, and in sheltered areas as far north as Zone 6 if covered with a heavy winter mulch such as salt hay or wood chips. Better success is assured from Zone 7 north if the corms are dug up in fall and stored at 55° to 60° in dry peat moss, vermiculite or perlite.

Baboonroots do best in full sun and well-drained soil that has been enriched with well-rotted cow manure. Corms that will remain in the ground through the winter should be planted in the fall and left undisturbed for two or three years; corms that must be dug up in fall should be planted in the spring. Set the corms 3 to 4 inches apart, covering them with 3 to 4 inches of soil. Dust with 5-10-5 fertilizer when the plants emerge and again a month later.

Plants grown indoors in pots do best in at least four hours of direct sunlight a day, night temperatures of 50° to 60° and day temperatures of 65° to 70°. For winter blossoms, pot in fall in a mixture of 1 part packaged potting soil, 1 part peat moss and 1 part sharp sand or perlite, with ground limestone added at a rate of 3 to 5 ounces per bushel. Plant five corms to a 4-inch pot, 12 corms to a 6-inch pot; cover the corms with 2 inches of soil. Keep moist and feed every three or four weeks from the time the plant emerges until the buds show color. After the leaves wither, store the corms in dry peat moss until fall.

Propagate in fall from the small corms that form around the old ones. Plants started from seeds require about 18 months to reach flowering size.

BABOONROOT See *Babiana*
BASKET FLOWER See *Hymenocallis*

BEGONIA
B. evansiana (hardy begonia), *B. tuberhybrida* (tuberous begonia, tuberous-rooted begonia)

Both these species of begonias, which grow from tubers, are unsurpassed as summer plants for shady places. They blossom profusely until frost, and make fine cut flowers when set afloat in shallow bowls. *B. evansiana* bears flesh-pink flowers an inch or less across above 3- to 6-inch leaves that are reddish underneath. Plants grow about 2 feet tall and die to the ground in winter. The free-blooming *B. tuberhybrida*, the tuberous begonia beloved by so many gardeners, produces 2- to 10-inch flowers in all colors except blue and green. Three types of this species are widely available: upright plants 12 to 18 inches tall; hanging-basket begonias, often called Pendula, with trailing stems 12 to 18 inches long; and Multiflora varieties, bushy 8- to 10-inch plants bearing great numbers of 2-inch flowers.

HOW TO GROW. Both species do best in light to medium shade. Set the tiny bulblike tubers of *B. evansiana* about 6 inches apart and cover them with 1 to 2 inches of soil. The plants can be left undisturbed in the ground for years in Zones 6-10, but in Zones 6-7 they require a winter mulch of salt hay or wood chips. Propagate in early spring from tiny bulbs that appear in the joints of the leaf stems.

B. tuberhybrida can be grown in gardens throughout Zones 2-10 but must be dug up each fall and replanted in spring. It can be planted directly in the garden or started indoors and transplanted outside. In the garden, plants do best in light shade in a 6-inch-deep soil mixture of 2 parts loam, 2 parts peat moss and 1 part well-rotted or dried cow manure. Plant the tubers 12 to 15 inches apart. Feed with a weak, all-purpose fertilizer such as 5-10-5 every two or three weeks from the time the first shoot appears until the foliage starts to wither. When the plants have died back to the ground, dig up the tubers, allowing some soil to cling to them; place the tubers in a sheltered frost-free spot for a few weeks, until they are so dry that their stems and the soil around them break away easily. Store the tubers over the winter in bags of dry vermiculite, perlite or peat moss at 40° to 50°.

To increase the length of the growing season, start tubers of *B. tuberhybrida* indoors about two months before the expected arrival of 50° nights; press them, hollow side up, into wooden flats or plastic trays filled with damp peat moss but do not cover them. When growth starts, pot in 5- or 6-inch pots in a mixture of 2 parts loam, 2 parts peat moss and 1 part well-rotted or dried cow manure. When night temperatures rise above 50° set the plants outdoors. Propagate *B. tuberhybrida* in early spring by taking cuttings from the shoots that arise from the tubers. Plants started from seed indoors in January will flower in June.

BELAMCANDA
B. chinensis, also called *Pardanthus chinensis* (blackberry lily, leopard lily)

The tuberous root of the blackberry lily is used in India as an antidote for cobra bites, but fortunately this handsome plant has less exotic uses in this country. Its slender

TOP: HARDY BEGONIA
Begonia evansiana   BOTTOM: TUBEROUS BEGONIA
B. tuberhybrida 'Double Picotee'

Illustration by Eduardo Salgado

BLACKBERRY LILY
Belamcanda chinensis

For climate zones and frost dates, see maps, pages 148-149.

flower stalks, 2½ to 3 feet tall, bear clusters of 2-inch, red-spotted orange flowers. Each blossom lasts only a day, but the many buds in each cluster guarantee a continuing display for several weeks in midsummer. The blossoms are followed by pods, which split open to reveal clusters of shiny black seeds that look like blackberries. The plants are attractive in flower borders, among shrubs or in a garden of wild flowers. If allowed to dry on the stalk, their seed clusters are splendid for winter arrangements.

HOW TO GROW. Hardy in Zones 5-10, blackberry lilies should be planted in spring or fall in full sun or light shade. Set the roots about 6 inches apart and cover them with 1 inch of soil. In Zones 5-6, apply a winter mulch such as salt hay or wood chips. Propagate by dividing the roots in spring or fall, or from seeds, which make flowering-sized plants the second year.

BELLEVALIA See *Hyacinthus*

BESSERA
B. elegans (coral drops)

Coral drops are admired for their clusters of drooping bell-shaped, 1-inch flowers, which bloom over a period of two months beginning in midsummer. The orange-red blossoms have white centers and white lines on the petals that contrast with the long, purple pollen-bearing stamens. The flowers appear in clusters of 10 to 20 atop 2- to 3-foot stems; sometimes as many as 10 stems rise from a single corm. The foliage is sparse, each corm sending out only two or three narrow leaves, 1 to 2 feet long, which usually flop on the ground. The plants are attractive when set in groups of a dozen or more in flower borders and when naturalized in open wooded areas or unmowed grass. The flowers are excellent for cutting.

HOW TO GROW. Coral drops do best in full sun in soil enriched with compost. In Zones 7-10, plant in early fall; from Zone 6 north, plant in early spring. Set the corms 8 to 12 inches apart and cover them with 4 inches of soil.

Coral drops can be grown in Zones 8-10 without winter protection, and in Zone 7 if covered with a winter mulch such as salt hay or wood chips. From Zone 6 north they must be dug up in fall after the foliage dies and stored over winter at 55° to 60° in dry peat moss, perlite or vermiculite. Propagate after the foliage dies by dividing the small corms that appear around large ones.

BLETILLA
B. striata, also called *B. hyacinthina*
(Chinese ground orchid, hardy orchid)

Chinese ground orchids grow from tuberlike stems called pseudobulbs, which send up 1- to 2-foot floral spikes bearing six to 10 blossoms about an inch across for a six-week period beginning in early summer. The flowers are generally pink to purple, except for those of the rarer *B. striata alba,* which are white. The narrow leaves, 10 to 12 inches long, have prominent lengthwise pleats. Chinese ground orchids make attractive long-lasting cut flowers and are highly decorative as pot plants.

HOW TO GROW. Chinese ground orchids can be grown outdoors in Zones 5-10. They do best in partial shade, in moist soil composed of 2 parts loam, 2 parts leaf mold or peat moss and 1 part coarse sand. Plant the roots about 6 inches apart in fall or early spring, covering them with 4 inches of soil. In Zones 5-7 apply a heavy winter mulch such as salt hay or wood chips. Move pot-grown plants into a cool, above-freezing location over winter. Propagate in fall or spring by dividing clumps of pseudobulbs into individual plants.

CORAL DROPS
Bessera elegans

CHINESE GROUND ORCHID
Bletilla striata

BLUE DICKS See *Brodiaea*
BLUEBELL, ENGLISH See *Scilla*
BLUEBELL, SPANISH See *Scilla*
BREVOORTIA See *Brodiaea*
BRIMEURA See *Hyacinthus*

BRODIAEA

B. elegans, also called *B. coronaria, B. grandiflora* (harvest brodiaea); *B. hyacinthina,* also called *Triteleia hyacinthina* (white brodiaea); *B. ida-maia,* also called *Brevoortia ida-maia, Dichelostemma ida-maia* (firecracker flower); *B. ixioides,* also called *B. lutea, Triteleia ixioides* (golden brodiaea, prettyface); *B. laxa,* also called *Triteleia laxa* (Ithuriel's-spear, grassnut); *B. pulchella,* also called *B. capitata, Dichelostemma pulchellum* (blue dicks, wild hyacinth)

Brodiaeas are beautiful natives of the western part of North America. Most species send up grasslike foliage and slender 1- to 3-foot flower stalks bearing clusters of ½- to 1½-inch blossoms. Brodiaeas are especially handsome planted in groups of a dozen or more in flower borders, rock gardens or naturalized in grass. They are also excellent for cutting.

Two species bloom from late spring to midsummer: *B. elegans* (5 to 20 inches tall, violet to purple flowers); *B. ida-maia* (about 1½ feet tall, green-tipped scarlet flowers). *B. ixioides* (1 to 3 feet tall, golden yellow flowers) and *B. laxa* (18 to 30 inches tall, blue or white flowers) bloom from early spring to early summer. *B. pulchella* (1 to 2 feet tall, pinkish violet flowers) blooms in early spring. *B. hyacinthina* (12 to 18 inches tall, purplish white flowers) blooms in early summer.

HOW TO GROW. The hardiness of brodiaeas varies according to species: *B. pulchella* can be left in the ground over winter in Zones 5-10; *B. elegans,* in Zones 7-10; all others in Zones 6-10. Brodiaeas need sun and exceptionally good drainage. Where rainfall is apt to be abundant in late summer, provide a 4-inch bed of coarse sand under the corms in the planting bed. Plant the corms in fall, spacing them 3 to 5 inches apart and covering them with 4 to 6 inches of soil. In Zones 5-6 apply a winter mulch such as salt hay or wood chips. Propagate brodiaeas in fall from the small corms that develop next to the large ones. They do best if left undisturbed for a number of years.

BRODIAEA UNIFLORA See *Ipheion*
BRUNSVIGIA See *Amaryllis*

BULBOCODIUM

B. vernum (spring meadow saffron)

Spring meadow saffron is among the first flowers of the new year, opening as early as December or January in southern zones. The 4-inch-tall flowers spring directly from the soil, two or three flowers often appearing from one corm; the flowers are followed by foliage that may become 5 or 6 inches tall before withering in early summer. The plants, which originated in Europe, make a bright splash of early spring color when planted in rock gardens or set out informally in rough grass or under trees.

HOW TO GROW. Spring meadow saffron can be left in the ground in Zones 3-10 and does best in full sun or light shade. Plant the corms in early fall, spacing them 4 inches apart and covering them with 3 inches of soil. Propagate every two to four years in midsummer after the foliage has died down by removing the small corms that develop around the large ones.

BUTTERCUP See *Ranunculus*
BUTTERCUP, BERMUDA See *Oxalis*

BRODIAEA
Brodiaea laxa

SPRING MEADOW SAFFRON
Bulbocodium vernum

For climate zones and frost dates, see maps, pages 148-149.

FANCY-LEAVED CALADIUM
Caladium hortulanum

MARIPOSA TULIP
Calochortus venustus

C

CALADIUM

C. hortulanum (fancy-leaved caladium)

Caladiums are grown for their decorative heart- or spear-shaped leaves, which may be anywhere from 6 to 24 inches long and which come in almost endless combinations of red, pink, silver, white and green. Most modern varieties are hybrids of *C. bicolor* and *C. picturatum,* species native to the riverbanks of the Amazon. Plants grow about a foot tall; their pale pink flowers, seemingly made of damp tissue paper, are usually hidden by the foliage. Widely grown as pot plants by florists for spring and summer sales, caladiums do well in gardens, window boxes or outdoor pots.

HOW TO GROW. Tolerant of varying light conditions from full sun to deep shade, fancy-leaved caladiums may be left in the ground throughout the year in Zone 10, but in the rest of the country they must be dug up just before frost. In Zones 8-10, plant them directly in the garden when daytime temperatures are 70° or higher. Space the tubers 12 inches apart and cover with 1 inch of soil. Elsewhere, start them indoors six to eight weeks before 70° temperatures are expected, pressing them upside down into damp peat moss or vermiculite; set them 1 inch deep and keep at 75° to 85°. As soon as leaves appear, shift the plants to 4-inch peat pots. Indoors or out, caladiums do best in a mixture of 2 parts loam, 2 parts peat moss, 1 part well-rotted or dried cow manure and 1 part coarse sand. Feed every two to three weeks during the growing season by dusting any mild all-purpose fertilizer around each plant.

In fall, when the foliage flops over, or frost threatens, dig up the roots with soil and tops clinging to them and let them dry in an airy place out of the sun for about a week or until the tops come away with a gentle tug. Shake off the soil, then dust the roots with a combination fungicide-insecticide, and store over the winter at about 55° to 60° in dry peat moss, perlite or vermiculite. Propagate by cutting tubers into pieces, leaving at least one eye, or bud, on each section *(drawing, page 22);* fuller plants with multiple stems will result if three to five eyes are left on each section. Dust the cut surfaces with a fungicide to prevent decay and let them air-dry for two days before planting.

CALADIUM ESCULENTUM See *Colocasia*
CALLICORE See *Amaryllis*

CALOCHORTUS

C. albus (white fairy lantern, satin bell); *C. amabilis,* also called *C. pulchellus* (golden fairy lantern); *C. amoenus* (purple globe tulip); *C. caeruleus* (cat's-ear); *C. venustus* (Mariposa tulip, butterfly tulip)

Of the 50 or so species of calochortus that grow wild from California east to Colorado, three types are widely cultivated for rock gardens or for cut flowers in spring and early summer. One type includes three species with globe-shaped flowers about 1½ inches across: *C. albus,* 12 to 24 inches tall with translucent greenish white globes; *C. amabilis,* about a foot tall with brown-marked yellow flowers; and *C. amoenus,* 18 to 24 inches tall with mauve-pink flowers. The second type, *C. caeruleus,* grows only 3 to 6 inches tall and bears upright 1-inch lilac-colored flowers lined and fringed with soft hairs. The third type, *C. venustus,* is most colorful—the strain Eldorado has 2- to 4-foot-tall stems bearing erect blossoms as much as 4 inches across in lilac, purple, rose, red, yellow or white, all with distinctive "eyes" that resemble markings on butterfly wings.

HOW TO GROW. All species listed above are hardy in Zones 5-10, except *C. venustus,* which should not be planted north of Zone 6. They do best in light shade, again excepting *C. venustus,* which requires full sun. All prefer particularly well-drained, gritty soil that remains dry in summer. Plant the bulbs in late fall, spacing them 4 to 6 inches apart and covering them with 2 inches of soil. Insert small twigs among the young plants of tall-growing types to provide support as they develop. To assure continued blooming, the bulbs of all calochortuses must dry out fully after the foliage dies in summer. In the East and Northwest, therefore, many gardeners dig up the bulbs in midsummer, storing them in a dry place and planting them again just before the ground freezes; this treatment prevents late, new growth that could be nipped by frost. Apply a heavy winter mulch such as salt hay or wood chips in Zones 5-7. Propagate in midsummer after the foliage dies down from the small bulbs that develop beside larger ones.

CAMASS See *Camassia*

CAMASSIA

C. cusickii (Cusick camass); *C. leichtlinii*
(Leichtlin camass); *C. quamash,* also called *C. esculenta* (common camass, quamash, wild hyacinth);
C. scilloides (Atlantic camass)

North American wild flowers, camasses were called quamashes by the Indians, who found that although the bulbs are poisonous when raw they could be eaten safely after cooking (a practice not recommended for home gardeners). For several weeks in spring, camasses bear spikes of starry 1¼-inch flowers set amid long, slender leaves. *C. cusickii* grows 2½ to 3 feet tall and produces spikes of 30 to 100 amethyst-blue flowers; *C. leichtlinii,* probably the handsomest species of all, grows 2 to 3 feet tall and has spikes of 20 to 40 dark blue, cream or white flowers; *C. quamash,* 2 to 3 feet tall, bears spikes of 10 to 40 blue to white flowers; and *C. scilloides,* 1½ to 2 feet tall, bears spikes of 15 to 35 light blue or white flowers.

HOW TO GROW. Camasses are hardy in Zones 3-10 and will grow in any normal to wet ground in full sun or light shade. Plant the bulbs in fall, spacing them 3 to 6 inches apart and covering with 3 to 4 inches of soil. Once planted, they need no care. Camasses can be propagated easily from seeds, but take four years to reach flowering size.

CANNA

C. generalis, also called *C. hybrida* (canna, Indian shot)

Modern cannas, hybridized from a number of mainly Central and South American species, vary in height from 1½ feet to nearly 5 feet; from early summer until frost they bear flower spikes about a foot tall made up of many 4- to 5-inch blossoms ranging in color from white through various shades of yellow and pink to scarlet. Their broad leaves, 6 to 12 inches long, may be bright green, blue-green or shiny bronze. Three notable strains are the Grand Opera Series, usually 3 to 4 feet tall; Pfitzer Hybrids, a little over 2 feet tall; and Seven Dwarfs, about 1½ feet tall. Groups of single colors are most effective beside pools or against walls or evergreens. Cannas also do well in tubs.

HOW TO GROW. In Zones 7-10, cannas can be left in the ground over the winter, but in the rest of the country they must be dug up in the fall. They do best in moist soil enriched with compost or well-rotted cow manure, full sun and hot weather. In Zones 7-10 plant the rhizomes in the garden in spring; elsewhere, you can start the rhizomes in peat pots indoors about a month before night temperatures stay above 50° to 60°. Space the rhizomes 15 to 18 inches apart and cover them with 1 to 2 inches of soil. Feed every two to four weeks with a dusting of 5-10-5 fertilizer during the growing season. From Zone 6 north, cut

COMMON CAMASS
Camassia quamash

CANNA
Canna generalis

For climate zones and frost dates, see maps, pages 148-149.

GLORY-OF-THE-SNOW
Chionodoxa luciliae

the stalks to the ground after they are blackened by frost. Dig the roots and let them dry a few days before storing them, upside down, in dry peat moss, perlite or vermiculite. In Zones 7-10, dig and reset every third year.

To grow cannas in containers, start rhizomes in spring. Plant in a mixture of 1 part peat moss, 1 part packaged potting soil and 1 part sharp sand or perlite, with ground limestone added at a rate of 3 to 5 ounces per bushel. Keep moist and feed with 5-10-5 fertilizer (*above*). Move the plants into an above-freezing location over winter.

Propagate by dividing rhizomes in spring. One strain —Seven Dwarfs—can also be grown from seeds, which take three to six months to reach garden size. Nick seed coats or soak seeds overnight before planting.

CAPE COWSLIP See *Lachenalia*
CARDINAL FLOWER See *Rechsteineria*
CAT'S-EAR See *Calochortus*
CHINCHERINCHEE See *Ornithogalum*
CHINESE GROUND ORCHID See *Bletilla*

CHIONODOXA
C. gigantea, also called *C. grandiflora; C. luciliae; C. sardensis.* (All called chionodoxa, glory-of-the-snow)

In Asia Minor only a little over a century ago, the Swiss botanist Pierre-Edmond Boissier discovered chionodoxas blooming at the edge of the retreating mountain snows. Today three species are widely available from bulb merchants. They bloom in early spring shortly after the first crocuses open and, in light shade, the flowers will last three to four weeks. The most common species is *C. luciliae,* a 6-inch gem that bears eight to 10 violet-blue, white-centered 1-inch flowers on each stem. The white *C. luciliae alba* and lilac-pink *C. luciliae rosea* bear two to three flowers on a stem. *C. sardensis* is also 6 inches tall and has ¾-inch porcelain-blue flowers with a touch of white at the throat; it bears six to eight blossoms on a stem. *C. gigantea* grows 10 inches tall and bears eight to 10 1½-inch pale purple-blue flowers with white centers on a stem. The white *C. gigantea alba* is rare, but *C. gigantea rosea* 'Pink Giant,' with eight to 10 blush-pink 1½-inch flowers per stem, is usually available; it is often listed in bulb catalogues as a form of *C. luciliae.* Chionodoxas are most effective in large groups under deciduous trees, in front of early-flowering shrubs, or on banks where they can be naturalized. Though short stemmed, the blossoms are also attractive and long lived in cut-flower arrangements.

HOW TO GROW. Chionodoxas can be grown in gardens in Zones 3-10, but do best in cool parts of the country. They flourish in an especially well-drained soil in full sun or light shade. Plant the bulbs in early fall as soon as they are available, spacing them 1 to 3 inches apart and covering them with 3 inches of soil. Once planted, they need no care. Fertilizer is not necessary in most garden soils. Bulbs are so inexpensive that it is not worthwhile to dig up and divide them. Plants often sow their own seeds, spreading slowly in the garden.

CHLIDANTHUS
C. fragrans (Peru chlidanthus, delicate lily)

Native to the Andes, chlidanthuses grow slender stalks just under a foot tall, each topped in summer by one to four 3-inch flowers that have a delightful lemon scent. The long narrow leaves may appear with the blossoms or slightly later. Excellent as cut flowers, chlidanthuses are well suited to rock gardens and make attractive pot plants.

HOW TO GROW. Chlidanthuses do best in full sun. Plant the bulbs as soon as they are available in spring, spacing

PERU CHLIDANTHUS
Chlidanthus fragrans

them 6 to 8 inches apart and covering them with 2 inches of soil. They can be left outdoors over winter in Zones 8-10, but elsewhere must be dug up before the first frost in fall. For cold-weather storage let them dry for about a week in an airy place out of the sun, then keep at 55° to 60° in dry peat moss, perlite or vermiculite.

One of the best ways to grow chlidanthuses, north and south, is in clay pots, which can be enjoyed outdoors in summer and moved indoors to a dry, frost-free place if necessary. Plant the bulbs about 2 inches deep in a mixture of 1 part peat moss, 1 part packaged potting soil and 1 part sharp sand or perlite, with ground limestone added at a rate of 3 to 5 ounces per bushel. When all danger of frost is past, move the pots to the garden, plunging them into the soil to their rims to conserve moisture and keep them from blowing over. Mulch with finely ground bark in and around the pots. Feed once after flowering with a light dusting of 5-10-5 fertilizer. Propagate in fall from the small bulbs that develop at the base of the large ones.

CLIVIA
C. hybrids, *C. miniata.* (All called Kafir lily)

Kafir lilies, natives of South Africa, have 12- to 15-inch-tall stems, each bearing clusters of 12 to 20 fragrant, long-lasting flowers as much as 3 inches wide. The straplike evergreen leaves, which arch out gracefully, grow 18 to 24 inches long. The chief species grown is *C. miniata,* which bears orange to scarlet flowers with yellow throats. The hybrid *C. cyrtanthiflora* produces salmon flowers; Belgian and Zimmerman hybrids bear blossoms in many blends of orange, yellow, salmon, scarlet and white. Spring-flowering garden plants in mild climates, Kafir lilies can be grown as winter-blooming house plants in all zones. And they all make excellent cut flowers.

HOW TO GROW. Although Kafir lilies are hardy in Zones 9-10, they are often grown in containers because they blossom most freely when their roots are crowded. Plant the bulbs any time in a partially shaded location, either directly in the garden or in pots. Space them 18 to 24 inches apart and barely cover them with soil. Feed every month or two from early spring to late summer with a light dusting of 5-10-5 fertilizer. For potted plants, indoors or out, use a mixture of 1 part packaged potting soil, 1 part peat moss and 1 part sharp sand or perlite, with ground limestone added at a rate of 3 to 5 ounces per bushel.

As house plants Kafir lilies do best in bright indirect or curtain-filtered sunlight, night temperatures of 50° to 55° and day temperatures of 68° to 72°. Move the plants outdoors to a shady place when night temperatures reach 50° and bring them indoors before the first fall frost. From midwinter until late summer, let the potting medium become slightly dry between thorough waterings and feed every month or two with a standard house-plant fertilizer. From late fall until midwinter, withhold fertilizer and water only enough to keep the leaves from wilting. Repot in February every three or four years. Propagate in late spring from the small bulbs that develop around the large ones.

COLCHICUM
C. autumnale; C. byzantinum, also called *C. autumnale major; C.* hybrids; *C. luteum,* also called *Synsiphon luteum; C. speciosum.* (All called colchicum, autumn crocus, meadow saffron)

Colchicums always bring a surprise to fall gardens, for their bright blossoms seem to appear out of nowhere, rising from the earth without foliage. Their unusual life cycle starts when the corms are planted in August. Within a few weeks they send up clusters of flowers that generally last

KAFIR LILY
Clivia miniata

COLCHICUM
Colchicum autumnale minor

For climate zones and frost dates, see maps, pages 148-149.

two to three weeks, then disappear. Leaves develop the following spring but wither away in early summer. The translucent flowers vary from 2 to 8 inches in diameter and look like crocuses, although the plants are only distantly related. Interestingly, an extract of colchicum called colchicine is an important tool in plant breeding; it induces startling mutations when placed on the buds of other kinds of plants.

Popular varieties include the 8-inch-tall *C. autumnale* and the 6-inch-tall *C. autumnale minor*, both of which bear pale rose to white flowers 2 inches across; *C. byzantinum*, which grows 6 inches tall and bears clusters of 10 to 20 rosy lilac flowers up to 4 inches across; *C. speciosum,* which grows 8 to 12 inches tall and bears 6- to 8-inch tuliplike flowers in rosy lavender or white. *C. luteum,* which blooms in early spring rather than in fall, grows 6 inches tall and bears bright yellow 2-inch flowers. Among the excellent hybrids are Lilac Wonder, 8 inches tall with 4- to 6-inch violet-mauve flowers; The Giant, 8 inches tall with 6- to 8-inch rosy lilac flowers; and Waterlily, 6 inches tall with 4- to 6-inch many-petaled pink flowers. Colchicums have coarse 6- to 10-inch-long leaves that take considerable time to develop fully and die, so the corms should be planted among shrubs or in woodland gardens where their withering foliage will not be conspicuous.

HOW TO GROW. *C. luteum* is hardy in Zones 7-10, but all the other species are hardy as far north as Zone 4. Colchicums do best in full sun or light shade, located in a place where they can be left undisturbed for years. Plant the corms in August, spacing them 6 to 9 inches apart and covering them with 3 to 4 inches of soil. Propagate in early summer, after the foliage has withered, from the small corms that develop at the base of the larger ones. Colchicums may also be grown from seeds, but take five years to reach flowering size.

COLOCASIA
C. antiquorum; C. antiquorum esculenta, also called *Caladium esculenta.*
(Both called elephant's-ear, taro, dasheen)

Both the descriptively named leaves of the elephant's-ear and its tuberous roots, commonly called taro, are used as food in tropical Asia as well as the Pacific and Caribbean islands. (Hawaiian poi, a sticky grayish dish for which an acquired taste seems important, is made by pounding the cooked roots to a paste.) The plants grow 4 to 6 feet tall and the leaves may reach 2 feet in length and 18 inches in width, hiding the lackluster yellow blossoms. Grouped with tree ferns and other tropical plants, the leaves provide bold accents for gardens.

HOW TO GROW. Elephant's-ears survive winters outdoors only in Zone 10. They do well in full sun or light shade if given moist soil, composed of 2 parts loam, 2 parts peat moss, 1 part well-rotted or dried cow manure, and 1 part coarse sand. Plant the tubers in spring, spacing them 2 to 4 feet apart and covering them with 4 inches of soil. North of Zone 10 start them indoors a month before 60° nights arrive, setting one tuber to a 6-inch pot, then transfer them out of the pots and into the garden when the nights become warm. In these cool climates dig up the tubers after the first fall frost and allow them to dry for about a week in an airy place out of the sun. Then store them over the winter at 55° to 60° in dry peat moss, perlite or vermiculite.

Start tub plants in spring, setting the tubers 2 to 3 inches deep in a mixture of 2 parts peat moss, 2 parts packaged potting soil, 1 part well-rotted or dried cow manure and 1 part coarse sand. Move the plants indoors before the first fall frost. While indoors, plants do best in bright indirect sunlight, night temperatures of 65° to 70° and day tem-

ELEPHANT'S-EAR
Colocasia antiquorum

peratures of 70° or higher. Keep the potting mixture moist and feed every three or four months with a standard house-plant fertilizer.

Propagate in spring by dividing the tubers, leaving at least one eye on each division. Dust the cut surfaces with a fungicide powder and air-dry for two days before planting.

CONVALLARIA
C. majalis (lily of the valley)

The sweetly fragrant snow-white bells of lilies of the valley are favorites in bridal bouquets, at least partly because the underground rootstalks, called pips *(page 11),* can be kept in cold storage and forced into bloom at any season. In late spring each pip sends up two 8-inch-long leaves and a slender flower stem carrying five to eight drooping ¼-inch bells; the flowers are followed occasionally by ¼-inch orange to red berries. A lesser known variety, *C. majalis rosea,* has pale purplish pink flowers. In gardens, lilies of the valley are most valuable as a low-maintenance ground cover in shade. The cut flowers make lovely, fragrant small arrangements indoors.

HOW TO GROW. Lilies of the valley do best in Zones 3-7 and are not satisfactory in warmer climates. They thrive in partial shade and moist, acid soil with a pH of 4.5 to 6.0. Plant the pips in fall or early spring, spacing them 3 to 4 inches apart and covering them with 1 inch of soil. For vigorous growth and abundant flowering, mulch lightly in fall with compost or well-rotted cow manure. Propagate by dividing the pips in fall when the foliage has developed fully and begun to yellow.

COPPERTIP See *Crocosmia*
CORAL DROPS See *Bessera*
CRIMSON FLAG See *Schizostylis*

CRINODONNA
C. corsii, also called *Amarcrinum howardii*

In late summer and early fall, each crinodonna bulb sends up two flower stalks, usually about 3 feet tall, bearing long-lasting clusters of fragrant 4-inch shell-pink blossoms above dark green straplike leaves that may become as much as 2 feet long. On garden plants the foliage is usually evergreen, but the leaves of container-grown plants may wither in late fall at the end of the growing season.

HOW TO GROW. Crinodonnas do best in Zones 7-10, but can be left in the earth through the winter as far north as Zone 6 if they are given a mulch such as salt hay or wood chips. Plant the bulbs in spring or fall in a sunny location. Space the bulbs 8 to 12 inches apart and cover them with 4 to 6 inches of soil.

Crinodonnas are often grown in pots even in mild climates because they bloom best when their roots become crowded and because they can be brought into view while in blossom and moved to an out-of-the-way spot during the rest of the season. Pot in a mixture of 1 part peat moss, 1 part packaged potting soil and 1 part sharp sand or perlite, with ground limestone added at a rate of 3 to 5 ounces per bushel. Plant one bulb to a 6- to 8-inch pot, leaving the top third of the bulb above the surface. Keep the mixture moist and feed monthly with a standard house-plant fertilizer during the growing season, early spring to late fall. Then withhold moisture and do not feed until new growth appears in spring. When grown indoors, crino-donnas do best in at least four hours of direct sunlight a day, night temperatures of 50° to 55° and day temper-atures of 68° to 72°. Repot every three or four years.

Propagate at any time from the small bulbs that de-velop beside the large ones.

LILY OF THE VALLEY
Convallaria majalis

CRINODONNA
Crinodonna corsii

For climate zones and frost dates, see maps, pages 148-149.

CRINUM
Crinum powellii

CRINUM

C. americanum (swamp crinum, Florida crinum); *C. asiaticum* (grand crinum); *C. bulbispermum,* also called *C. capense; C. longifolium* (hardy crinum); *C.* hybrids; *C. moorei* (longneck crinum)

Crinums, majestic bulb plants with straplike evergreen leaves, produce massive clusters of 3- to 6-inch lilylike flowers, usually fragrant, atop leafless 2- to 3-foot stems. Most bloom in late summer and fall, although some types bloom in late spring in mild climates.

C. americanum and *C. asiaticum* have white flowers; *C. bulbispermum* bears rosy red flowers that are white inside; *C. moorei* has white flowers with pink stripes. Particularly handsome hybrids are *C. powellii,* with reddish pink or white flowers; Ellen Bosanquet, an especially good plant to grow in tubs with deep wine-red flowers; and Cecil Houdyshel, a profusely flowering pink variety.

HOW TO GROW. The crinums listed above may be grown in protected spots as far north as Zone 6 if covered with a heavy winter mulch such as salt hay or wood chips, but the foliage may die back or suffer severely. They do best in Zones 8-10, and gardeners north of those zones generally grow them in large containers that can be put in a frost-free location during the winter. All crinums except *C. moorei* need moist, well-drained soil in full sun with light shade during the hottest hours. In southern gardens, the bulbs can be planted any time; space them 12 to 18 inches apart and cover them with 6 inches of soil. Garden plantings can be left undisturbed indefinitely.

As house plants, crinums do best in at least four hours of direct sunlight a day, with indirect or curtain-filtered sunlight during the hottest part of the summer. Night temperatures of 50° to 55° and day temperatures of 68° to 72° are ideal. Plant the bulbs any time in a potting mixture of 1 part peat moss, 1 part packaged potting soil and 1 part coarse sand or perlite, with ground limestone added at a rate of 3 to 5 ounces per bushel, and set them so that their tips are barely covered. Keep moist and fertilize monthly with a house-plant fertilizer from April through September. Let the soil become slightly dry and withhold fertilizer while the plants are dormant in winter. Crinums flower most abundantly when the roots become crowded, so do not repot more often than every three to four years.

Propagate at any time of the year from the small bulbs that develop beside the larger ones.

CROCOSMIA

C. aurea, also called *Tritonia aurea* (coppertip); *C. crocosmiiflora,* also called *Montbretia crocosmiiflora, Tritonia crocosmiiflora* (montbretia); *C. masonorum,* also called *Tritonia masonorum.* (All called crocosmia)

In late summer and fall crocosmias, relatives of the gladiolus from South Africa, bear slender 2- to 4-foot flower stalks with spikes of 1½-inch blossoms set amid sword-shaped foliage. *C. aurea,* with golden yellow flowers, is exceedingly handsome but has been largely superseded by the hybrid *C. crocosmiiflora,* whose colors range from yellow and orange to brilliant orange scarlet. *C. masonorum* bears erect orange-yellow flowers on arching spikes. All crocosmias make excellent and long-lived cut flowers, and provide garden color late in the season after most other flowering plants have faded.

HOW TO GROW. Hardy in Zones 6-10, crocosmias must be lifted and protected from the cold elsewhere. They do best in full sun. Plant the corms in spring, spacing them 3 inches apart and covering them with 2 inches of soil. Apply a light dusting of 5-10-5 fertilizer when the plants emerge and again three to four weeks later.

MONTBRETIA
Crocosmia crocosmiiflora

In Zones 6-7 in fall, apply a heavy winter mulch such as salt hay or wood chips. North of Zone 6, lift the corms after cutting off the tops that have been frosted. Since the corms never become completely dormant, lift several together with the soil clinging to them. Allow them to dry for a few days in an airy place out of the sun, then store them at 55° to 60° in dry peat moss, perlite or vermiculite, without removing the dry soil, until planting time in the spring. Where they are hardy, dig them up and divide the crowded corms every third spring.

Propagate from the small corms that develop next to the large ones. Crocosmias can also be grown from seeds, but take about three years to reach flowering size.

CROCUS
Many species and varieties commonly called crocus.

To many gardeners the very name crocus is a synonym for spring, yet all crocuses do not blossom then; there are also species that bloom in fall and even some that flower in winter in mild climates. All are wild flowers native to southern Europe and Asia Minor, and they send up 1- to 2-inch wineglass-shaped flowers on stems 2 to 6 inches tall before the leaves are fully developed. The arching, grasslike foliage continues to grow after the flowers fade and may become 8 to 10 inches long before it matures and finally withers away. Flower colors for species and hybrid crocuses run through shades of lavender to deepest purple, as well as yellow and white; many varieties are attractively striped, and all of them have prominent yellow stamens.

Spring-flowering species include *C. biflorus*, Scotch crocus (shades of purple); *C. chrysanthus*, golden crocus (orange yellow); *C. etruscus*, Tuscan crocus (lilac or cream); *C. fleischerii*, Fleischer crocus (white with lilac stripes); *C. imperati*, early crocus (lilac or white with purple stripes); *C. korolkowii*, Korolkow crocus (orange yellow); *C. moesicus (C. aureus)*, Moesia crocus (bright yellow); *C. sieberii*, Sieber crocus (lilac); *C. susianus*, cloth-of-gold crocus (bright orange yellow inside, brown outside); *C. tomasinianus*, Tomasinian crocus (reddish blue); and *C. vernus*, common crocus (lilac or white with purple stripes).

Spring crocuses also include early-blooming, large-flowered Dutch varieties such as Jeanne d'Arc, Kathleen Parlow and Blizzard (white); Yellow Mammoth and Golden Goblet (yellow); Little Dorrit, Queen of the Blues and Early Perfection (lilac); The Sultan, Paulus Potter and Remembrance (deep purple); and Cinderella, Pickwick and Striped Beauty (striped pale and deep lilac).

Autumn-flowering species include *C. cancellatus*, the cross-barred crocus (lilac or white); *C. longiflorus*, the long-flower crocus, *C. medius*, the intermediate crocus and *C. pulchellus*, the pretty crocus (all bright lilac); *C. sativus*, the saffron crocus (lilac or white); *C. speciosus*, the showy crocus (lilac and purple to blue); and *C. zonatus*, the banded crocus (rose lilac with a yellow throat).

For the earliest spring bloom, plant crocuses in a sunny protected spot; for later bloom, plant them on the north side of a wall, hedge or building, or under very light shade. The Dutch crocuses do well naturalized in grass; the species crocuses have shorter stems and are better suited to rock gardens. Crocuses may also be grown in pots for midwinter bloom indoors.

HOW TO GROW. Hardy in Zones 3-10, crocuses do best in parts of the country that have cool or cold winter temperatures, especially from Zone 7 northward. Plant the corms in full sun or light shade as early in the fall as possible, spacing them 2 to 6 inches apart and covering them with 2 to 4 inches of soil. Heavy fertilizing is not necessary; apply a light dusting of bone meal or 5-10-5 fertilizer on the

SPRING-FLOWERING CROCUS
CLOCKWISE FROM TOP LEFT: *Crocus chrysanthus hybrid,*
C. chrysanthus 'Zwanenburg Bronze,' *C. imperati, C. moesicus,*
C. tomasinianus, C. susianus

For climate zones and frost dates, see maps, pages 148-149.

107

AUTUMN-FLOWERING CROCUS
TOP: *Crocus speciosus* CENTER: *C. sativus*
BOTTOM: *C. cancellatus*

soil each fall so that it can work in during the winter months. Some gardeners dig up and separate the corms in early summer every three or four years, but undisturbed clumps fed as noted above will increase in beauty from year to year. Propagation is by natural increase of corms, which multiply rapidly in rich soil.

Plants can also be grown from seeds, but since they require three to four years to reach flowering size, and because the corms are so inexpensive to purchase, most gardeners prefer to buy additional corms.

As house plants, crocuses do best in at least four hours of direct sunlight a day, night temperatures of 40° to 50° and day temperatures of 68° or lower. They are often bought as fully blossoming plants from florists or nurseries in midwinter, but they can also be started from large-sized dormant corms in October. Pot the corms in a mixture of 1 part peat moss, 1 part packaged potting soil, and 1 part sharp sand or perlite, with ground limestone added at a rate of 3 to 5 ounces per bushel. Keep them in a cold frame until mid-January or later, then bring them indoors. Keep the mixture moist as long as the foliage is green but do not fertilize.

CROCUS, AUTUMN See *Colchicum*
CROWN IMPERIAL See *Fritillaria*

CYCLAMEN
C. cilicicum (Sicily cyclamen); *C. coum*, also called *C. atkinsii, C. caucasicum, C. hyemale, C. ibericum, C. orbiculatum, C. vernum* (Cos cyclamen); *C. europeum* (European cyclamen); *C. neapolitanum* (Neapolitan cyclamen); *C.* 'Puck'; *C. persicum* (Persian or florists' cyclamen)

The large-flowered cyclamens, whose bright 2- to 4-inch blossoms beckon through florists' windows during the winter months, are well known to most gardeners, but not everyone is as familiar with the charming little wild, or species, cyclamens that may be grown in gardens throughout most of the country. Compared to their hot-house sisters, these species could be called miniatures because they grow only 4 to 5 inches tall, bearing ¾- to 1-inch butterflylike flowers in shades of pink or white.

Cyclamens are native to the islands and shores of the Mediterranean. In this country they blossom, according to their species, in spring or fall. In Zone 9 spring-flowering species come into blossom from January through March; elsewhere they open in April and May. Fall-flowering species bloom for four to six weeks, beginning as early as August in warmer areas and lasting into October in cooler regions. Flowers of every species bloom for many weeks. Most species lose their foliage for a brief period each year, usually in midsummer.

Among the species commonly available, *C. cilicicum* has pale rose flowers and marbled leaves and blossoms in the fall; *C. coum,* which blossoms in the spring, comes in red, pink and white and has plain green or marbled foliage; *C. europeum* has marbled foliage and fragrant crimson-rose flowers in the fall; *C. neapolitanum* has marbled foliage and rose-to-white flowers in the fall.

The small-flowered cyclamens are best grown where they can be enjoyed close at hand, beneath the shade of a tree sheltering an intimate entrance garden or in a protected nook beside a favorite chair on a patio.

C. persicum, the winter-blooming florists', or Persian, cyclamen, has pink, red, lavender or white flowers and plain or marbled foliage; plants grow about a foot tall. Puck, a hybrid that blooms almost continuously, bears 2-inch flowers on 6- to 8-inch plants. Florists' cyclamens are generally bought as flowering pot plants.

HOW TO GROW. Most small-flowered cyclamens are suited for gardens in Zones 5-9—Zone 10 is too hot for them, and Zone 4 is generally too cold, although some gardeners grow them by covering the beds with a winter mulch such as salt hay or wood chips.

All small-flowered cyclamens do best in light shade in soil enriched with compost. An annual spring mulch of about ½ inch of compost gives enough nourishment. Plant the tubers in midsummer, spacing them 6 to 8 inches apart. Cover the tubers of Neapolitan cyclamens with 2 inches of soil; set the tubers of others just beneath the soil.

Florists' cyclamens and Puck can be planted in fall in Zones 9-10 for winter and spring bloom. Set growing plants 12 to 18 inches apart with the tubers half above the soil level. Discard after flowering.

As house plants, cyclamens do best in bright indirect or curtain-filtered sunlight, night temperatures of 40° to 55° and day temperatures of 65° or lower. Pot in a mixture of 2 parts peat moss to 1 part packaged potting soil and 1 part sharp sand or perlite, with ground limestone added at a rate of 3 to 5 ounces per bushel. Keep the potting medium well moistened and feed every two weeks with a standard house-plant fertilizer.

Cyclamens may be propagated from seeds, which usually take about 18 months to reach flowering size (Puck will bloom in about four to six months).

CYPELLA
C. herbertii, C. peruviana, C. plumbea

Cypellas are South American wild flowers, rare enough to appeal to gardeners who want unusual plants. These summer-flowering bulbs produce irislike blossoms, 3 inches across, above sword-shaped leaves 1 to 3 feet tall. Each flower lasts only a day, but the flower spikes bear enough buds to extend the blooming season over a period of several weeks. C. herbertii has mustard-yellow flowers; C. peruviana has bright yellow flowers with brown bases; C. plumbea has grayish lilac flowers and its variety C. plumbea platensis has bright blue flowers.

HOW TO GROW. In Zones 9-10, cypellas may be left in the garden year round, but farther north they must be dug up in fall after the foliage turns brown. Let the bulbs dry for about a week in an airy place out of the sun; then store them over the winter at 55° to 60° in dry peat moss, perlite or vermiculite.

Cypellas do best in full sun. Plant the bulbs in early spring, spacing them 6 inches apart and covering them with 3 to 4 inches of soil. Apply a dusting of 5-10-5 fertilizer every two to three weeks from the time the shoots appear until the buds show color.

Propagate from the small bulbs that develop around large ones, or from seeds. Seedlings sown in spring usually produce flowering plants during their second season.

D

DAFFODIL See *Narcissus*
DAFFODIL, PERUVIAN See *Hymenocallis*
DAFFODIL, SEA See *Pancratium*

DAHLIA
D. hybrida

Dahlias are among the most accommodating of all garden plants and can easily be grown virtually anywhere in the United States and Canada if the roots are protected from frost. Their blossoms, which come in every flower color except clear blue, range from miniatures less than an inch across to giants more than a foot in diameter; they bloom from midsummer until frost on stiff, erect stems 1

NEAPOLITAN CYCLAMEN
Cyclamen neapolitanum

CYPELLA
Cypella herbertii

For climate zones and frost dates, see maps, pages 148-149.

to 7 feet tall, providing constant color in the garden and superb cut flowers indoors. The plants grow from tuberous roots and die back each fall either from maturity in warm climates or from frost elsewhere.

The horticultural name, *D. hybrida,* alludes to the fact that modern dahlias are descended from several species native to Mexico. New hybrids are introduced frequently and go in and out of popularity—almost like automobile styles. They vary so much in flower and stature that they are classified in 16 categories, each of which spans the full color range and most of which include the full gamut of heights and blossom sizes. The descriptions that follow include the standard abbreviations by which the classes are often listed in flower catalogues.

ANEMONE-FLOWERED DAHLIAS (An) are distinguished by pincushionlike clusters of tiny tubular flowers, surrounded by a single row of flat petals radiating outward. BALL DAHLIAS (Ba) have ball-shaped flower heads, 4 or more inches in diameter, consisting of short, closely set, spirally arranged petals. CACTUS-FLOWERED DAHLIAS (C) produce flowers consisting of a profusion of petals, many of them rolled or quill-shaped. INCURVED CACTUS DAHLIAS (IC) have blossoms similar to those of the cactus dahlias, but with petals that curve inward instead of radiating outward.

SEMICACTUS DAHLIAS (SC) have blossoms with petals that become tubelike at their ends for less than one third of the petal's length. STRAIGHT CACTUS DAHLIAS (St-C) have blossoms with petals that are tubelike at their ends for more than half of the petal's length. COLLARETTE DAHLIAS (Coll) have flowers that consist of a single row of petals radiating outward around an inner row of shorter petals, often of a contrasting color, which in turn surround the open center of the flower. DWARF DAHLIAS (Dwf) may become up to 2½ feet tall and usually bear great numbers of 3- to 4-inch-wide flowers consisting of a single row of petals. FORMAL DECORATIVE DAHLIAS (FD) have blossoms with a profusion of equal-length, symmetrically arranged petals. INFORMAL DECORATIVE DAHLIAS (ID) have blossoms whose abundant petals are long, often twisted and unevenly spaced. MINIATURE DAHLIAS (M) bear flowers in all of the dahlia shapes except the ball and the pompon; the blossoms are only 2½ to 4½ inches in diameter; the plants seldom grow more than 4 feet tall. MINIATURE BALL DAHLIAS (M Ba) have ball-shaped flower heads, with closely set, spirally arranged petals, and blossoms are less than 4 inches across. ORCHID DAHLIAS (O) have star-shaped flowers with open centers; the long petals curve backward at their ends. PEONY DAHLIAS (P) bear flowers whose open centers are surrounded by two or three rows of petals, often twisted or curled, that radiate outward. POMPON DAHLIAS (Pom) have lushly petaled blossoms similar to those of ball dahlias, but the flower heads are not quite so round and most are only about 2 inches in diameter. SINGLE DAHLIAS (S) have flowers with open centers that are surrounded by a row of outward-radiating petals.

Flower catalogues not only abbreviate dahlia classes but also often abbreviate dahlia blossom sizes, as follows: A. more than 8 inches across; B, 6-8 inches across; BB, 4-6 inches across; M, less than 4 inches across.

HOW TO GROW. Named varieties of dahlias are sold by growers in three forms: root divisions, pot roots and so-called green plants, which are young plants, 4 to 6 inches high, that have been grown from stem cuttings.

A root division consists of a single root shaped much like that of a sweet potato, one end of which has been cut so that it contains a bit of the stem of the mother plant; from this stem end arise the buds that will form the stems of the growing plant.

TOP: CACTUS-FLOWERED DAHLIA   CENTER: FORMAL DECORATIVE DAHLIA
BOTTOM: POMPON DAHLIA
Dahlia hybrida

Pot roots are produced by the grower by letting stem cuttings mature in small pots containing potting soil, in which they make tiny clusters of roots; such clusters have the advantage of having a number of buds and no cut surfaces, which are possible areas of decay. Generally speaking, however, root divisions are every bit as good as pot roots for the average gardener.

In Zone 10 dahlias may be planted in late summer for winter bloom provided no frosts occur. Everywhere else they must be treated as tender plants—planted in the spring, and dug up in the fall and stored in a frost-free location during the winter months. They like bright sunshine, but will do creditably in light shade if they receive at least three or four hours of sunshine a day; the more sun they get, the sturdier the plants will be.

Dahlias may be grown in any garden soil, but will do best in one that is rich in organic matter, phosphorus and potash. Dig in compost, well-decayed manure or peat moss, and a fertilizer such as 0-20-20 at a rate of 5 to 6 pounds per 100 square feet.

Set green plants or pot roots in the garden as you would any plant. Root divisions should be laid on their sides in holes 7 inches deep and covered with 2 inches of soil; add more soil as they grow until the hole is filled (*drawings, page 20*). Space green plants, root divisions or pot roots 15 to 30 inches apart, depending upon the size of the variety being grown. When the plants have become well established, feed with a complete garden fertilizer, such as 5-10-10, spread lightly and evenly, then scratched into the surface of the soil and well watered.

Most gardeners support the growing plants with stakes, set beside them as they are planted; some gardeners, especially in windy areas, simply pinch off the top of the stems to produce low-growing, stocky plants.

When cutting dahlias for the house, dip the ends of the stems into an inch of boiling water for a second, or sear them with a candle flame. This will make the blossoms last longer without wilting. As an alternative, cut them in the early morning and immediately put the stems in 2 inches of hot water (100°) and allow them to sit for four to six hours before arranging them.

When dahlias have finished flowering in the fall, dig up the roots, allow them to dry for an hour or so, then put them into boxes lined with plastic and fill in around them with dry peat moss, perlite or vermiculite. In order to keep the roots from sprouting, put them in the coldest part of the cellar. But in the heated cellars of today's homes, this requires special attention (*drawing, page 76*).

Dahlias may be propagated from root divisions or from stem cuttings. They also produce flowers the first year when grown from seeds; the dwarf strains, such as Coltness, Unwin, Early Bird or Border Jewels, are often treated as annuals. Seeds should be sown indoors six to eight weeks before the last frost is due. Seedlings of named varieties are usually markedly inferior to the parent plants; the excellence of named varieties results from the selection of the best out of many thousands of seed-grown plants.

DASHEEN See *Colocasia*
DESERT CANDLE See *Eremurus*
DICHELOSTEMMA See *Brodiaea*
DIETES See *Morea*
DOUBLE-DECKER PLANT See *Rechsteineria*

E

EDELWEISS, BRAZILIAN See *Rechsteineria*
ELEPHANT'S-EAR See *Colocasia*
ENDYMION See *Scilla*

TOP: COLLARETTE DAHLIA   CENTER: SINGLE DAHLIA
BOTTOM: ANEMONE-FLOWERED DAHLIA
Dahlia hybrida

For climate zones and frost dates, see maps, pages 148-149.

WINTER ACONITE
Eranthis hyemalis

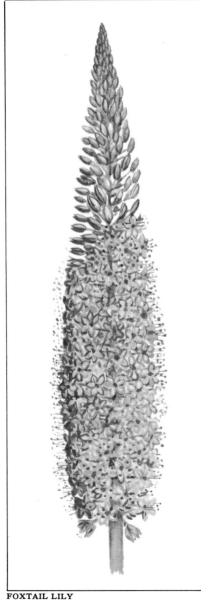

FOXTAIL LILY
Eremurus 'Shelford Hybrid'

ERANTHIS

E. cilicica (Cilician winter aconite), *E. hyemalis* (winter aconite), *E. tubergenii* (Tubergen winter aconite)

In earliest spring, winter aconites send up bright yellow honey-scented flowers that cover the ground like a golden carpet. Each 2- to 4-inch stem bears a single blossom above a ruff of finely divided green or bronze-green leaves that mature quickly and soon disappear until the following spring. Both *E. cilicica* and *E. hyemalis* have flowers about an inch across. *E. tubergenii* and its hybrids, Glory and Guinea Gold, have 2-inch flowers. Winter aconites are especially lovely in rock gardens. They are relatives of the buttercup and should not be confused with true aconites (*Aconitum*), which are summer-flowering perennials.

HOW TO GROW. Hardy in Zones 4-9, winter aconites do well in full sun or light shade; they thrive in any soil that does not dry out severely in summer, but should be planted where they are protected from wind. Purchase the twiglike tubers as soon as they are available in late summer, and soak them in water for 24 hours before planting. Space the tubers 3 to 4 inches apart and cover them with 2 to 3 inches of soil. Plants can be moved even when in bloom, but make sure to dig up sods of the tubers and divide and replant them with the soil still clinging to them. Winter aconites can also be propagated easily from seeds (they often spread by sowing their seeds; seedlings take two to three years to flower).

EREMURUS

E. himalaicus (Himalayan foxtail lily), *E. robustus* (giant foxtail lily), *E.* 'Shelford Hybrids.'
(All called foxtail lily, desert candle)

Foxtail lilies are spectacular tuberous-rooted plants that tower as much as 9 feet high. The top 3 or 4 feet of each leafless stalk bears hundreds of ¾- to 1-inch flowers in late spring or early summer, making them impressive against tall evergreens or at the back of a perennial border. When cut, the flowers last up to three weeks. Shortly after the flowers fade, the slender 1- to 3-foot leaves at the bases of the plants wither away. The Himalayan foxtail lily grows 8 to 9 feet tall and bears white flowers; the giant foxtail lily grows 6 to 8 feet tall and bears pink flowers; Shelford Hybrids grow 3 to 4 feet tall and bear white, orange, yellow, cream, rose or peach-pink flowers.

HOW TO GROW. Foxtail lilies can be grown in gardens in Zones 5-9 and do best in full sun. Plant them any time from September to December in a rich sandy loam supplemented with compost or decayed or dried cow manure, spacing them 1½ to 3 feet apart and covering each brittle root with 6 inches of soil. Mulch each fall with compost and salt hay or wood chips. Remove the mulch early in spring, but leave it beside the plants until all danger of frost is past so that you can easily cover the tender new growth on cold nights. Foxtail lilies can be left untouched for 10 to 15 years; because they resent being disturbed, it is better to buy new roots than to divide plantings. Seedlings take about six years to reach flowering size.

ERYTHRONIUM

E. albidum (white fawn lily), *E. americanum* (adder's-tongue), *E. californicum* (California fawn lily), *E. citrinum* (lemon fawn lily), *E. dens-canis* (dog's-tooth violet), *E. grandiflorum* (lamb's-tongue fawn lily), *E. hendersonii* (Henderson fawn lily), *E. oregonum* (Oregon fawn lily), *E. purpurascens* (Sierra fawn lily), *E. revolutum* (mahogany fawn lily)

North American species of these dainty woodland flowers are sometimes known by such picturesque names as avalanche lily, alpine lily or glacier lily, but they are most commonly called fawn lilies or trout lilies because their leaves are often mottled with brown. The one European species grown in the United States is known as dog's-tooth violet because its bulb is shaped something like a dog's tooth. Fawn lilies bear delicately scented, 1- to 3-inch flowers in spring, and look most natural when grown in generous clumps beside a shady path or in a shaded rock or wild-flower garden. *E. citrinum* grows 8 inches tall and has lemon-yellow flowers; *E. dens-canis* grows 6 inches tall and has rose-purple flowers; and *E. grandiflorum* grows 24 inches tall, bearing unmottled green foliage and bright yellow flowers. Most other species grow about a foot tall; these include *E. albidum*, with plain or mottled leaves and white-to-pink flowers; *E. americanum*, with rather sparse yellow flowers; *E. californicum*, with cream-white flowers; *E. hendersonii*, with purple flowers; *E. oregonum*, with creamy white flowers; *E. purpurascens*, with plain leaves and purple-tinged yellow flowers; and *E. revolutum*, with cream-colored flowers that turn purplish as they age.

HOW TO GROW. Fawn lilies survive winters outdoors in Zones 3-9, but cannot stand extreme heat or dryness and are seldom grown in Zone 10. They do best in light shade. Plant the bulbs any time in summer or fall, spacing them 4 to 6 inches apart and covering them with 2 to 3 inches of soil. Apply a mulch of coarse peat moss every two or three years in fall. Fawn lilies may be left undisturbed indefinitely. Propagate in summer or fall from the small bulbs that develop around larger ones, replanting immediately so the bulbs do not dry out. Plants started from seeds require two or three years to reach flowering size.

EUCHARIS

E. grandiflora, also called *E. amazonica* (Amazon lily)

Amazon lilies, whose fragrant 2-inch blossoms look much like white daffodils, are favorites for wedding bouquets, as well as for potted plants and cut flowers. They have alternate periods of growth and rest and may bloom at any time, sending up 1- to 2-foot stems that bear clusters of three to six blossoms above shiny evergreen leaves.

HOW TO GROW. Amazon lilies cannot survive frost and are most successfully grown in containers even in warm climates because they bloom most profusely when their roots are confined. Indoors or out, they do best in bright light but not direct sun. Night temperatures of 65° to 70° and day temperatures of 75° or higher are ideal. Pot the bulbs any time in a mixture of 2 parts peat moss, 1 part packaged potting soil, 1 part sharp sand or perlite, with ground limestone added at a rate of 3 to 5 ounces per bushel. Plant three or four bulbs to an 8-inch flowerpot, setting the tips flush with the surface of the mixture. While the plants are growing, keep very moist and feed every two weeks with a standard house-plant fertilizer. After flowers have faded, withhold fertilizer and water only enough to prevent the foliage from withering. Let the plants rest for a few weeks. When new growth appears, resume regular watering and feeding. Do not repot the bulbs more often than every two or three years. Propagate any time from the small bulbs that develop around the large ones.

EUCOMIS

E. autumnalis, also called *E. undulata; E. bicolor; E. comosa,* also called *E. punctata; E. zambesiaca.* (All called pineapple lily, pineapple flower)

These natives of South Africa, which look strangely like pineapples sprouting flowers, bloom for several weeks in midsummer, bearing masses of ½-inch blossoms on 1- to 2-foot stalks that rise above rosettes of leaves as long as 2

LEFT: ADDER'S-TONGUE
Erythronium americanum
RIGHT: WHITE FAWN LILY
E. albidum

OREGON FAWN LILY
Erythronium oregonum 'White Beauty'

AMAZON LILY
Eucharis grandiflora

For climate zones and frost dates, see maps, pages 148-149.

PINEAPPLE LILY
Eucomis comosa

feet. *E. autumnalis* grows about a foot tall and has greenish white flowers; *E. bicolor* grows up to 1½ feet tall and has greenish yellow flowers edged with purple. *E. comosa* grows 1½ to 2 feet tall and bears fragrant creamy white flowers with violet brown in their centers; the leaves are spotted purple. *E. zambesiaca* grows a foot tall with greenish white blossoms. All make attractive cut flowers.

HOW TO GROW. Pineapple lilies survive winters in Zones 7-10, but are sometimes left outdoors in Zone 6 when set at the base of a sunny wall and given ample protection with a heavy mulch such as salt hay or wood chips. Even in the South, however, they are often grown in containers that can be moved indoors at the season's end. Plant bulbs in the garden in early fall, spacing them about a foot apart and covering them with 5 to 6 inches of soil. Apply a dusting of 5-10-5 fertilizer in the spring when new growth is visible. When grown in pots or tubs, the bulbs should be set just beneath the soil surface in spring. Wherever grown, they do best in full sun. Growth appears rather late in spring and is not apt to be nipped by late frosts when potted plants are set outdoors. Garden plantings can be left undisturbed for years, but container-grown plants should be repotted in fresh soil each year. Keep container-grown plants moist from spring to fall and dry during winter, when they must be stored in a frost-free location. Propagate from the small bulbs that develop beside large ones or from seeds. Seedlings require about five years to flower.

F

FAIR-MAID-OF-FEBRUARY See *Galanthus*
FAIRY LANTERN See *Calochortus*
FIRECRACKER FLOWER See *Brodiaea*
FLOWER OF THE WEST WIND See *Zephyranthes*

FREESIA
F. armstrongii, F. hybrida, F. refracta

Freesias are so strongly scented that even a few potted or cut blossoms will bring fragrance to an entire room. The 2-inch blossoms of *F. armstrongii* are pink; those of *F. refracta* are white or yellow; freesia hybrids range from white to blends of lilac, mauve, purple, blue, yellow, orange, pink or vermilion. Freesias have slender sword-shaped leaves and wiry stems 1 to 1½ feet long that may need support. Most freesias bloom in winter or early spring. But specially treated corms from Holland are summer blooming.

HOW TO GROW. Hardy in Zones 9-10, freesias—except for the treated corms—are grown as house plants elsewhere. In Zones 9-10 they do best in a sunny location in the garden, or one with light shade during midday. Plant the corms in fall, spacing them 2 to 4 inches apart and covering them with 2 inches of soil. Feed monthly from the time the plant emerges until the buds take on color with a dusting of 5-10-5 fertilizer.

North of Zone 9, plant treated corms in spring for midsummer bloom. These plantings are most successful in areas where summer evenings are cool. After the foliage withers, dig up the corms and store in a dry place until fall, then pot for indoor blooming in winter.

All freesias can be grown as house plants. Set the corms barely beneath the surface in a mixture of 1 part peat moss, 1 part packaged potting soil and 1 part sharp sand or perlite, with ground limestone added at a rate of 3 to 5 ounces per bushel. Keep the plants outside in a cool, sunny location in summer, moving them indoors before frost. They do best in at least four hours of direct sunlight a day, night temperatures of 55° to 60° and day temperatures of 68° to 72°. Keep the mix moist during the growing season and fertilize monthly until the buds show color.

FREESIA
TOP: *Freesia hybrida*   CENTER: *F. armstrongii*
BOTTOM: *F. refracta*

When the foliage withers, withhold water. After the leaves die, propagate from the small corms that develop beside large ones and store them in a dry place until the following planting season. Plants can also be grown from seeds. Rub the seeds together to loosen the outer coating, then soak them for 24 hours before planting. Seedlings take from six months to a year to flower.

FREESIA, FLAME See *Tritonia*

FRITILLARIA

F. imperialis (crown imperial), *F. meleagris* (checkered fritillary, guinea-hen flower, snake's-head), *F. lanceolata* (riceroot fritillary), *F. pluriflora* (pink fritillary), *F. pudica* (yellow fritillary), *F. recurva* (scarlet fritillary)

Leaping from the earth in spring, unmarred by frosty weather, the 2½- to 4-foot stems of the crown imperial are topped by a crest of leaves beneath which hang great clusters of 2-inch reddish orange, bronze, red or yellow flowers. Because the flowers' odor is musky and the lilylike leaves die down in early summer, crown imperial is best planted in perennial or shrub borders where neither its scent nor its fading foliage will be objectionable. The only other species that is widely grown in the United States is the spring-blooming *F. meleagris*. It grows about 12 inches tall with drooping bell-shaped 1½-inch flowers checkered purple and white; *F. meleagris alba* is pure white. Both make good borders or random plantings in rough grass.

There are many species of fritillaria native to western North America, but these usually do not succeed elsewhere. Among them are *F. lanceolata*, which grows 1 to 2 feet tall and has yellow-mottled dark purple 1-inch flowers; *F. pluriflora*, which grows 6 to 12 inches tall and has pinkish purple 1-inch flowers; *F. pudica*, which grows 6 to 9 inches tall and has purple-tinged yellow 1-inch flowers; and *F. recurva*, which grows 24 to 30 inches tall and has yellow-checkered scarlet 1-inch flowers. All bloom in spring.

HOW TO GROW. *F. meleagris* and *F. pudica* are hardy in Zones 3-10; *F. imperialis*, *F. lanceolata* and *F. pluriflora* are hardy in Zones 5-10 and *F. recurva* is hardy in Zones 6-10. All do best in a soil with a pH of 6.0 to 7.5 and in light shade or in a place that is shaded during the hottest part of the day. Plant the bulbs in summer or fall as soon as they are available. Set *F. imperialis* bulbs 8 inches apart and cover them with 6 inches of soil. Set the others 3 to 4 inches apart and cover them with 3 to 4 inches of soil. Apply a dusting of 5-10-5 fertilizer when new growth emerges in spring. Plantings may be left undisturbed for years where they can survive winters outdoors.

When the foliage dies in early summer, dig up the plants. Separate and replant the bulbs immediately. Propagate from the small bulbs around the large ones. Seedlings take four to six years to flower.

FRITILLARY See *Fritillaria*

G

GALANTHUS

G. elwesii (giant snowdrop), *G. nivalis* (common snowdrop). (Both called fair-maid-of-February)

Snowdrops are among the first flowers to open in spring and can also be grown indoors for midwinter bloom. Each translucent blossom is composed of three green-tipped inner petals and three longer, all-white outer petals; the slender leaves grow 3 to 8 inches long and wither away in late spring. Snowdrops grow particularly well beneath deciduous trees and are well suited to random planting amidst rough grass. The only species usually available from bulb

TOP: CROWN IMPERIAL
Fritillaria imperialis

BOTTOM: CHECKERED FRITILLARY
F. meleagris

sellers are the giant snowdrop, 6 to 9 inches tall, and the common snowdrop, 4 to 6 inches tall; both have 1-inch flowers. The latter has several varieties; two merit special note: *G. nivalis* 'S. Arnott,' which grows 6 to 10 inches tall with sweetly scented flowers, is considered the finest variety. Another notable variety is *G. nivalis flore pleno,* which grows 4 to 6 inches tall with many-petaled globe-shaped flowers.

HOW TO GROW. Snowdrops can be grown outdoors in Zones 3-9 but do better in northern gardens than in warm climates. They grow best in light shade. Plant the bulbs in early fall, spacing them 2 to 4 inches apart and covering them with 2 to 3 inches of soil. Do not fertilize. Snowdrops may be left undisturbed for years. Bulbs can be dug up and divided soon after flowering, then replanted immediately so the roots do not dry out. But since they are inexpensive, most gardeners simply buy new ones. Snowdrops can also be started from seeds; indeed, the plants often spread by casting their own seeds. Seedlings take three to four years to flower.

To grow indoors, plant the bulbs in fall. Set them ½ inch deep in the mixture recommended for *Freesia (page 114).* Put the pots in a cold frame, then bring them indoors any time after the first of the year. They do best in indirect or curtain-filtered sunlight in the coolest room —ideally under 50°. Keep moist but do not fertilize. After the flowers fade, set the plants in the garden.

GALTONIA

G. candicans, also called *Hyacinthus candicans* (summer hyacinth)

Summer hyacinths bear 20 to 30 fragrant bell-shaped flowers on 3- to 4-foot spikes for a month in midsummer. The strap-shaped leaves grow 2 to 3 feet long and die down in fall. Because of their height, plant summer hyacinths at the back of a garden or among low shrubs. Their flowers open when gladioluses do and combine well with them in cut-flower arrangements.

HOW TO GROW. Summer hyacinths do best in full sun. Plant in fall in Zones 8-10, in spring north of Zone 8, spacing the bulbs about 15 inches apart and covering them with 6 to 7 inches of soil. Plants may be left in the garden year round in Zones 5-10, but from Zones 5-7 they need a winter mulch such as salt hay or wood chips. North of Zone 5—and in Zones 5-7 if you do not want to risk losing them—dig the bulbs up after the first frost and store them over the winter at 55° to 60° in open-mesh bags. Propagate from the small bulbs that develop beside large ones, or from seeds. Seedlings take several years to flower.

GARLIC See *Allium*
GARLIC, SOCIETY See *Tulbaghia*

GLADIOLUS

G. blandus (snowpink gladiolus); *G. byzantinus* (Byzantine gladiolus); *G. colvillii,* also called *G. colvillei; G. hybridus; G. tristis* (evening-flower gladiolus)

Gladioluses are grown primarily for cutting, and few if any other plants offer such a wide variety or mass of color for bouquets. Plants range from 1 foot to over 5 feet in height, depending upon the variety and growing conditions. Although individual plants bloom only for a week to 10 days, a staggered planting schedule will assure flowers for about three months. All have sword-shaped foliage that may remain green until cut down by frost.

Of the 150 or more wild forms of the genus, plant breeders have used about a dozen South African species in developing *G. hybridus,* the familiar modern "glads." Because of their complex ancestry, these hybrids are classified by

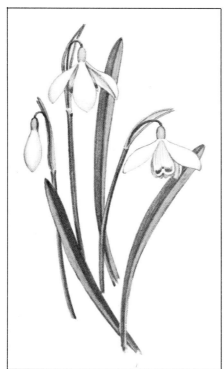

COMMON SNOWDROP
Galanthus nivalis

SUMMER HYACINTH
Galtonia candicans

116

color and flower size. The North American Gladiolus Council recognizes 28 different basic colors and lists them in a numerical sequence beginning with white (coded 00-01) through green, cream, yellow, buff, orange, salmon, scarlet, pink, red, rose, lavender, purple and blue to smoky, tan and brown (96-97). Numbers have been reserved in the ranges where new colors are expected to be developed. The flower size is also coded: In the 100, or miniature, series, the small flowers, or florets, that make up the flower spike are under 2½ inches wide; the 200 series (small) has florets 2½ to 3½ inches wide; the 300 series (medium) has florets 3½ to 4½ inches wide; the 400 series (large) has florets 4½ to 5½ inches wide; and the 500 series (giant) has florets over 5½ inches wide. Some varieties now have florets as much as 8 inches in diameter.

In many bulb catalogues, the color and size codes are combined into a three-digit number following the varietal name, for example, Landmark (510). The 5 indicates that it is of the 500, or giant, series, with florets over 5½ inches wide; the 10 means they are cream colored. The catalogues usually have descriptions of the plants. (The 100 series varieties are seldom catalogued; "miniature" is usually applied to the 200 series.)

In addition to varieties of G. hybridus, one other hybrid and three species of gladiolus are sometimes grown. G. colvillii, reported to be the first hybrid gladiolus, grows 18 inches tall and has bright red flowers marked with yellow on the lower petals. G. blandus grows 12 to 18 inches tall and has pink flowers; G. byzantinus grows 2 feet tall and has red flowers; and G. tristis grows 18 inches tall and its fragrant creamy white flowers open in the evening.

HOW TO GROW. Although G. hybridus can be left in the garden year round in Zones 8-10, the plants will flower more profusely if the corms are dug and reset annually, as they must be in the colder zones. The species G. byzantinus is hardy in Zones 5-10 and G. blandus, G. colvillii and G. tristis are hardy in Zones 7-10, but even these bloom better if dug up and reset annually.

All gladioluses do best in full sun. A light sandy loam is ideal, but they will grow satisfactorily in almost any garden soil that has been enriched with compost, leaf mold or peat moss. Add 5-10-5 fertilizer, one cup to a 25-foot row. Avoid animal manures; they encourage bulb rot.

To extend the season of bloom, plant gladiolus corms at intervals of seven to 10 days, starting after the last spring frost and continuing until two months before the first fall frost is expected. In Zones 9 and 10—except along the coast of California—the summer months are so hot that the corms should be planted only from November to February to bloom from January to May.

Plant the corms 4 to 6 inches apart, covering them with 4 to 6 inches of soil. Many gardeners place a double row of bulbs in the same 8-inch-wide trench, staggering the bulbs to achieve the proper spacing. Fertilize just as the spikes appear, and then after the flowers are picked, by scratching 5-10-5 fertilizer around the plants at the rate of 1 cup to a 25-foot row and watering it into the soil.

When plants are about 12 inches tall, hold them erect by mounding, or "hilling up," earth around the stems to a height of about 6 inches. Otherwise the gladioluses should be supported with stakes or with stake-supported cords down each side of the row. At this time, mulch around the plants with a 1-inch layer of sawdust or grass clippings to avoid further weeding and to conserve moisture.

Pick the spikes when two or three flowers on the stem have opened. The best times of day are early morning and late afternoon, when the stems are full of moisture. Separate the leaves slightly if necessary and, pulling gently on

LEFT: GLADIOLUS HYBRID   RIGHT: BYZANTINE GLADIOLUS
Gladiolus 'Cerulean'   G. byzantinus

For climate zones and frost dates, see maps, pages 148-149.

the stem, cut it with a sharp knife. But leave four or five leaves on the plant so that the corm can mature.

Dig up the corms four to six weeks after the flowers fade, or after frost. Lift them with a spading fork, cut off the tops and let the corms dry in a shallow container set in an airy place out of the sun for two or three weeks. Pull off the dried remnants of the old corms and save both the fresh corms and the cormels at their bases. (Cormels will reach flowering size in two years.) Dust the corms and cormels with a combination insecticide-fungicide and store them over the winter at 40° to 50°. Old nylon stockings make ideal storage bags because they can be hung up to allow air circulation around the corms. New plants can also be grown from seeds but, since the parent plants are hybrids, flower color and size are not predictable. Seedlings usually take three years to reach flowering size.

GLADIOLUS PLICATUS See *Babiana*

GLORIOSA
G. rothschildiana, G. superba (glory lily, climbing lily)
Climbing by tendrils on the ends of their slender leaves, glory-lily vines bear impressive 3- to 4-inch flowers and usually grow 3 to 4 feet tall, though some reach 6 feet in rich soil. In the mild climates of Zones 8-10, or when grown indoors in pots, they may produce flowers at any season. In cold climates, they flower in summer if planted outdoors. Two popular species are *G. rothschildiana,* with yellow petals turning scarlet at the ends, and *G. superba,* with orange petals that darken to red. Both are widely used in small bouquets and corsages.

HOW TO GROW. Glory lilies survive winters outdoors only in Zones 8-10. There they can be planted any time of the year, preferably in spring. They do best in full sun or very light shade and soil enriched with well-rotted cow manure. Lay the tubers on their sides 8 to 12 inches apart and cover them with 4 to 5 inches of soil. Give them a light support, such as a small trellis. Feed monthly during the growing season with a dusting of 5-10-5 fertilizer. North of Zone 8 plant in spring; dig up in fall and store over winter at 55° to 60° in dry peat moss, perlite or vermiculite.

As house plants, glory lilies need at least four hours of sunlight a day, night temperatures of 65° to 70° and day temperatures above 75°. Pot them in spring in the mixture recommended for *Freesia (page 114).* Keep moist and feed with a house-plant fertilizer every two weeks until the flowers fade; withhold moisture and food when dormant, normally October through January. Propagate by dividing the tubers in spring or by separating small tubers that develop beside the large ones. Plants started from seeds take two to three years to flower.

GLORY LILY
Gloriosa rothschildiana

GLORY-OF-THE-SNOW See *Chionodoxa*
GLOXINIA See *Sinningia*
GRASSNUT See *Brodiaea*
GUINEA-HEN FLOWER See *Fritillaria*

H

HAEMANTHUS
H. albiflos, H. coccineus, H. hybridus, H. katherinae, H. multiflorus. (All called blood lily)
Blood lilies produce masses of red, pink or white flowers in 6- to 12-inch clusters. The 8- to 20-inch stalks are leafless, but each plant bears two or more leaves that grow as much as 6 inches wide and 18 inches long, then die in fall. *H. albiflos* (white) and *H. coccineus* (coral red) blossom in early fall; *H. katherinae* (pink) and the hybrids Andromeda (salmon pink) and King Albert (scarlet) bloom

in late spring or early summer; *H. multiflorus* (blood red) flowers in summer. All make attractive pot plants.

HOW TO GROW. Blood lilies cannot survive frost, and even in the warmth of Zones 9-10 they blossom more freely when their roots are confined in pots. Pot in spring, placing one bulb to a container that is 2 inches wider than the diameter of the bulb. Use the mixture recommended for *Freesia (page 114)*. Set the bulb so its tip is just above the surface. Move the plants outside when night temperatures remain above 50°. During the growing season, keep moist and feed monthly with a house-plant fertilizer. While the plants are resting in fall and winter, keep the mixture nearly dry and do not feed. Each spring, use a hose to wash out part of the soil without disturbing the roots, and add fresh soil. As house plants, blood lilies do best in four hours of sunlight a day, night temperatures of 50° to 55° and day temperatures of 68° to 72°. Propagate in spring from the small bulbs that appear beside the large ones.

HARDY ORCHID See *Bletilla*
HARLEQUIN FLOWER See *Sparaxis*

HIPPEASTRUM
H. hybrids (amaryllis)

Hippeastrum has been known as amaryllis for so long that many gardeners think that is the generic name; to compound the confusion, plants of the true genus *Amaryllis* are more familiar as belladonna lilies *(page 94)*. The so-called amaryllis is characterized by clusters of three to four enormous lilylike flowers—some as much as 8 to 10 inches in diameter—borne at the top of leafless 1- to 2-foot stems in winter and spring. The flower stalks grow with amazing speed, usually before or at the same time that new leaves arise from the bulbs. Most large bulbs send up a second flower stalk about the time that the first one begins to fade. The dark green straplike leaves grow 18 to 24 inches long. In some hybrids the foliage is evergreen or nearly evergreen, but most amaryllis foliage is deciduous and must be allowed to grow until late summer or early fall, when it withers and dies. Seed-grown plants are sold by color; superior varieties that are propagated from cuttings are sold by name. Notable varieties, all of which are often sold as Dutch Hybrids, are Appleblossom (blush pink); Beautiful Lady (salmon orange); Fire Dance (bright red); Scarlet Admiral (deep scarlet); and White Giant (snowy white).

HOW TO GROW. Amaryllises grow well outdoors in Zones 9-10. They do best in light shade and rich moist soil. Plant in fall, spacing the bulbs 12 to 15 inches apart and covering them with 2 to 3 inches of soil. North of Zone 9, amaryllises should be treated as house plants and do best in at least four hours of direct sunlight a day. Night temperatures of 60° to 65° and day temperatures of 70° or higher are ideal. Plant any time from fall to early spring, setting each bulb in a big enough pot to allow 2 inches of space between the bulb and the sides. Use the mixture recommended for *Freesia (page 114)*. Water thoroughly once, then withhold water until the flower stalk appears. From that point on, keep the plant moist and feed monthly with a standard house-plant fertilizer until the leaves yellow in late summer. Reduce the water and omit fertilizer through the fall and winter until about a month before flowers are desired. Each year, before starting bulbs into growth, wash away some of the old soil with a hose and replace with fresh soil. Repot every three to four years. Propagate in fall from the small bulbs that develop beside the large ones, or from seeds. Seedlings take three to four years to reach flowering size.

BLOOD LILY
Haemanthus coccineus

AMARYLLIS
Hippeastrum 'Appleblossom'

For climate zones and frost dates, see maps, pages 148-149.

119

HYACINTH See *Hyacinthus*
HYACINTH, GRAPE See *Muscari*
HYACINTH, SUMMER See *Galtonia*
HYACINTH, WILD See *Brodiaea, Camassia*
HYACINTHELLA See *Hyacinthus*
HYACINTHOIDES See *Scilla*

HYACINTHUS

H. amethystinus, also called *Brimeura amethystina* (amethyst hyacinth); *H. azureus,* also called *Hyacinthella azurea, Muscari azureum* (fringed hyacinth); *H. orientalis* (large-flowered hyacinth); *H. orientalis albulus* (French-Roman hyacinth); *H. romanus,* also called *Bellevalia romana* (Dutch-Roman hyacinth, Roman squill)

Hyacinths have a sweet, haunting fragrance that gardeners everywhere associate with spring. The most familiar species is the large-flowered hyacinth, *H. orientalis,* which grows 8 to 12 inches tall and bears 6- to 10-inch pomponlike clusters of single or double flowers. Notable varieties are Amsterdam (salmon pink), Bismarck (pale blue), City of Haarlem (primrose yellow), L'Innocence (pure white), King of the Blues (rich indigo blue) and Pink Pearl (deep pink). *H. orientalis albulus* varieties have slender 6- to 8-inch stalks of graceful, widely spaced blue, pink or white flowers. Bulb catalogues usually list three additional species as hyacinths. *H. amethystinus* has 4- to 10-inch stalks of tiny pale blue or white bell-shaped flowers that appear after other hyacinths have faded; *H. azureus* has 4- to 8-inch stalks lined with tiny dark blue flowers and looks much like the grape hyacinth *(Muscari); H. romanus* has 6- to 12-inch stalks and ¼-inch blue or white flowers. All three are excellent bulbs for rock gardens or for naturalizing in rough grass.

HOW TO GROW. Most hyacinths survive winters outdoors in Zones 4-10, but *H. orientalis albulus* and *H. romanus* varieties are not hardy north of Zone 6. Hyacinths are also among the most popular house plants for midwinter flowering indoors. All species do best in full sun. Plant them directly in the garden in September or October in Zones 4-7, from late October through December in Zones 8-10. Space *H. orientalis* bulbs 5 to 6 inches apart and cover them with 5 inches of soil; space the smaller hyacinths' bulbs 3 to 4 inches apart and cover them with 3 inches of soil. In Zones 4-6, apply a winter mulch such as salt hay or wood chips. Left undisturbed, plants will continue to blossom for years.

The blooms of *H. orientalis* become smaller the second year because their large bulbs split into two or more small ones. To have beds of large flowers every spring, dig up the old bulbs after the leaves turn yellow and replace them.

To grow hyacinths as house plants, pot them in fall in a mixture of 1 part peat moss, 1 part packaged potting soil and 1 part sharp sand or perlite with ground limestone added at a rate of 3 to 5 ounces per bushel. Keep the potting mixture very moist while the plants are growing, then dry after the foliage matures. Do not fertilize. Save the bulbs for planting in the garden in fall. Propagation of hyacinths is a lengthy, complicated task best left to experts.

Keep the pots in a cool dark place (50° or below) for about 12 weeks, until the plant is about 2 inches tall. Then bring it into indirect light in the coolest room in the house —night temperatures of 50° or lower assure long-lasting bloom. After about a week to 10 days, give the plant at least four hours of direct sunlight a day until the buds show color; then shield the plant from direct sun with a light curtain or shade.

HYACINTHUS CANDICANS See *Galtonia*
HYACINTHUS NONSCRIPTUS See *Scilla*

LEFT: LARGE-FLOWERED HYACINTH
Hyacinthus orientalis

RIGHT: FRENCH-ROMAN HYACINTH
H. orientalis albulus

HYMENOCALLIS

H. hybrids; *H. narcissiflora,* also called *H. calathina, Ismene calathina.*

(All called spider lily, Peruvian daffodil, basket flower)

The fragrant, 3- to 4-inch, intricately designed flowers of these plants are borne along one side at the top of 18- to 24-inch-tall leafless stalks in midsummer. Their strap-like leaves grow up to 2 feet long and may be deciduous or evergreen, depending upon the species. The most common species, *H. narcissiflora,* has white blossoms with green stripes; in the variety Advance the striping is very faint. Three outstanding hybrids are Sulfur Queen, with yellow flowers; Festalis, with white flowers; and Daphne, with white flowers that are borne in a circle around the top of the flower stalks instead of at one side, as is usual.

HOW TO GROW. Spider lilies survive winters outdoors in Zones 8-10. They do best in full sun or very light shade in a soil enriched with well-rotted or dried cow manure. Plant the bulbs outdoors in spring or fall, spacing them 12 to 15 inches apart and covering them with 3 to 5 inches of soil. From Zone 7 north, plant the bulbs in spring after night temperatures average above 60°; just before frost, dig up the bulbs and put them in a well-ventilated shady place on their sides until the leaves wither; cut off the leaves and store the bulbs upside down over winter in dry vermiculite, perlite or peat moss at 65° to 70°. In Zones 8-10 dig up and divide the bulbs in spring every four or five years.

To grow spider lilies in containers, plant in fall or spring in the mixture recommended for *Hyacinthus (page 120).* Keep moist and feed monthly with a standard house-plant fertilizer from spring to fall. Move the plants outdoors when night temperatures average above 60°. Over the winter, keep the plants in a well-lighted frost-free place and water them just enough to prevent the foliage from wilting.

Propagate in fall from the small bulbs that develop at the base of large ones.

I

INDIAN SHOT See *Canna*

IPHEION

I. uniflorum, also called *Brodiaea uniflora, Milla uniflora* and *Triteleia uniflora* (spring starflower)

This little spring-flowering plant, a native of Peru and Argentina, sends up from among its grassy leaves 6-inch stems, each bearing a bluish white flower an inch or more across. The blossoms have a mintlike scent, but the leaves, when crushed, smell like onion. Although each stem carries only one flower, a single bulb sends up several stalks over a period of many weeks. The foliage appears in fall and lies on the ground over winter, withering in early summer. The low growth of spring starflowers makes them especially attractive in rock gardens, at the edge of borders or walks, beneath shrubs or naturalized in rough grass.

HOW TO GROW. Spring starflowers survive winters outdoors in Zones 6-10 and make fine midwinter-flowering house plants indoors. They will grow in full sun or light shade. Plant the bulbs in late summer or early fall, spacing them 6 inches apart and covering them with 3 inches of soil. No fertilizer is necessary; usually the bulbs multiply so fast they can be dug up at the midsummer planting season every few years and the divisions shared with friends.

Indoors, plants do best in at least four hours of direct sunlight a day, night temperatures of 50° to 65° and day temperatures of 68° or higher. Pot them 1 inch deep in fall in the mixture recommended for *Hyacinthus (page 120).* Keep this potting mixture moist until the foliage finally withers in late spring, then keep the bulbs dry until

SPIDER LILY
Hymenocallis narcissiflora 'Festalis'

SPRING STARFLOWER
Ipheion uniflorum

For climate zones and frost dates, see maps, pages 148-149.

TOP: NETTED IRIS
Iris reticulata

BOTTOM: DUTCH IRIS
I. 'Lemon Queen'

late summer or early fall, when they should be separated and repotted in fresh potting mixture.

IRIS

The Reticulata group: *I. bakeriana* (Baker iris), *I. danfordiae* (Danford iris), *I. histrioides major* (Harput iris), *I. reticulata* (netted iris); the Xiphium group: *I.* hybrids (Dutch iris), *I. xiphioides* (English iris), *I. xiphium* (Spanish iris); the Juno group: *I. bucharica* (Bokhara iris), *I. magnifica*

Among the more than 200 kinds of wild irises that grow in various parts of the world, those that are truly bulb plants fall into three groups. Reticulata irises are low growing—usually only 4 to 8 inches tall—and each bulb bears one flower 1 to 3 inches across in very early spring, just about when snowdrops, crocuses and winter aconites appear; the leaves are short or just beginning to grow when the flowers open, but eventually become 12 to 18 inches long before fading away in early summer. Four Reticulata irises are especially lovely in rock gardens and along paths. The violet-scented *I. bakeriana* has three deep violet erect petals and three purple-spotted hanging outer petals; it grows 4 inches tall. *I. danfordiae* and *I. histrioides major* bloom when their leaves first pierce the soil; *I. danfordiae* has lemon-yellow flowers and grows 2 to 3 inches tall, and *I. histrioides major* has blue flowers and grows 4 inches tall. *I. reticulata* has fragrant, deep violet-purple flowers and grows 6 inches tall. *I. reticulata* has also been crossed with other species to produce the fine Reticulata hybrids, whose colors run from deep purple to light blue.

Xiphium irises grow 1 to 2 feet tall, each bulb usually bearing two flowers 3 to 4 inches across in late spring. The group takes its name from the botanical name of the fragrant Spanish iris, *I. xiphium,* a species that comes in white, yellow, orange, bronze or blue. The Dutch iris hybrids, obtained from a crossing of the Spanish iris and several other species, come in white, yellow, orange, bronze, blue, purple or bicolor mixtures. The English iris, *I. xiphioides,* ranges in color from white through shades of blue to violet purple. All Xiphium irises are most effective when planted in groups and are excellent for cutting.

Juno irises look somewhat like immature corn plants until they blossom in the early spring. They grow about 2 feet tall and bear blossoms 3 to 4 inches across. Each bulb usually produces five to seven blossoms on its stalk; the flowers appear along the stalk as well as at the top. Two attractive species are *I. bucharica,* with small white erect petals and large golden yellow hanging outer petals, and *I. magnifica,* with pale lilac erect petals and white outer petals topped by orange crests.

HOW TO GROW. Juno and Reticulata irises are hardy in Zones 5-10; the Xiphium group is hardy in Zones 7-10. English irises do well only in coastal areas of the Pacific Northwest, where the climate is relatively cool and moist. All do best in full sun, with light shade at midday in the hot areas of Zones 9 and 10. Plant the bulbs early in the fall as soon as they become available. Space the bulbs of Reticulata irises about 4 inches apart and cover them with about 3 inches of soil. Space the bulbs of Xiphium irises and Juno irises 4 to 6 inches apart and cover them with about 5 inches of soil; be careful not to break off the thick roots below the bulbs of Juno irises. Apply a dusting of 5-10-10 fertilizer when the plants emerge in spring. Leave iris bulbs undisturbed for three to five years until blossoming slackens, then dig them up when dormant in midsummer, and reset them farther apart. Danford iris bulbs split into small ones during their first two seasons in the ground. Propagate irises from small bulbs at the base of the old bulbs.

IRIS, BUTTERFLY See *Morea*
IRIS, PEACOCK See *Morea*
IRIS, VILLOSA See *Morea*
IRIS BICOLOR See *Morea*
IRIS PAVONIA See *Morea*
ISMENE See *Hymenocallis*
ITHURIEL'S-SPEAR See *Brodiaea*

IXIA

I. hybrids (African corn lily, ixia)

The handsome hybrids called African corn lilies are so mixed genetically that botanists cannot be sure which species are involved in the strains grown today. The plants grow about 18 inches tall, and in late spring and early summer the wiry stems bear flowers about 2 inches across. The colors are red, pink, orange, yellow and cream, most with dark centers. The blossoms open fully to a flat position only in sunshine, forming an attractive cup shape when partly open. The swordlike foliage dies down to the ground in midsummer. The plants are most attractive planted in groups in the garden and make good house plants and cut flowers.

HOW TO GROW. Ixias are best suited to gardens in the dry regions of Zones 8-10 in the West and Southwest. They can also be grown outdoors in other sections of Zones 8-10, but even in warm Florida they last only a season or two; wherever the soil is moist in the summer the corms fail to ripen properly. Plant outdoors in late November (if they are planted earlier they are likely to make top growth that will be nipped by frost). Space the corms 3 to 6 inches apart and cover them with 3 inches of soil. Apply a dusting of 5-10-5 fertilizer when the plants emerge in spring. Though ixias can be left in the ground for several years in the mildest, driest areas, it is usually better to dig them up in summer after the foliage withers and store them in a dry place before resetting them in late fall.

Indoors, ixias do best in at least four hours of direct sunlight a day, night temperatures of 50° to 55° and day temperatures of 68° to 72°. Pot in fall in a mixture of 1 part packaged potting soil, 1 part peat moss and 1 part sharp sand or perlite, with ground limestone added at a rate of 3 to 5 ounces per bushel. Keep the mix moist and feed monthly with a standard house-plant fertilizer as long as the foliage is green. Store the corms in a dry place until the next planting season. Repot in fresh potting mixture.

Propagate by removing the small corms that develop beside the large ones. Ixias may also be started from seeds; they take about three years to reach flowering size.

IXIOLIRION

I. montanum, also called *I. ledebourii, I. pallasii* and *I. tataricum*

Ixiolirions are 12- to 16-inch-tall bulb plants from central Asia that bear sprays of faintly fragrant 2-inch lavender-blue flowers in late spring or early summer. Because they have weak, spindly stems and sparse grasslike foliage that dies down in summer, they are often planted among low ground covers. The flowers are excellent for cutting.

HOW TO GROW. Ixiolirions do best in full sun. In Zones 7-10 plant the bulbs in fall, setting them 3 to 4 inches apart and covering them with about 3 inches of soil. Since they start growth very early in spring, protect them from late frosts in Zone 7 with a mulch. Do not fertilize. From Zone 6 north, plant in spring and dig up the bulbs before frost in fall. Pack them in dry peat moss, vermiculite or perlite and store them at 55° to 60° over winter.

Propagate in fall by removing the small bulbs that develop beside the large ones.

AFRICAN CORN LILY
Ixia hybrids

IXIOLIRION
Ixiolirion montanum

For climate zones and frost dates, see maps, pages 148-149.

CAPE COWSLIP
Lachenalia aloides lutea

LAPEIROUSIA
Lapeirousia laxa

J
JONQUIL See *Narcissus*

L
LACHENALIA
L. aloides lutea; L. bulbifera, also called *L. pendula;*
L. aloides, also called *L. tricolor.*
(All called Cape cowslip, leopard lily)

Cape cowslips bear 6-inch spikes of inch-long flowers in winter or early spring. Their weak ribbonlike leaves, often spotted with purple, are 9 to 12 inches long. *L. aloides lutea* bears golden yellow flowers; the flowers of *L. bulbifera* combine coral red, yellow and purple; and *L. aloides* has green flowers banded with red and yellow.

HOW TO GROW. Cape cowslips are sometimes grown in rock gardens or garden nooks in Zones 9-10; elsewhere —and even in Zones 9-10—they are usually grown as house plants. Cape cowslips planted outdoors do best in full sun with light shade at midday. Plant the bulbs in fall, spacing them 3 to 5 inches apart and covering them with 1 to 2 inches of soil. To grow Cape cowslips indoors, plant six bulbs to a 5-inch pan as soon as they are available in August or September. Pot in 1 part packaged potting soil, 1 part peat moss and 1 part sharp sand or perlite, with ground limestone added at a rate of 3 to 5 ounces per bushel. Water once, then withhold water until foliage appears. Cape cowslips do best in at least four hours of direct sunlight a day, but keep them cool—night temperatures of 50° or lower assure long-lasting blooms. During the growing season keep moist and feed monthly with a standard house-plant fertilizer. After the leaves wither in spring, withhold water and food until fall. Propagate in the fall from the small bulbs that develop around the larger ones.

LAPEIROUSIA, also called LAPEYROUSIA
L. grandiflora, also called *Anomatheca grandiflora; L. laxa,*
also called *L. cruenta* and *Anomatheca cruenta*

Lapeirousias look much like freesias, but blossom in summer and fall. They have sparse sword-shaped leaves and 6- to 12-inch spikes of four to 12 tubular flowers, 1 to 2 inches across. *L. grandiflora* bears 2-inch red flowers on 12-inch stems; *L. laxa* bears 1-inch red flowers on 6- to 12-inch stems. Both species are excellent for cutting; grown indoors they provide midwinter blooms.

HOW TO GROW. In Zones 7-10, plant lapeirousias in fall; elsewhere, plant them in spring. They do well in full sun or very light shade. Set the corms 3 to 4 inches apart and cover them with 4 inches of soil. In Zones 7-10 they can be left undisturbed for two or three years; they will by then have multiplied greatly and need resetting. From Zone 6 north they must be dug up in fall and stored at 55° to 60° in dry peat moss, vermiculite or perlite over winter.

Indoors, lapeirousias do best in at least four hours of direct sunlight a day, night temperatures of 50° to 55° and day temperatures of 65° or lower. Pot in the mixture recommended for *Lachenalia (above)*. Keep moist and feed monthly with house-plant fertilizer from the time the first shoot appears until the leaves wither, then withhold moisture and food over the summer. Propagate in fall from the small corms that grow around the larger ones.

LAPEYROUSIA See *Lapeirousia*

LEUCOJUM
L. aestivum (summer snowflake), *L. autumnale* (autumn snowflake), *L. vernum* (spring snowflake)

The common name snowflake indicates how well these European wild flowers withstand frost. Their delicate white blossoms, less than an inch across, provide quiet surprises in rock gardens or beneath deciduous trees. The larger plants make unusual cut flowers. The slender foliage dies when flowering ends. The spring snowflake has green-tipped flowers, usually borne singly on 6- to 9-inch stems in early spring. The summer snowflake bears four to eight blossoms, also green tipped, on 12-inch stems in late spring or early summer; a variety called Gravetye grows about 18 inches tall and has up to nine flowers on each stem. The autumn snowflake bears two to three tiny pink-based flowers on 4- to 6-inch stems and blossoms in early fall.

HOW TO GROW. *L. aestivum* grows well in Zones 4-10; *L. autumnale* in Zones 5-10; and *L. vernum* in Zones 4-8. All do best in full sun or light shade. Plant the bulbs as soon as they are available in fall, setting them 4 inches apart and covering them with 3 to 4 inches of soil. Late-planted bulbs may not bloom until the second year. Leave the bulbs undisturbed. They can be propagated from the small bulbs that develop around larger ones, but are so inexpensive that most gardeners simply buy new ones. Plants started from seed take about three years to flower.

LILIUM

Many species and hybrids commonly called lily.

A few years ago, only wild species of lilies were grown in gardens. This is no longer true; a revolution in lily culture has produced hybrids that are more vigorous and colorful, adapt to a greater variety of growing conditions and are freer of disease than their forebears. As a result, gardeners can have a succession of fragrant, blooming lilies from late spring until early fall. Except for a few tried and true species, listed below, the new hybrids are the only ones to be recommended.

Lilies can be used anywhere their striking beauty is desired to create a focal point in the garden. They are most effective in small groups, along a hedge or fence or against a dark background of evergreens. Plant at least three bulbs in each group. Colonies of bulbs can be left undisturbed for years, but the bulbs should be lifted and divided when the plants become overcrowded. Easter lilies bought as house plants can be planted outdoors to flower during summer in following years. Certain Asiatic Hybrids *(below)* can also be grown as house plants.

The Royal Horticultural Society and the North American Lily Society divide lilies into nine horticultural groups. The classifications are based on origin—geographical in some, ancestral in others—and on flower form. Blooming time for any given type is remarkably uniform throughout the country; southern and northern flowering times rarely differ by more than three or four weeks and are affected more by the amount of sunlight than by temperature.

ASIATIC HYBRIDS are generally early flowering, most varieties blooming in June. They range from 2 to 5 feet tall with 4- to 6-inch flowers in bright reds, yellows and orange as well as delicate shades of pink, lavender and creamy white. There are three subdivisions: one includes hybrids with upright flowers (examples are Mid-Century Hybrids such as Enchantment and Harmony); another includes outward-facing flowers (Corsage, Prosperity, Paprika); the third includes those with pendant flowers of a form commonly called Turk's-cap, with sharply backswept petals (Harlequin Hybrids, Citronella, Fuga).

MARTAGON HYBRIDS, which bloom in June, bear quantities of 3- to 4-inch flowers like those of the Turk's-cap lilies described above. Examples are Achievement, which grows from 3 to 4 feet tall and bears yellowish white flowers, and Paisley Hybrids, which reach a height of 6 or more feet and come in white, yellow, orange, brown, lav-

SUMMER SNOWFLAKE
Leucojum aestivum

ASIATIC HYBRID LILIES
TOP: *Lilium* 'Enchantment'
CENTER: *L.* 'Paprika' BOTTOM: *L.* 'Harlequin'

For climate zones and frost dates, see maps, pages 148-149.

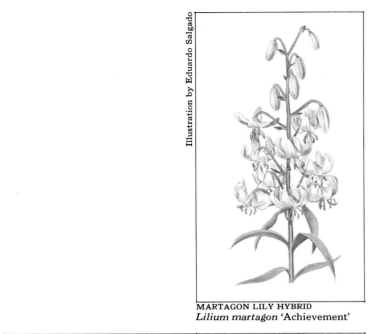

MARTAGON LILY HYBRID
Lilium martagon 'Achievement'

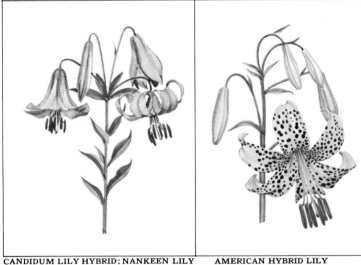

CANDIDUM LILY HYBRID: NANKEEN LILY
Lilium testaceum

AMERICAN HYBRID LILY
Lilium 'Buttercup'

LONGIFLORUM LILY
Lilium longiflorum eximium

ender and purple, all of them with tiny maroon dots.

CANDIDUM HYBRIDS, which grow 3 to 4 feet tall and bear 4- to 5-inch flowers in June and July, are crosses between *L. candidum* and *L. chalcedonicum*. From these species came the first recorded hybrid lily, *Lilium testaceum*, also known as the nankeen lily, which bears up to a dozen pale yellow to buff flowers. The petals curve sharply back.

AMERICAN HYBRIDS, 4 to 8 feet tall with 4- to 6-inch blossoms, bloom in late June or early July. The best known strains are the Bellingham Hybrids, which make especially fine cut flowers. The pyramidal flower heads, with up to 20 nodding, backswept flowers, may be cut when the first buds open and the other buds will open indoors. Colors range from yellow to orange red and have many brown or reddish brown spots. One outstanding Bellingham Hybrid is Buttercup, which grows as tall as 6 feet and bears many large yellow flowers heavily spotted with maroon.

LONGIFLORUM HYBRIDS is a category set aside for descendants of *L. longiflorum*, the popular Easter lily, and *L. formosanum;* various hybrids are under development.

AURELIAN HYBRIDS, which include lilies formerly called Trumpet Hybrids, are derived from Asiatic species. They flower in July and August and generally grow between 4 and 6 feet tall. Colors range from white through yellow to pink and copper. Aurelian Hybrids have four basic flower shapes. Chinese Trumpets bear trumpet-shaped flowers 6 to 8 inches long (examples are Black Dragon, Green Magic, Golden Splendor, Pink Perfection). Bowl-shaped lilies (Heart's Desire, First Love) bear 8-inch outward-facing flowers. Pendant types (Golden Showers) bear downward-facing bowl-shaped flowers 8 inches wide. Sunburst types (Golden Sunburst, Bright Star, Lightning, Thunderbolt) bear star-shaped flowers often 10 inches in diameter.

ORIENTAL HYBRIDS, generally August flowering, grow 2 to 8 feet in height. The extremely fragrant flowers, which may grow as large as 12 inches across, come in white, white with golden stripes, pink and crimson. There are three flower forms: bowl-shaped (Empress of India, Crimson Beauty, Little Rascal), flat-faced (Pink Glory, Imperial Crimson, Imperial Gold, Imperial Silver) and sharply backswept petals (Jamboree, Sprite). A fourth category, trumpet shaped, has been set up for future hybrids.

UNCLASSIFIED HYBRIDS. The eighth division is reserved for future hybrids not covered in the preceding categories.

TRUE SPECIES OF LILIES, the ninth group, includes *L. auratum* (gold-band lily), 5 to 6 feet tall with 10- to 12-inch yellow-banded white flowers in late July and August; *L. canadense* (meadow lily), 2 to 5 feet tall with 2- to 3-inch generally yellow, purple-brown-spotted flowers in late June and July; *L. candidum* (Madonna lily), 2 to 4 feet tall with 3- to 4-inch white flowers in late June and July; and *L. chalcedonicum* (scarlet Turk's-cap lily), 2 to 4 feet tall with 2- to 3-inch bright red flowers in July. Varieties of *L. longiflorum*, which are widely grown in greenhouses for sale at Easter, also do well in gardens; they grow 2 to 3 feet tall and bear their fragrant 6- to 8-inch white trumpets in July. Other species lilies include *L. martagon* (martagon or Turk's-cap lily), 3 to 6 feet tall with 2- to 3-inch pink flowers in June and July; *L. philadelphicum* (wood lily), 1 to 3 feet tall with 3- to 4-inch orange-red, purple-spotted flowers in late June and July; *L. regale* (regal lily), 3 to 6 feet tall with 4- to 6-inch white flowers in July and early August; *L. speciosum* (showy Japanese lily), 4 to 6 feet tall with 4- to 6-inch flowers in August and September (two well-known varieties are *L. speciosum album*, with white flowers, and *L. speciosum rubrum*, with red flowers); *L. superbum* (American Turk's-cap lily), 3 to 8 feet tall with 3- to 4-inch orange-scarlet brown-spotted flowers from late July to early September; and *L. tigrinum* (tiger lily), 2 to 4 feet tall with 3- to 5-inch black-spotted orange flowers in July and August.

HOW TO GROW. Most lilies can be left in the ground over winter throughout Zones 3-10. Lilies do best in at least five or six hours of sun a day, but tiger lilies and wood lilies tolerate light shade. In the South, lilies do best with shade at midday, to prevent colors from bleaching and to lengthen the period of bloom. They cannot stand wet soil about their roots (on level sites where water does not drain quickly, plant lilies in raised beds). Mix up to one third organic matter such as peat moss or leaf mold into the soil to a depth of at least 1 foot. Lilies can be planted in the fall or in early spring. Plant the bulbs as soon as they are purchased to keep them from drying out. Set the bulbs 9 to 18 inches apart, depending on the ultimate height of the variety, and cover them with 4 to 6 inches of soil; the only exception is the Madonna lily, whose bulbs should be covered with 1 inch of soil. Spread a 5-10-5 fertilizer evenly and water it in around the plants in early spring and again two months later. To prevent the roots from drying, apply a 3-inch mulch of peat moss, leaf mold, well-rotted manure or other organic matter. In areas of Zones 9-10 where no frost is common, dig up the bulbs and refrigerate them for eight weeks to give them their required rest period. In areas that are exposed to high winds and heavy rains, support the stems with stakes.

Easter lilies and Mid-Century Hybrids can be grown as house plants but only from bulbs that have been precooled (and are so designated by bulb dealers). They do best in night temperatures of 40° to 50° and day temperatures of 68° or lower. Give them bright indirect or curtain-filtered sunlight while they are blooming; when the flowers fade, the plants will need full sun until the leaves wither. Pot in 1 part packaged potting soil, 1 part coarse peat moss and 1 part sharp sand or perlite. Keep moist until the foliage matures. Feed monthly with a standard house-plant fertilizer until the buds show color. When the flowers fade, remove them to prevent the formation of seeds. Lilies are difficult to keep indoors for more than one season; as soon as night temperatures remain above 40°, plant them in the garden.

Propagate lilies in fall from the small bulbs that develop around the large ones, from the bulbils that develop on the stems of some varieties *(drawings, page 18)*, or from the scales that comprise the bulb *(drawings, page 19)*. Plants propagated by any of these methods will reach flowering size in two or three years. Lilies grown from seeds require about four years to reach flowering size.

LILY See *Lilium*
LILY, AFRICAN CORN See *Ixia*
LILY, AMAZON See *Eucharis*
LILY, AVALANCHE See *Erythronium*
LILY, AZTEC See *Sprekelia*
LILY, BELLADONNA See *Amaryllis*
LILY, BLACKBERRY See *Belamcanda*
LILY, BLOOD See *Haemanthus*
LILY, BLUE AFRICAN See *Agapanthus*
LILY, BUGLE See *Watsonia*
LILY, CALLA See *Zantedeschia*
LILY, CLIMBING See *Gloriosa*
LILY, CORSICAN See *Pancratium*
LILY, CUBAN See *Scilla*
LILY, DELICATE See *Chlidanthus*
LILY, FAIRY See *Zephyranthes*
LILY, FAWN See *Erythronium*
LILY, FORTNIGHT See *Morea*
LILY, FOXTAIL See *Eremurus*

AURELIAN LILY HYBRIDS
TOP: *Lilium* 'Pink Perfection'
CENTER LEFT: *L.* 'Green Magic'
CENTER RIGHT: *L.* 'Sunburst' BOTTOM: *L.* 'First Love'

ORIENTAL HYBRID LILIES
TOP: *Lilium* 'Crimson Beauty' BOTTOM: *L.* 'Imperial Gold'

For climate zones and frost dates, see maps, pages 148-149.

SPECIES LILIES
TOP: MADONNA LILY *Lilium candidum*
BOTTOM: JAPANESE LILY *L. speciosum* 'Red Champion'

HARDY AMARYLLIS
Lycoris squamigera

LILY, GLACIER See *Erythronium*
LILY, GLORY See *Gloriosa*
LILY, GOLDEN SPIDER See *Lycoris*
LILY, GUERNSEY See *Nerine*
LILY, JACOBEAN See *Sprekelia*
LILY, KAFIR See *Clivia, Schizostylis*
LILY, LEOPARD See *Belamcanda, Lachenalia*
LILY, NERINE See *Nerine*
LILY, PERUVIAN See *Alstroemeria*
LILY, PINEAPPLE See *Euchomis*
LILY, RAIN See *Zephyranthes*
LILY, RESURRECTION See *Lycoris*
LILY, ST.-BERNARD'S See *Anthericum*
LILY, ST.-BRUNO'S See *Paradisea*
LILY, ST.-JAMES'S See *Sprekelia*
LILY, SCARBOROUGH See *Vallota*
LILY, SEA See *Pancratium*
LILY, SPIDER See *Hymenocallis*
LILY, SPIRIT See *Pancratium*
LILY, STAR See *Milla*
LILY, TROUT See *Erythronium*
LILY, ZEPHYR See *Zephyranthes*
LILY OF THE INCAS See *Alstroemeria*
LILY OF THE NILE See *Agapanthus*
LILY OF THE VALLEY See *Convallaria*

LYCORIS

L. aurea, also called *Amaryllis aurea* (golden lycoris, golden spider lily); *L. radiata,* also called *Amaryllis radiata* (short-tube lycoris); *L. sanguinea* (orange lycoris); *L. squamigera,* also called *Amaryllis hallii* (hardy amaryllis, resurrection lily, magic lily of Japan)

Plants of the *Lycoris* genus bear clusters of 3- to 4-inch trumpet-shaped, often fragrant blossoms in late summer and early fall. In very early spring the plants send up slender leaves that grow up to 2 feet long and wither in early summer. *L. aurea* has yellow flowers, *L. radiata* has deep pink to scarlet flowers, *L. sanguinea* has orange-crimson flowers and *L. squamigera* has rosy lilac flowers.

HOW TO GROW. *L. aurea* is hardy in Zones 9-10; *L. radiata* and *L. sanguinea* in Zones 8-10; *L. squamigera* in Zones 5-10. All can be grown in containers anywhere. They do best in full sun or light shade. Plant in midsummer as soon as the bulbs are available and space them 5 to 8 inches apart. Cover *L. squamigera* with 5 inches of soil, the other species with 3 to 4 inches of soil.

Container-grown plants blossom more profusely than those planted in the garden. Pot in the mixture recommended for *Lachenalia (page 124).* Set the bulbs so that their tips are at the surface. Water once thoroughly, then do not water again until the flower stalks appear. Keep moist until a month after the blossoms fade, then withhold moisture until leaves sprout. Feed every two weeks with house-plant fertilizer. After the foliage fades, keep the soil nearly dry until late summer when flower stalks appear. Protect pot-grown plants from freezing. Propagate, after foliage dies, from the small bulbs around the large ones.

M

MAGIC FLOWER See *Achimenes*
MAGIC LILY OF JAPAN See *Lycoris*
MARIPOSA See *Calochortus*
MEXICAN STAR See *Milla*

MILLA

M. biflora (star lily, Mexican star)

Although the wild star lily usually bears only two flowers to each stem, the 12- to 20-inch stalks of the cultivated kinds are topped by as many as six sweetly fragrant 2½-inch blossoms. The flowers open sporadically from spring until fall. The grassy foliage, shorter than the flower stalks, dies down after the flowers fade. Star lilies are most attractive in rock gardens and as edgings for garden paths or borders in mild climates, and as house plants for late winter and spring bloom elsewhere.

HOW TO GROW. Star lilies do best in full sun. In Zones 8-10, plant the bulbs in fall, spacing them 3 to 4 inches apart and covering them with 3 inches of soil. From Zone 7 north they can be grown in pots. They do best in at least four hours of direct sunlight a day, night temperatures of 55° to 65° and day temperatures of 68° or higher. Pot in the mixture recommended for *Lachenalia (page 124)*. Keep moist and feed monthly with a standard house-plant fertilizer. After the flowers and leaves fade, withhold food and moisture until the next growing season. Repot every two to three years. Propagate in fall from the small bulbs that develop around the large ones.

MILLA UNIFLORA See *Ipheion*
MONTBRETIA See *Crocosmia, Tritonia*

MOREA

M. bicolor, also called *Dietes bicolor, Iris bicolor* (yellow morea); *M. glaucopsis,* also called *Iris pavonia,* and *M. pavonia* (both called peacock iris); *M. iridioides,* also called *Dietes vegeta* (fortnight lily, butterfly iris)

Moreas are irislike plants with 2- to 4-inch blossoms whose three outer petals are often blotched with dark "eyes" shaped like the markings on peacock feathers. The flowers, borne atop branching stems 1½ to 3 feet tall, bloom intermittently throughout the year in frost-free areas; they appear repeatedly on the same stems that have blossomed before, each flower lasting about two days. The plants have sword-shaped evergreen leaves and are attractive in rock gardens, borders and among shrubs.

Four species of moreas are commonly grown. *M. bicolor* bears 2-inch yellow flowers with a brownish black spot at the base of each outer petal; *M. glaucopsis* bears 1-inch white flowers with bluish black spots; *M. pavonia* and its variety *M. pavonia villosa* bear red, purple, yellow or white 3½-inch flowers with a darker blotch at the center. *M. iridioides,* also grown as a house plant, bears 3-inch white flowers with brownish yellow and purplish blue spots; the *M. iridioides johnsonii* variety has 4-inch blossoms.

HOW TO GROW. Moreas, which can be grown in gardens in Zones 8-10 without winter protection, do best in full sun. *M. bicolor* thrives in a moist soil, *M. glaucopsis* and *M. pavonia* blossom most freely in dry soil. *M. iridioides* is not choosy—it can stand dryness or moisture. Growing plants can be purchased and planted 12 to 24 inches apart any time of year. Since the foliage is evergreen and the stems flower for years, do not cut the plants back. Feed once in early spring with a dusting of 5-10-5 fertilizer.

Indoors *M. iridioides* does best in at least four hours of direct sunlight a day, night temperatures of 60° to 65° and day temperatures of 70° or higher. Pot in the mixture recommended for *Lachenalia (page 124)*. Keep damp and feed monthly with house-plant fertilizer.

Propagate moreas any time by dividing the rhizomes or corms from which different species grow. Plants started from seeds take about 18 months to reach flowering size.

MUSCARI

M. armeniacum (Armenian grape hyacinth); *M. botryoides* (common grape hyacinth); *M. comosum* (tassel grape hyacinth); *M. macrocarpum,* also called *M. moschatum fla-*

STAR LILY
Milla biflora

PEACOCK IRIS
Morea pavonia 'Magnifica'

TOP: TUBERGEN GRAPE HYACINTH
Muscari tubergenianum
BOTTOM: ARMENIAN GRAPE HYACINTH
M. armeniacum 'Heavenly Blue'

For climate zones and frost dates, see maps, pages 148-149.

TRUMPET DAFFODIL
TOP: *Narcissus* 'King Alfred'
CENTER: *N.* 'Music Hall' BOTTOM: *N.* 'Beersheba'

LARGE-CUPPED DAFFODIL
TOP: *Narcissus* 'Aranjuez' CENTER LEFT: *N.* 'Scarlet Leader' CENTER RIGHT: *N.* 'Flower Record'
BOTTOM: *N.* 'Mrs. R. O. Backhouse'

vum (golden musk grape hyacinth); *M. moschatum* (musk grape hyacinth); *M. tubergenianum,* also called *M. aucheri tubergenianum* (Tubergen grape hyacinth)

Few spring-flowering bulbs grow as well with as little care as grape hyacinths, and few supply such a wealth of bright flowers. Their tiny, sweetly scented blossoms appear on spikes that generally grow 6 to 9 inches tall; the grasslike leaves appear in the fall and lie on the surface of the soil uninjured by winter cold, then wither away in early summer. The plants are attractive in rock gardens and borders, among shrubs and under trees or naturalized in short grass. When cut, they make appealing miniature indoor arrangements, and they can also be grown as house plants. Outstanding selections are the Armenian grape hyacinth, including its variety Heavenly Blue, and the common grape hyacinth, all with sky-blue flowers; a variety of the common grape hyacinth, *M. botryoides album,* with white flowers; the taller-growing (8 to 12 inches) tassel grape hyacinth, with purplish green flowers, and its variety *M. comosum monstrosum;* the plume grape hyacinth, with fuzzy mauve-blue flowers; the golden musk grape hyacinth, with bright yellow flowers on the lower parts of its spikes that blend to purple at the top; the musk grape hyacinth, with purple flowers; and the Tubergen grape hyacinth, with two-toned blue flowers which are pale at the bottom of its spikes and darker at the top.

HOW TO GROW. Grape hyacinths, which can be grown throughout Zones 2-10 without winter protection, do best in full sun or light shade. Plant the bulbs as soon as they are available in late summer or early fall, setting them 3 inches apart and covering them with 3 inches of soil. Do not fertilize. Leave the bulbs in the ground indefinitely to form a carpet of spring color—they can be dug up and divided in midsummer every few years but are so inexpensive that most gardeners simply buy more when they want to plant them elsewhere. Grape hyacinths also spread through the garden by self-sown seeds; the seedlings usually blossom in their third growing season.

Plants grown in pots do best in at least four hours of direct sunlight a day, night temperatures of 40° to 45° and day temperatures of 68° or lower. For winter bloom, plant in early fall using a mixture of 1 part packaged potting soil, 1 part coarse peat moss and 1 part sharp sand or perlite, with ground limestone added at a rate of 3 to 5 ounces per bushel. Keep the soil moist until the leaves wither, but do not fertilize. Propagate in midsummer from the small bulbs that develop around the large ones.

MUSCARI AZUREUM See *Hyacinthus*

N

NAEGELIA See *Smithiantha*

NARCISSUS
Many species and varieties commonly called narcissus, daffodil or jonquil

No flowers speak of springtime with more eloquence than narcissuses, nor can any other spring flowers be planted with more assurance of success; given a minimum of care, most kinds not only will endure in a garden for many years but will increase abundantly each growing season.

Much of the confusion over names in the *Narcissus* genus results from extensive interbreeding, which has obliterated many of the differences that used to separate the plants. All may correctly be called narcissuses. The name daffodil applies primarily to the types with large trumpet-shaped flowers, but has come to be commonly used for all members of the genus. The name jonquil originally applied only to the species *N. jonquilla* but is now used for all its descendants *(below)*.

Narcissuses are among the most useful of bulbs, filling all garden needs. The low-growing types do well in rock-garden niches. All are excellent for cutting, and trumpet and tazetta types are among the most satisfactory of all bulbs for winter bloom indoors.

Narcissuses are classified into 11 basic types in a system established by the Royal Horticultural Society of Great Britain and followed by bulb growers throughout the world. Plant heights vary from 3 inches for the smallest types to nearly 2 feet for the largest ones, with a wide range included in most classifications. Similarly, flower sizes range from less than 1 inch to more than 3 inches across.

TRUMPET NARCISSUSES, commonly called trumpet daffodils, bear one flower to a stem; the cup, or trumpet, is as long as or longer than the petals. The four color subdivisions are: yellow (Flower Carpet and King Alfred), bicolor (Music Hall), white (Beersheba) and "other colors," which includes buff and orange.

LARGE-CUPPED NARCISSUSES also bear one flower to a stem; the cup is more than one third but less than the total length of the petals. The four color subdivisions are: yellow petals with a colored cup such as yellow or orange (Helios Aranjuez and Scarlet Leader); white petals with a colored cup (Duke of Windsor and Flower Record); white petals, white cup (White Butterfly); and other colors. Pink large-cupped daffodils fall into this division but are often listed separately in catalogues; among the best are Mrs. R. O. Backhouse, Chiffon, Debutante, Easter Bonnet, Irish Rose, Passionale and Salmon Trout.

SMALL-CUPPED NARCISSUSES bear one flower per stem; the cup is not more than one third the length of the petals. The four color subdivisions are: yellow petals, colored cup (Edward Buxton, Chungking); white petals, colored cup (Amateur, Polar Ice, Verger); white petals, white cup (Cushendall); and other colors.

DOUBLE NARCISSUSES include all types with more than one layer of petals, regardless of the number of flowers on each stem. Excellent varieties are Golden Ducat, all yellow; Snowball, all white; and Cheerfulness, white with yellow deep within the petals.

TRIANDRUS NARCISSUSES are hybrids or varieties descended from the species *N. triandrus.* They are characterized by slender foliage and have one to six flowers per stem. There are two subdivisions based on whether the cup is less or more than two thirds the length of the petals. Recommended varieties include Liberty Bells, all yellow; Dawn, white petals, yellow cup; and Tresamble, all white.

CYCLAMINEUS NARCISSUSES are hybrid descendants of the species *N. cyclamineus.* Each stem bears one nodding flower, the petals curve back away from the cup, and the edges of the cup are wavy. There are two subdivisions of this type based on whether the cup is less or more than two thirds the length of the petals. Recommended are February Gold and Peeping Tom, all yellow; Jack Snips, cream petals, yellow cup; and March Sunshine, light yellow petals, deep yellow cup.

JONQUILS, descendants of the species *N. jonquilla,* have slender leaves and stems bearing two to six flowers each. There are two subdivisions based on whether the cup is less or more than two thirds the length of the petals. Recommended varieties are Sweetness and Trevithian, all yellow; Cherie, ivory petals, pale pink cup; Sweet Pepper, golden yellow petals, red cup.

TAZETTA NARCISSUSES, sometimes called Poetaz narcissuses (not to be confused with the Poeticus narcissuses, described below), are descendants of the species *N. tazetta.*

For climate zones and frost dates, see maps, pages 148-149.

SMALL-CUPPED DAFFODIL
TOP: *Narcissus* 'Edward Buxton' CENTER: N. 'Verger'
BOTTOM: *N.* 'Polar Ice'

DOUBLE DAFFODIL
Narcissus 'Cheerfulness'

TRIANDRUS DAFFODIL
Narcissus 'Liberty Bells'

CYCLAMINEUS DAFFODIL
TOP: *Narcissus* 'February Gold'
BOTTOM: *N.* 'Peeping Tom'

JONQUILLA DAFFODIL
Narcissus 'Trevithian'

TAZETTA DAFFODIL
Narcissus 'Laurens Koster'

POETICUS DAFFODIL
Narcissus 'Actaea'

SPLIT-CUP DAFFODIL
Narcissus 'Estella de Mol'

Each stem bears a cluster of four to eight fragrant white flowers, usually with colored cups. Recommended varieties are Cragford, scarlet cup; Geranium, orange cup; and Laurens Koster, yellow cup. Also in this division are such tender narcissuses as Paper White, Chinese Sacred Lily and Soleil d'Or, which can be grown outdoors in Zones 8-10 but are often forced into winter bloom indoors *(page 83)*.

POETICUS NARCISSUSES usually bear one flower per stem, a fragrant white blossom with a shallow cup of a contrasting color. Recommended varieties are Pheasant's Eye, deep red cup; Actaea, bright yellow cup edged with red; Winifred Van Graven, citron-yellow cup edged with red.

SPECIES NARCISSUSES, WILD FORMS AND WILD HYBRIDS include *N. bulbocodium,* the petticoat daffodil (8 inches tall); *N. cyclamineus,* the cyclamen-flowered daffodil (4 inches tall); *N. gracilis,* the graceful daffodil (12 inches tall); *N. juncifolius,* the rush-leaved daffodil (6 inches tall); *N. pseudo-narcissus minimus,* the dwarf daffodil (3 inches tall); and *N. triandrus,* angel's-tear (8 inches tall). All bear single yellow flowers; petticoat daffodil and angel's-tear also come in white.

MISCELLANEOUS: The 11th division consists of all narcissus hybrids that do not fall into the other 10 categories. It includes varieties with split cups such as Estella de Mol, Square Dancer, Gold Collar and Cassata, as well as hybrids of the petticoat daffodil *N. bulbocodium (above).*

HOW TO GROW. All narcissuses can remain in the ground over winter in Zones 4-10 except for the tazetta types, which are hardy only in Zones 8-10, and the petticoat, cyclamen-flowered, graceful, and rush-leaved daffodils, which are hardy only in Zones 6-10. All grow well in full sun or the light shade of deciduous trees.

Plant the bulbs as soon as possible after they become available in late summer, before the ground freezes and hardens in the fall—the earlier the bulbs are planted, the better roots they will make in preparation for the nourishment of next spring's blossoms. Large-flowered types should be set 6 to 8 inches apart, smaller varieties proportionately closer. Set the bulbs three times as deep as their diameter, measuring not to the tip of the bulb, but where the tip swells to form a shoulder; large bulbs may have to be covered with 5 to 6 inches of soil, smaller species with only 3 inches. Apply bone meal at a rate of 5 to 6 pounds to each 100 square feet of bed area, and work it into the soil before setting the bulbs. Where bulbs are planted amidst grass rather than in beds, work a teaspoonful of bone meal into each hole. When the shoots appear in spring apply a dusting of bone meal around the plants.

Narcissuses grown as house plants do best in bright indirect or curtain-filtered sunlight while in blossom; night temperatures should be as cool as possible (50° to 55° is ideal) and day temperatures should be 68° or lower. Trumpet and hardy tazetta varieties are generally bought in pots when already in bud; they bloom in winter and spring. Tender tazettas are usually sold unpotted as dry bulbs and should be set shallowly in pebbles, pearl chips or coarse sand, so that only their bases are anchored *(page 83).* Keep the growing medium moist without letting the water reach the bulb base; do not fertilize. Set the bulbs in a cool, dark place until new growth is about 4 inches tall, then expose them to the light gradually to bloom. Discard tender tazettas after they flower. The bulbs of trumpet and hardy tazetta types can be set outdoors after the leaves have yellowed, and will bloom normally in spring.

Propagate garden-grown narcissuses in midsummer from the small bulbs that develop around the larger ones.

NASTURTIUM See *Tropaeolum*

NERINE

N. bowdenii, N. filifolia, N. hybrids, *N. sarniensis* (Guernsey lily), *N. undulata.* (All called nerine lily)

Nerine lilies bear clusters of long-lasting flowers on 12- to 24-inch leafless stalks in late summer or fall. The 12- to 18-inch strap-shaped leaves start to grow in fall, usually about the time the flowers open; the leaves continue to grow through the winter and spring and, in the case of the deciduous *N. bowdenii* and *N. sarniensis,* wither away by July. The 1- to 3-inch blossoms have prominent pollen-bearing stamens; the petals are accented by dark center lines and seem iridescent, especially in artificial light.

Nerine lilies are widely grown in containers and make excellent cut flowers. Several fine selections are available from bulb sellers. *N. bowdenii* bears 3-inch-long magenta-pink flowers in clusters of eight to 12; its variety Pink Triumph has silvery pink flowers. *N. filifolia* and *N. undulata* bear rose-pink flowers—*N. filifolia* in clusters of five to 10, with grasslike evergreen leaves; *N. undulata* in clusters of 10 to 15, with almost evergreen leaves. *N. sarniensis* bears red, pink, rose or white flowers in clusters of four to 10. *N. sarniensis* has been crossed with several other species to produce many bright-colored hybrids; one of the loveliest is the plant often sold as *N. curvifolia* 'Fothergillii Major,' whose scarlet flowers seem burnished with gold.

HOW TO GROW. *N. bowdenii* can be grown in gardens in Zones 8-10, the other species and hybrids only in Zones 9 and 10; all can be grown in containers in any zone and moved indoors over winter. Nerine lilies do best in light shade. Plant the bulbs in midsummer or early fall, spacing them 6 to 8 inches apart and covering them with 3 to 6 inches of soil. Apply a dusting of 5-10-5 fertilizer monthly while the leaves are growing. Because they blossom most freely when crowded, nerine lilies are often grown in pots even in mild climates. Pot them in a mixture of 1 part coarse peat moss, 1 part packaged potting soil and 1 part sharp sand or perlite, adding ground limestone at a rate of 3 to 5 ounces per bushel. After applying a dusting of bone meal, set the bulbs so that only the bottom half of each is below the surface. Do not water until the flower stalks appear, then keep the mix moist and feed monthly with a standard house-plant fertilizer while the leaves continue to grow throughout winter and spring. In summer, stop watering and feeding deciduous species when their leaves wither; for evergreen species, keep the soil just moist enough to prevent the leaves from wilting. Except in frost-free climates, containers must be brought indoors to a cool (under 60°), brightly lighted location in winter. Repot every four or five years. Propagate from the small bulbs that develop beside large ones, or from seeds; seedlings take three to four years to reach flowering size.

NUT ORCHID See *Achimenes*

O

ONION See *Allium*
ONION, FALSE SEA See *Ornithogalum*

ORNITHOGALUM

O. arabicum (Arabian star-of-Bethlehem),
O. caudatum (false sea onion), *O. nutans* (nodding star-of-Bethlehem), *O. pyramidale* (pyramid star-of-Bethlehem), *O. thyrsoides* (chincherinchee),
O. umbellatum (common star-of-Bethlehem)

Many species of *Ornithogalum* are called star-of-Bethlehem because they bear stalks of star-shaped white flowers, which are usually fragrant and often have a green stripe or greenish coloration on the backs of the petals. All bloom

SPECIES DAFFODIL
TOP LEFT: *Narcissus bulbocodium*
TOP RIGHT: *N. triandrus albus* BOTTOM LEFT: *N. cyclamineus*
BOTTOM RIGHT: *N. juncifolius*

Illustration by Eduardo Salgado

GUERNSEY LILY
Nerine sarniensis

For climate zones and frost dates, see maps, pages 148-149.

133

in spring and have slender leaves that die away shortly after the flowers fade. *O. arabicum* grows 12 to 24 inches tall and bears spikes of six to 12 fragrant 2-inch flowers, each of which has a conspicuous black pollen-receiving pistil at its center. *O. caudatum* grows 18 to 36 inches tall and has spikes of 50 to 100 half-inch flowers. *O. nutans* grows 12 inches tall and has pendant clusters of 2-inch flowers. *O. pyramidale* grows 24 to 36 inches tall and has spikes of 20 to 50 half-inch flowers. *O. thyrsoides* grows 6 to 18 inches tall and has spikes of 12 to 30 fragrant white or yellow 2-inch flowers. *O. umbellatum* grows 9 to 12 inches tall and has flat-topped clusters of 12 to 20 one-inch flowers. Stars-of-Bethlehem can be left undisturbed for years in the garden. *O. arabicum, O. caudatum* and *O. thyrsoides* make dramatic house plants. *O. caudatum* looks best in pots because its fat bulbs must be planted nearly out of the ground. All species, but particularly *O. thyrsoides,* are among the longest lasting of cut flowers.

HOW TO GROW. *O. caudatum* survives winters outdoors in Zones 8-10, *O. arabicum* and *O. thyrsoides* in Zones 7-10, *O. nutans* and *O. pyramidale* in Zones 5-10, *O. umbellatum* in Zones 4-10. All do well in sun or light shade in almost any soil. *O. umbellatum* can spread so fast as to become a nuisance. For garden planting, space the bulbs 6 to 8 inches apart in fall. Cover bulbs up to 1½ inches wide with 2 to 3 inches of soil; set larger bulbs (except *O. caudatum,* noted above) 4 to 6 inches deep.

As house plants, stars-of-Bethlehem need at least four hours of direct sunlight a day, night temperatures of 50° to 60° and day temperatures of 68° to 72°. Pot in fall in the mixture recommended for *Oxalis (below).* Keep moist and feed monthly with a standard house-plant fertilizer as long as the leaves are green; after the growing season, withhold moisture and food to let bulbs rest. Propagate in fall from small bulbs that develop around large ones.

OXALIS

O. adenophylla (Chilean oxalis); *O. bowieana,* also called *O. bowiei, O. purpurata bowiei* (Bowie oxalis); *O. brasiliensis* (Brazilian oxalis); *O. cernua,* also called *O. pes-caprae* (Bermuda buttercup); *O. crassipes; O. deppei* (rosette oxalis); *O. purpurea,* also called *O. variabilis* 'Grand Duchess'

Oxalises grow in neat mounds of foliage 4 inches to a foot across topped by five-petaled 1-inch flowers. Colors are pink, red and yellow as well as white. Most blossoms open in sunshine and close at night or on cloudy days, but *O. deppei* closes in hot sun and opens in the cool parts of the day. Oxalises are popular house plants; Chilean oxalis is well suited to rock gardens.

HOW TO GROW. Chilean oxalis can be left in the ground year round in Zones 6-10; it bears rosy pink flowers from late spring to midsummer. Bowie oxalis, hardy in Zones 7-10, bears purplish pink flowers indoors but chiefly in winter outdoors. Brazilian oxalis, hardy in Zones 8-10, bears rosy red flowers in spring. Oxalises hardy in Zones 9-10 are Bermuda buttercup (yellow flowers in fall, winter and spring); *O. crassipes* (pink or white flowers all year); rosette oxalis (red or white flowers in spring); and Grand Duchess (pink or white flowers in winter).

Oxalises do best in full sun, but can tolerate very light shade. As outdoor plants, set them directly into the garden in fall, spacing the bulbs 4 to 6 inches apart and covering them with 2 inches of soil. They need no further care than a dusting of 5-10-5 fertilizer when new growth starts.

For indoor plants, pot the bulbs in fall in a mixture of 1 part peat moss, 1 part packaged potting soil, 1 part sharp sand or perlite, with ground limestone added at a rate of 3

NODDING STAR-OF-BETHLEHEM
Ornithogalum nutans

CHILEAN OXALIS
Oxalis adenophylla

to 5 ounces per bushel; cover with 1 inch of mixture. Plants do best in at least four hours of direct sunlight a day, night temperatures of 50° to 60° and day temperatures of 68° to 72°. Keep moist and feed monthly with house-plant fertilizer except when the plants are dormant.

Propagate in late summer or early fall from the masses of small bulbs that develop around large ones. Even small bulbs will produce flowering plants the first year.

P

PANCRATIUM

P. illyricum (Corsican lily, spirit lily),
P. maritimum (sea daffodil, sea lily)

Two species of *Pancratium* bear exceedingly fragrant 3-inch flowers in summer. The blossoms resemble large white daffodils and are borne in clusters on 1- to 1½-foot stalks above twisted straplike leaves about 2 feet long. *P. illyricum* blooms in early summer and its leaves usually are deciduous. *P. maritimum* blooms in late summer and its leaves are evergreen.

HOW TO GROW. Corsican lilies and sea daffodils survive winters only in Zones 8-10 and are generally grown farther north as summer-flowering pot plants for the patio. They do best in full sun. Plant the bulbs in spring. For garden planting, space them 8 to 10 inches apart and cover with about 3 inches of soil. Feed once with a light dusting of 5-10-5 fertilizer just as new leaves begin growth. Bulbs in pots, also planted in spring, are set so that their tips are level with the surface. Use a mixture of 1 part peat moss, 1 part packaged potting soil and 1 part sharp sand or perlite; add ground limestone at a rate of 3 to 5 ounces per bushel. Keep the mix moist and feed monthly with a standard house-plant fertilizer while the leaves are green. Before frost, bring the plants indoors and set them in a sunny window. Water and feed the plants until the deciduous leaves wither or the evergreen leaves reach full growth; then withhold moisture and food. Propagate from the small bulbs that develop around large ones.

PARADISEA

P. liliastrum (St.-Bruno's-lily)

St.-Bruno's-lily blooms in early summer, sending up 1- to 2-foot spikes that bear five to eight fragrant 2-inch flowers distinguished by a small green spot at the tip of each petal. The slender, grasslike leaves grow 12 to 18 inches long and die down to the ground in fall. *P. liliastrum major* is a bit larger than *P. liliastrum,* but otherwise identical. Both are pleasant additions to lightly shaded borders or rock gardens and wooded areas.

HOW TO GROW. St.-Bruno's-lilies can be grown in Zones 3-7 and do best in partial shade. Their roots are brittle and must be handled carefully. Plant the roots in early fall or spring, spacing them 12 to 18 inches apart and covering them with about 3 inches of soil. St.-Bruno's-lilies may be left undisturbed for years, but a mulch of well-rotted cow manure, applied each fall, will help keep the soil cool and damp as well as nourish the roots. Propagate by dividing the roots in fall or spring. Plants started from seeds take two to three years to reach flowering size.

PARDANTHUS See *Belamcanda*
PINEAPPLE FLOWER See *Eucomis*

POLIANTHES

P. tuberosa (tuberose)

The superbly fragrant tuberoses, once grown in enormous quantities by florists, became so closely identified with funerals that they eventually lost favor and have near-

SEA DAFFODIL
Pancratium maritimum

ST.-BRUNO'S-LILY
Paradisea liliastrum

TUBEROSE
Polianthes tuberosa

For climate zones and frost dates, see maps, pages 148-149.

135

STRIPED SQUILL
Puschkinia scilloides

DOUBLE-FLOWERED PERSIAN BUTTERCUP
Ranunculus asiaticus

ly disappeared from cultivation. Two varieties usually available are Mexican Everblooming, which grows nearly 4 feet tall and bears 2-inch flowers, and The Pearl, which grows about 15 inches tall and bears 2-inch many-petaled flowers. Both send up two to five flower stalks over a period of several weeks in late summer and fall. Tuberoses are so fragrant that they should be grown in small groups in the garden and mixed with other flowers in bouquets.

HOW TO GROW. Even in Zones 9-10, where tuberoses survive winters outdoors, it is best to dig up the bulbs each fall and reset them in spring. Do not set them into the garden until the weather is reliably warm (60° or higher at night). Tuberoses do best in full sun. Space the bulbs 6 to 8 inches apart and cover with about 3 inches of soil. Feed monthly from the time the plants emerge until the buds show color with a dusting of 5-10-5 fertilizer scratched into the soil. Since tuberoses require such a long flowering season, gardeners north of Zone 5 generally start bulbs in pots indoors four to six weeks before warm nights are expected to be sure to have flowers before frost. Bulbs should be dug up in fall after the tops have been turned brown by frost. Cut the stems off close to the bulbs and let them dry in a warm airy place for two weeks. Store them in dry peat moss, perlite or vermiculite at 55° to 65° over winter.

Tuberose bulbs are unique in that large-sized ones divide into several smaller ones during the year they are planted. Since these smaller bulbs require one or two years of good growing conditions to reach flowering size, buy bulbs that are not quite full size to get at least two years' flowering from the bulbs before they split up. By that time they will have multiplied so that there are bulbs of all sizes in your collection, providing flowering-sized bulbs for each future year. Because the bulbs are inexpensive, some gardeners buy new large bulbs each year and do not bother to save those that were planted in the spring.

PRETTYFACE See *Brodiaea*

PUSCHKINIA
P. scilloides, also called *P. libanotica, P. sicula*
(striped squill, Lebanon squill)

The striped squill is a relative of the true squill, *Scilla (page 138).* In very early spring it sends up 4- to 8-inch stalks that bear as many as six lushly petaled ½- to 1-inch flowers. *P. scilloides* has blue-striped, bluish white blossoms. *P. scilloides-alba* has all-white blossoms. The leaves grow 4 to 6 inches long and die to the ground in early summer. Striped squill is an excellent bulb for rock gardens and can be set at random in rough grass.

HOW TO GROW. Striped squills are hardy in Zones 3-10, but do best in cool climates where they can be planted in full sun or partial shade. Plant the bulbs in fall, spacing them 2 to 3 inches apart and covering them with 2 or 3 inches of soil. You can propagate in midsummer from the small bulbs that develop around large ones, but striped squills blossom most abundantly when left undisturbed, and most gardeners prefer to buy additional bulbs.

Q
QUAMASH See *Camassia*

R
RANUNCULUS
R. asiaticus (Persian buttercup, French buttercup, Dutch buttercup, Scotch buttercup, turban buttercup, double buttercup)

Ranunculuses, commonly called Persian buttercups, bear 2- to 5-inch flowers crowded with petals over a long period

—three to four months—and are usually grown as cutting flowers. They come in every color except green and blue, mainly in subtle shades and combinations of yellow, orange, pink, red and white. Each plant bears several flowers on 18-inch stalks and may produce up to 75 flowers a season. The fernlike foliage withers in early summer.

HOW TO GROW. Persian buttercups do best in full sun. In Zones 8-10, plant in November to blossom from February until May. From Zone 7 north, plant early in spring to blossom in late spring through early summer.

Soak the tubers in water for three or four hours before planting. Persian buttercups flower best in a soil that is dry around the crowns of the plants but moist under the roots. To provide such conditions, knock the bottoms out of clay pots and set the pots directly into the garden with their rims raised about 1½ inches above the soil. Set the tubers in the pots, claw side down, and cover the tops with about 1½ inches of soil. Water thoroughly once, then withhold moisture until sprouts appear unless the soil becomes excessively dry.

Although the bulbs survive winters outdoors in Zones 8-10, it is advisable in all climates to dig them up after the foliage withers and store over winter at 50° to 55° in dry peat moss, perlite or vermiculite. Propagate by dividing the tubers after the foliage dies. Seeds sown in spring will produce blossoming plants the second year.

RECHSTEINERIA
R. cardinalis (cardinal flower), *R. leucotricha* (Brazilian edelweiss), *R. verticillata* (double-decker plant)

Rechsteinerias make unusually fine long-flowering house plants. Most species have hairy heart-shaped 4- to 6-inch leaves topped by 12- to 18-inch flower stalks. Cardinal flowers bear bright red 2-inch flowers throughout the year if old flower stems are removed. Brazilian edelweiss, which has silvery haired leaves, bears pinkish 1-inch flowers nine months after planting. The double-decker plant bears pink-spotted purple 1-inch flowers seven months after planting.

HOW TO GROW. Rechsteinerias do best indoors in bright indirect or curtain-filtered sunlight but can have direct sun in winter; cardinal flower and Brazilian edelweiss also thrive under 14 to 16 hours a day of artificial light from the special fluorescent lamps used for house plants. Night temperatures of 65° to 70° and day temperatures of 75° or higher are ideal. Pot in 2 parts peat moss, 1 part packaged potting soil and 1 part sharp sand or perlite, add ground limestone at a rate of 3 to 5 ounces per bushel. Place pots in a humidifying tray; water from the bottom so no moisture touches the leaves. Allow to become slightly dry between thorough waterings and feed monthly with a house-plant fertilizer while growing. Withhold moisture and food while dormant. Propagate cardinal flowers and double-decker plants from stem cuttings in late winter or early spring; all three species can be propagated from seeds, taking about seven months to flower.

RICHARDIA See *Zantedeschia*

S

SAFFRON, MEADOW See *Colchicum*
SAFFRON, SPRING MEADOW See *Bulbocodium*
SATIN BELL See *Calochortus*

SCHIZOSTYLIS
S. coccinea (crimson flag, Kafir lily)

Crimson flags—sometimes called Kafir lilies, a name more commonly used for clivias *(page 103)* bear 1½- to 2-foot spikes of 2-inch flowers in late fall. *S. coccinea* has

CARDINAL FLOWER
Rechsteineria cardinalis

Illustration by Eduardo Salgado

CRIMSON FLAG
Schizostylis coccinea

For climate zones and frost dates, see maps, pages 148-149.

LEFT: SPANISH BLUEBELL
Scilla hispanica
TOP RIGHT: TUBERGENIAN SQUILL
S. tubergeniana
BOTTOM RIGHT: SIBERIAN SQUILL
S. sibirica 'Spring Beauty'

GLOXINIA
Sinningia speciosa

scarlet flowers; the hybrids Mrs. Hagarty and Viscountess Byng have pink flowers. The foot-long leaves are evergreen. Crimson flags are most effective as cut flowers.

HOW TO GROW. Hardy in Zones 8-10, crimson flags do best in full sun—they can be grown in light shade in hot areas—and thrive in wet, even boggy, soil. Set growing plants in the garden in spring, spacing them 9 inches apart and covering the rhizomes with 2 inches of soil. Propagate by digging up clumps of four to six shoots in spring.

SCILLA

S. bifolia (two-leafed squill); *S. hispanica*, also called *S. campanulata, Endymion hispanicus, Hyacinthoides hispanica* (Spanish bluebell); *S. nonscripta*, also called *S. nutans, Endymion nonscriptus, Hyacinthoides nonscripta, Hyacinthus nonscriptus* (English bluebell); *S. peruviana*, also called *S. ciliaris* (Peruvian squill, Cuban lily); *S. pratensis* (meadow squill); *S. sibirica* (Siberian squill); *S. tubergeniana* (Tubergenian squill)

Blue is the color most often associated with squills, but there are pink, reddish, purple, lavender and white varieties as well. The many species grow from 6 to 12 inches tall and bear spiky clusters that may hold anywhere from three to 100 half-inch to 1-inch flowers. The ribbonlike leaves wither away in early summer. All species are effective in rock gardens or massed under trees or spring-blossoming shrubs. They are also easy to grow in pots for midwinter bloom indoors, and they make pleasing miniature cut flowers.

HOW TO GROW. *S. bifolia* and *S. hispanica* survive winters outdoors in Zones 4-10; *S. nonscripta* and *S. pratensis* are hardy in Zones 5-10; *S. peruviana* is hardy in Zones 9-10; *S. sibirica* and its varieties, as well as *S. tubergeniana*, which do not grow in hot climates, are hardy in Zones 1-8. Squills do well in any light from full sun to deep shade.

S. peruviana is nearly evergreen; plant it in early summer, immediately after its brief dormant period. In Zones 9-10, put the bulbs directly into the garden, spacing them 8 to 10 inches apart and covering them with 5 or 6 inches of soil. North of Zone 9, *S. peruviana* must be treated as a pot plant and protected from freezing temperatures. All other squills should be planted in the garden in fall. Space *S. hispanica* and *S. nonscripta* 6 to 8 inches apart, and cover them with 3 to 4 inches of soil. Space the others 3 to 6 inches apart and cover them with 2 to 3 inches of soil.

For winter-blooming house plants, pot bulbs in early fall (except Peruvian squill, which is planted in early summer) in a mixture of 1 part peat moss, 1 part packaged potting soil and 1 part sharp sand or perlite, with 3 to 5 ounces of ground limestone added per bushel. Put them in a cool dark place for eight to 10 weeks before bringing them into indirect light. Keep the pots in the coolest room in the house—night temperatures of 50° or lower assure long-lasting bloom. Keep the soil moist during active growth. Do not fertilize. After flowers fade and foliage withers, save the bulbs for planting in the garden in fall.

Once planted, squills may be left undisturbed and will increase in beauty for many years. Propagate in early summer from the small bulbs that develop around large ones. Seedlings take about three years to reach flowering size.

SHELLFLOWER See *Tigridia*

SINNINGIA

S. pusilla, S. speciosa (gloxinia)

Gloxinias, tuberous-rooted gesneriads that are grown exclusively as house plants, are compact and about a foot high and equally wide with hairy 4- to 6-inch leaves; their 3-

to 6-inch blossoms may be bell- or slipper-shaped, erect or nodding, and range in color from red, pink, lavender and purple to white and multicolored. Plants go through alternate periods of growth and dormancy and may bloom at any time of the year. When the flowers fade, the leaves wither away completely to reappear a few months later. A fascinating species, *S. pusilla,* is a miniature house plant that grows only about 2 inches tall and bears ½-inch violet flowers continuously throughout the year.

HOW TO GROW. Gloxinias do best in bright indirect or curtain-filtered sunlight and also thrive with 14 to 16 hours of artificial light from the special fluorescent lamps used for house plants a day. Night temperatures of 65° to 70° and day temperatures of 75° or higher are ideal. Pot in the mixture recommended for *Scilla (opposite).* Keep *S. pusilla* moist and well humidified and feed monthly with a standard house-plant fertilizer all year. Water and fertilize *S. speciosa* from the time the sprouts appear until the leaves begin to wither, then withhold food and reduce watering gradually until the leaves die; let plants rest undisturbed until new growth starts two to four months later, then replant in a fresh potting mixture and resume watering and feeding. Propagate both species at any time from leaf cuttings, from divisions of the tuberous roots, or from seeds. Seedlings take six to seven months to flower.

SMITHIANTHA, formerly known as NAEGELIA
S. 'Carmel,' *S. cinnabarina, S. zibrina* hybrids.
(All called temple bells)

Temple bells are grown exclusively as house plants. From late summer until midwinter, they bear 1½-inch red, pink, orange, yellow or white flowers often streaked or spotted inside with contrasting colors. The stalks grow 8 to 24 inches tall from a cluster of heart-shaped leaves, usually hairy and often mottled with red and purple. *S. cinnabarina* has rose, red and orange-red flowers, and its leaves are covered with dark red hairs. The hybrid Carmel has red flowers with red-spotted ivory throats. *S. zebrina* hybrids have yellow, pink or red spotted flowers.

HOW TO GROW. Temple bells do best in bright indirect or curtain-filtered sunlight and also thrive with 14 to 16 hours a day of artificial light from special fluorescent lamps used on house plants. Night temperatures of 65° to 70° and day temperatures of 75° or higher are ideal. Pot in the mixture recommended for *Scilla (opposite).* Keep moist and feed monthly with a house-plant fertilizer. While the plants are dormant in late winter and spring, withhold fertilizer and water just often enough to keep the rhizomes from drying out. (Alternatively, remove the rhizomes from the pots, store them in barely damp peat moss or vermiculite, and repot them in early summer.)

Propagate by dividing the rhizomes in spring after the blooming season, by taking leaf cuttings at any time of year, or from seeds. Seeds sown in early spring produce flowering plants by late fall.

SNAKE'S-HEAD See *Fritillaria*
SNOWDROP See *Galanthus*
SNOWFLAKE See *Leucojum*

SPARAXIS
S. *tricolor* and its hybrids.
(All called harlequin flower, wandflower)

In spring, harlequin flowers produce 12- to 18-inch spikes of 2-inch flowers, distinguished by bright yellow throats and a three-cornered black spot near the base of each petal. They are suited to rock gardens or borders and make fine cut flowers. *S. tricolor* bears red, yellow, blue, purple,

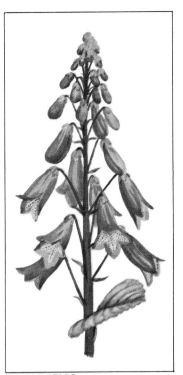

TEMPLE BELLS
Smithiantha hybrid

HARLEQUIN FLOWER
Sparaxis tricolor

For climate zones and frost dates, see maps, pages 148-149.

mauve or white blossoms. Hybrids, which make up most of the mixtures sold, have an even wider color range, including pastels. All have sword-shaped foliage, which appears in late fall and dies in early summer.

HOW TO GROW. Harlequin flowers are winter hardy in Zones 9-10 but do best in the West and Southwest where the soil dries out in summer. They flourish in full sun. From Zones 8 northward and in areas of Zones 9-10 that have rain in summer, they should be grown in containers. Whether grown in garden beds or in pots, they require well-drained soil, and must be kept dry after the foliage has turned yellow in summer. Plant the corms in fall, spacing them 2 to 3 inches apart and covering them with 2 to 3 inches of soil. Pot-grown plants in cold regions must be kept from freezing. After all frost danger is past, set them outdoors in their pots. Garden plants may be left undisturbed for years; pot plants may be grown for two or three years without repotting if given a standard house-plant fertilizer monthly while the foliage is green. Propagate in the fall from the small corms that develop beside large ones. Seedlings take about three years to reach flowering size.

SPREKELIA
S. formosissima, also called *Amaryllis formosissima*
(Aztec lily, Jacobean lily, St.-James's-lily)

Aztec lilies bloom in summer outdoors, but can be grown as house plants for spring flowers. Each plant generally produces a 12- to 18-inch stem topped with a long-lasting 4-inch blossom, but sometimes a bulb sends up a second flower stalk from among its 8- to 12-inch straplike leaves.

HOW TO GROW. Aztec lilies do best in full sun. In Zones 8-10, plant the bulbs any time, spacing them about 8 inches apart and covering them with 3 to 4 inches of soil. In Zones 8-10 the bulbs will flower several times during the summer if allowed to become crowded and to dry out occasionally. From Zone 7 north, plant the bulbs in spring after all danger of frost is past; they will blossom in six to eight weeks. In these colder regions, dig up the whole plants before the first fall frost, and let them dry thoroughly. Then remove the foliage and store the bulbs over winter at 55° to 60° in dry peat moss, perlite or vermiculite.

As house plants, Aztec lilies do best in at least four hours of direct sunlight a day, night temperatures of 60° to 65° and day temperatures of 72° or higher during their growing season. Plant the bulbs at any time in the potting mixture recommended for *Scilla (page 138)* and set them so that their necks protrude above the surface. Keep moist and feed monthly with house-plant fertilizer from February to September; from October to January, withhold moisture and food and store plants at 40° to 45°. Each year, wash away some of the old soil with a hose and replace with fresh soil. Repot every three or four years. Propagate any time from the small bulbs that form around large ones, or from seeds. Seedlings take six to seven years to flower.

SQUILL See *Scilla*
SQUILL, LEBANON See *Puschkinia*
SQUILL, ROMAN See *Hyacinthus*
SQUILL, STRIPED See *Puschkinia*
STAR OF PERSIA See *Allium*
STARFLOWER, SPRING See *Ipheion*
STAR-OF-BETHLEHEM See *Ornithogalum*

STERNBERGIA
S. lutea, also called *Amaryllis lutea*

At first glance, a sternbergia might be mistaken for a fall-blooming crocus. Its flowers are about 2 inches long and the petals seem made of waxen burnished gold. They open

AZTEC LILY
Sprekelia formosissima

STERNBERGIA
Sternbergia lutea

in September on 4-inch stems among grasslike leaves that eventually become 6 to 12 inches long. The leaves keep their color through winter and wither the following spring. Sternbergias are excellent for rock gardens or any part of the yard that becomes very dry during the summer.

HOW TO GROW. Sternbergias survive winters outdoors in Zones 6-10. They do best in full sun and extremely well-drained soil. Plant the bulbs as soon as they are available in midsummer. Space the bulbs about 3 inches apart and cover them with 5 inches of soil. Scratch a dusting of bone meal around the plants each spring. In areas where frost is common, sternbergias should have a winter mulch of salt hay. Sternbergias can be left undisturbed for years. If they fail to blossom freely, the usual cause is not overcrowding but too much summer moisture, and the cure is relocation to a site with better drainage. It is possible to dig up and divide the bulbs in midsummer, but most gardeners buy bulbs rather than disturb successful plantings.

SYNSIPHON See *Colchicum*

T

TARO See *Colocasia*
TEMPLE BELLS See *Smithiantha*
TIGERFLOWER See *Tigridia*

TIGRIDIA
T. pavonia (tigerflower, shellflower)

Tigridias bear 5- to 6-inch blossoms whose colors range from white to yellow, orange, scarlet, pink, lilac and buff and, except for varieties of the 'Immaculata' strain, have spotted inner petals. The flowers bloom in summer, sitting like huge butterflies atop 18- to 30-inch stems. Each blossom lasts only one day, but each stem sends out about six flowers over a period of six to eight weeks.

HOW TO GROW. Tigridias will survive winters outdoors in Zones 7-10 and do best in full sun, with light noontime shade. Plant the bulbs in spring when night temperatures stay above 60°, setting them 4 to 8 inches apart and covering them with 4 inches of soil. Feed with 5-10-5 fertilizer every two weeks and keep the soil moist. From Zone 7 north, tigridias must be dug up in fall after the leaves yellow. Dry thoroughly, then store the bulbs over winter in dry peat moss, vermiculite or perlite at 50° to 55°. In Zones 6-10, dig up and reset the bulbs every three to four years. Propagate from the small bulbs that develop beside the large ones. Tigridias started from seeds may blossom the first year if planted very early in spring.

TRITELEIA See *Brodiaea, Ipheion*

TRITONIA
T. crocata (saffron tritonia, flame freesia), *T. hyalina.* (Both called montbretia)

The arching flower spikes of tritonias provide brilliant summer color in rock gardens and borders and make long-lasting cut flowers. The 2-inch cuplike blossoms come in pink, salmon, yellow, apricot, orange, red, purple and white. Tritonias grow from corms, but are not to be confused with other cormous plants in the genus *Crocosmia (page 106),* with which they share the common name montbretia. The saffron tritonia, which grows 1 to 2 feet tall and bears orange-yellow flowers, is the most widely grown species; outstanding varieties include the bright red *T. crocata miniata,* the coppery orange Orange Delight, and the deep orange Princess Beatrix. Another fine species, *T. hyalina,* has pinkish orange flowers and grows about a foot tall.

HOW TO GROW. Tritonias, which will survive winters out-

TIGERFLOWER
Tigridia pavonia

SAFFRON TRITONIA
Tritonia crocata

For climate zones and frost dates, see maps, pages 148-149.

WREATH NASTURTIUM
Tropaeolum polyphyllum

doors in Zones 7-10, do best in full sun. Plant corms that are to be left in the garden in fall, spacing them about 3 inches apart and covering them with 2 to 3 inches of soil. Feed them every two weeks with a dusting of 5-10-5 fertilizer. Dig and reset the corms every three years. North of Zone 7, tritonias should be planted in early spring. In fall, after the tops have turned brown from frost, dig up the corms, allowing some soil to cling to them. Let them dry, then store them over winter, soil and all, in dry peat moss, vermiculite or perlite at 50° to 55°. Propagate from the small corms that develop around large ones. Tritonias started from seeds take three years to reach flowering size.

TROPAEOLUM

T. polyphyllum (wreath nasturtium),
T. tuberosum (tuber nasturtium)

These tuberous-rooted species of nasturtiums bear blossoms about an inch across above decorative, deeply lobed leaves; each blossom has the long taillike spur typical of nasturtiums. The flowers bloom in summer and the leaves die after flowering ceases. The wreath nasturtium has yellow flowers and trailing stems about 2 feet long. The tuber nasturtium has yellowish orange flowers with long red spurs, and climbs up to 6 feet high by twining.

HOW TO GROW. Wreath nasturtiums will survive winters outdoors in Zones 7-10; tuber nasturtiums are hardy only in Zones 8-10. Both need light shade. Plant in spring, spacing the tubers about 12 inches apart and covering them with 3 inches of soil. Where these plants are not hardy, the tubers should be dug in the fall and stored over winter in dry peat moss, vermiculite or perlite at 50° to 55°. Propagate in fall by dividing the tubers. Plants started from seeds in spring reach flowering size in two to three years.

TUBEROSE See *Polianthes*

TULBAGHIA

T. fragrans, also called *T. pulchella* (fragrant tulbaghia);
T. violacea (violet tulbaghia, society garlic)

Tulbaghias are deservedly popular—their flowers are less than an inch across but bloom in clusters for many months in gardens and throughout the year indoors. The flower stalks are leafless, the leaves evergreen and almost a foot long. The fragrant tulbaghia grows about a foot tall and bears clusters of 20 to 30 sweetly scented, lavender flowers in gardens from October to April. The violet tulbaghia grows 1 to 2 feet tall and bears clusters of eight to 20 purplish violet flowers from March to November; its leaves give off an onion scent when bruised.

HOW TO GROW. Tulbaghias are grown outdoors only in Zones 9-10, where they do best in full sun. They may be planted outdoors in these zones at any season. Set the bulbous roots 8 to 12 inches apart, with the tops at the surface of the soil. The foliage will be damaged by frost if temperatures dip to 25°, but new growth will appear quickly. The bulbous roots multiply rapidly and should be dug up and reset every four or five years.

Indoors, tulbaghias do best in at least four hours of direct sunlight a day, night temperatures of 40° to 45° and day temperatures of 60° or lower. Pot in the mixture recommended for *Scilla (page 138)*. Keep moist and feed monthly with house-plant fertilizer. Divide and repot the bulbs when they become overcrowded. Propagate from the small bulbs that develop around large ones.

TULIP See *Tulipa*
TULIP, BUTTERFLY See *Calochortus*
TULIP, GLOBE See *Calochortus*

FRAGRANT TULBAGHIA
Tulbaghia fragrans

TULIP, MARIPOSA See *Calochortus*

TULIPA
Many species and varieties commonly called tulips

Tulips, a mainstay of spring gardens everywhere, can provide abundant flowers in a wide spectrum of colors from March through May, and many varieties can be enjoyed as house plants in midwinter. Dwarf varieties are excellent in rock gardens, and tall-growing ones are indispensable in borders. Most tulips make excellent cut flowers.

More than 4,000 named varieties of tulips are now in existence; several hundred are available commercially. They are grouped into 15 classes, which are subject to almost constant revision.

Garden tulips are classed not only by their ancestry and flowering characteristics, but also by their time of bloom. In Zone 6, for example, so-called early-flowering tulips such as *T. kaufmanniana* and *T. fosteriana* bloom in mid- to late April, midseason tulips (Mendel, triumph, Darwin hybrid) bloom in late April to early May, and late-flowering tulips (Darwin, lily-flowered, cottage, Rembrandt, parrot, double late, *T. greigii*) bloom throughout May. Tulip flowers usually have cups about 2 or 3 inches deep but those that have been developed to bear unusually large flowers may have cups more than 4 inches deep. Some of the species tulips have cups as small as 1 inch deep.

SINGLE EARLY TULIPS grow about 9 to 16 inches tall and their single, six-petaled blossoms, which are the first of the ordinary garden tulips to appear in spring, are often pleasantly scented. Many varieties will flower indoors in winter. Recommended varieties include Brilliant Star, scarlet; Diana, white; Bellona, golden yellow; and Pink Perfection, soft pink with a white base.

DOUBLE EARLY TULIPS also grow 9 to 16 inches tall, but produce many-petaled, long-lasting flowers on stout stems about the same time as single early tulips. All varieties will flower indoors in winter. Recommended varieties include Peach Blossom, rosy pink; Scarlet Cardinal, orange scarlet; and Thunderbolt, lemon yellow.

MENDEL TULIPS, which flower in midseason, are vigorous plants that stand up well to wind and rain; they grow 16 to 26 inches tall and produce blossoms in many colors. All varieties will flower indoors in winter. Recommended varieties include Apricot Beauty, soft yellowish pink; Golden Olga, deep red with yellow edges; Olga, red with white edges; and Van der Eerden, bright red.

TRIUMPH TULIPS also grow 16 to 26 inches tall and produce large flowers in midseason about 10 days before Darwin tulips *(below)*. Many varieties will flower indoors in winter. Especially recommended are Aureola, red with golden yellow edges; Her Grace, white with pink edges; and Sulphur Glory, chrome yellow.

DARWIN HYBRID TULIPS, which bloom in midseason, grow 22 to 30 inches tall. The largest, most spectacular and among the most weather resistant of all garden tulips, they were bred by crossing the colorful Darwin varieties with the huge-flowered, early-blooming *T. fosteriana*. Many varieties will flower indoors in winter. Recommended varieties include Apeldoorn, orange red with purple-black bases; Gudoshnik, creamy peach, dusted rosy red; and Jewel of Spring, sulphur yellow with red edges.

DARWIN TULIPS, late flowering and the best known of all tulips, grow 22 to 30 inches tall and produce large, deep-cupped, solid-colored flowers on strong stems. Many varieties flower indoors during winter. The so-called "orchid-flowering" tulips with fringed petals are in this category. Recommended varieties include Aristocrat, violet rose; La Tulipe Noire, blackish purple; and Zwanenburg, white.

For climate zones and frost dates, see maps, pages 148-149.

SINGLE EARLY TULIP
Tulipa 'Brilliant Star'

DOUBLE EARLY TULIP
Tulipa 'Peach Blossom'

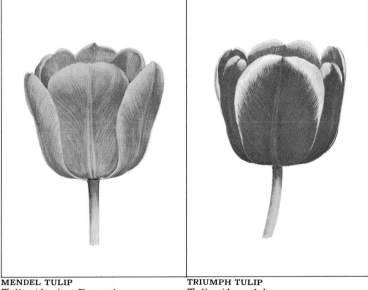

MENDEL TULIP
Tulipa 'Apricot Beauty'

TRIUMPH TULIP
Tulipa 'Aureola'

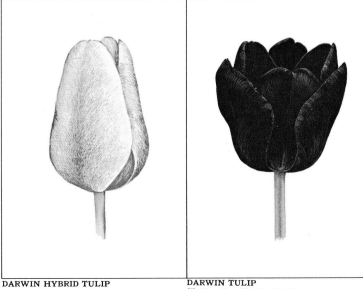

DARWIN HYBRID TULIP
Tulipa 'Gudoshnik'

DARWIN TULIP
Tulipa 'La Tulipe Noire'

LILY-FLOWERED TULIP
Tulipa 'Golden Duchess'

COTTAGE TULIP
Tulipa 'Rosy Wings'

REMBRANDT TULIP
Tulipa 'Cordell Hull'

DOUBLE LATE TULIP
Tulipa 'Nizza'

PARROT TULIP
Tulipa 'Pierson'

LILY-FLOWERED TULIPS, late flowering, like the Darwins, grow 18 to 26 inches tall and produce blossoms characterized by long pointed petals that arch outward at the tips. Their distinctive shape is interesting both in gardens and in flower arrangements. Some varieties will flower indoors in midwinter. Recommended varieties include Astor, salmon; Golden Duchess, deep yellow; Mariette, salmon pink; and Maytime, purplish violet with white edges.

COTTAGE TULIPS, late flowering, grow 16 inches to nearly 3 feet tall and produce large, usually egg-shaped flowers in a wide range of colors. Many of the multiflowered tulips, which bear clusters of blossoms, are in this category. Some varieties will flower indoors in midwinter. Recommended varieties include Georgette, clear yellow with red edges, four or more blossoms on a branching stem; Mrs. John T. Scheepers, enormous, soft yellow flowers; and Rosy Wings, pink shading to white at the base.

REMBRANDT TULIPS, late flowering, were formerly called Bizarre or Bybloemen tulips and are often referred to as "broken tulips." Virus-caused mutations have made their petals streaked, flushed, striped, feathered, splashed or veined with contrasting colors. Recommended varieties include Cordell Hull, which grows about 2 feet tall and has red and white flowers; Black Boy, which grows about 20 inches tall and has rounded mahogany-black flowers with clear yellow feathering; Madame Dubarry, which grows about 20 inches tall and has yellow flowers with apricot blotches; and Zomerschoon, which grows about 20 inches tall and has red flowers with white splashes.

PARROT TULIPS, late flowering, grow 20 to 28 inches tall and produce blossoms with twisted petals, the edges of which are cut into featherlike segments. Parrot tulips originated as "sports," or chance mutations, of other varieties. Some will flower indoors in winter. Recommended varieties include Pierson, a sport of the Darwin tulip Allard Pierson, that is blood red with a blue base; Blue Parrot, a lavender-blue sport of the Darwin tulip Bleu Aimable; Fantasy, a sport of the Darwin tulip Clara Butt that has green markings on a soft rose-pink background; Red Parrot, a sport of the Darwin tulip Gloria Swanson with deep scarlet flowers; and Texas Gold, a sport of the cottage tulip Inglescombe Yellow with golden yellow petals edged in red.

DOUBLE LATE TULIPS are late flowering and are often referred to as "peony-flowered" tulips because the shape and size of their many-petaled blossoms are similar to those of peonies. These tulips, which grow 18 inches to about 2 feet tall, are effective as cut flowers. Some types will flower indoors in winter. Recommended varieties include Eros, rose pink; Mount Tacoma, white; Nizza, yellow with red stripes; and Symphonia, red, a double-flowered sport of the Darwin tulip Pride of Haarlem.

TULIPA KAUFMANNIANA varieties and hybrids are very early flowering and often open in March in Zone 6. Sometimes referred to as "water-lily tulips" because their pointed petals open horizontally like those of water lilies, they grow 4 to 8 inches tall and produce wide flowers that are frequently bicolored. The leaves of the hybrids are often marked with brown stripes. Delightful additions to rock gardens, they may be left in the ground to multiply for many years. Recommended varieties include Ancilla, white with red centers; Daylight, scarlet with black bases; Heart's Delight, red petals with rosy white edges; and Shakespeare, a blend of salmon, apricot and orange.

TULIPA FOSTERIANA varieties and hybrids. In more than four centuries of crossing tulips, breeders have never developed larger flowers than those of the early-flowering wild species *T. fosteriana*, whose varieties and hybrids produce blossoms as large as 4 inches and grow 8 to 20 inches tall. All will flower indoors in winter. Recommended varieties include Pinkeen, a blend of orange, red and pink; Red Emperor, also called Madame Lefeber, vivid red with black bases; White Emperor and Purissima, also called White Empress, with white flowers; and Yellow Emperor, also called Summit, with pale yellow flowers.

TULIPA GREIGII varieties and hybrids are late-flowering tulips with very long-lasting blossoms, usually scarlet and yellow, borne on stout 8- to 12-inch stems. The hybrids have handsome leaves, usually mottled with purple or brown. Many can be grown indoors in winter. Recommended varieties (all with red petals) include Oriental Beauty (brown bases), Oriental Splendour (black bases, yellow edges) and Margaret Herbst, also called Royal Splendour.

OTHER WILD OR SPECIES TULIPS. The final class of tulips consists of the species, varieties and hybrids of the hundreds of wild tulips. Early to late flowering, depending on the type, they do well in rock gardens and other sunny, well-drained sites. Many varieties bear three to nine flowers on a stem. Most varieties will live for many years, even in hot regions such as southern California, if the bulbs remain dry in summer. Many can be grown indoors for winter bloom. Recommended varieties include *T. biflora*, the two-flowered tulip, 8 inches tall with white and yellow flowers; *T. chrysantha*, the golden tulip, 8 inches with bright yellow and red flowers; *T. clusiana*, the Clusius tulip, 8 inches with fragrant rose and white flowers with violet bases; *T. dasystemon*, the Kuenlun tulip, 3 to 6 inches with yellow and white flowers; *T. hageri*, the Hager tulip, 6 inches tall with deep red flowers; *T. patens*, the Persian tulip, 6 to 9 inches with fragrant white and yellow flowers; *T. praestans*, the leatherbulb tulip, 12 to 18 inches with light red flowers; and *T. pulchella*, the dwarf Taurus tulip, 4 to 6 inches with pale purplish flowers.

HOW TO GROW. Large-flowered garden tulips do best in Zones 3-7, where they can be left in the ground year round. Plant the bulbs in early fall as soon as they are available, working 5 to 6 pounds of bone meal per 100 square feet into the soil; when the shoots appear in spring, scratch a dusting of 5-10-5 fertilizer into the surface. Since tulip bulbs multiply and in the process produce smaller and less uniform flowers each successive year, some gardeners discard the bulbs after the flowers fade. In this case the bulbs are spaced 4 to 6 inches apart and covered with 5 or 6 inches of soil. When the bulbs are planted more deeply, however, they tend to multiply to a lesser extent and will produce beautiful flowers for up to eight years. If you use this method, dig up the soil to a depth of 15 to 18 inches, space the bulbs 4 to 6 inches apart and cover them with about 10 inches of soil. To hide maturing foliage after the flowers fade, some gardeners plant annuals above such deep-set bulbs without fear of interfering with their roots.

Large-flowered tulips can also be grown successfully in Zones 8-10 if the bulbs are refrigerated for about eight weeks at 40° to 45° from the time they are purchased in fall until late November or December, then planted beneath 6 to 8 inches of soil to keep the bulbs as cool as possible. Since most bulbs do not multiply well in the heat of southern summers, dig up and discard after flowers fade.

The smaller-flowered species or wild tulips are winter hardy outdoors in Zones 3-7, and in the West and Southwest in Zones 8-10. Plant in fall, spacing the bulbs 3 to 6 inches apart and covering them with 3 to 6 inches of soil.

Outdoors, all tulips do best in full sun but will bloom well if they receive five to six hours of direct sunlight a day. For indoor culture, see pages 82-85. Propagate tulips in midsummer after the leaves wither, from the small bulbs that develop beside large ones.

For climate zones and frost dates, see maps, pages 148-149.

SPECIES TULIP
TOP: *Tulipa kaufmanniana* CENTER: *T. fosteriana* 'Red Emperor'
BOTTOM: *T. greigii* 'Oriental Splendour'

V

VALLOTA

V. speciosa, also called *V. purpurea, Amaryllis purpurea* (Scarborough lily)

Scarborough lilies produce clusters of three to 10 spectacular 3- to 4-inch flowers on 2-foot stalks in late summer and fall. The flowers are usually red, but bulb sellers occasionally offer white or pink varieties. The 12- to 18-inch straplike foliage is evergreen and can serve as a ground cover. Scarborough lilies also thrive in pots indoors or out.

HOW TO GROW. Scarborough lilies survive winters outdoors only in Zone 10 and do best in light shade. Plant the bulbs in early summer before growth starts, or in fall after flowers fade. Space the bulbs 15 to 18 inches apart and set them so that the tips are barely covered with soil.

As house plants, Scarborough lilies do best in at least four hours of direct sunlight a day, night temperatures of 50° to 55° and day temperatures of 68° to 72°. Plant in early summer or fall in the mixture recommended for *Scilla (page 138),* in pots no more than 2 inches larger in diameter than the bulb. Keep moist and feed monthly from spring until fall with a house-plant fertilizer. Keep the soil slightly dry through the winter. Early each summer, hose away some of the old soil without disturbing the roots and replace it with fresh soil. Move the bulbs and roots intact to a larger container when necessary, or divide and repot every three to four years. Propagate in early summer from the small bulbs that develop beside large ones.

VIOLET, DOG'S-TOOTH See *Erythronium*

W

WANDFLOWER See *Sparaxis*

WATSONIA

W. beatricis; W. hybrids; *W. rosea,* also called *W. pyramidata.* (All called bugle lily, watsonia)

In summer bugle lilies bear masses of 2- to 3-inch flowers on gracefully branched stems 3½ to 6 feet tall. Two species are widely grown: *W. beatricis,* with evergreen foliage and bright red flowers, and *W. rosea,* with deciduous foliage and pink or red flowers. The numerous hybrids also come in pure white, salmon, orange and lavender.

HOW TO GROW. Bugle lilies survive winters outdoors in Zones 8-10. Plant the corms in late summer or early fall, spacing them 6 inches apart and covering them with 4 inches of soil. Keep moist during the growing season, but let the soil become dry in late summer when the corms are dormant. Feed once a month with a dusting of 5-10-5 fertilizer. North of Zone 8 watsonias should be planted early in the spring and dug up after the foliage has been browned by frost. Store the corms in dry peat moss or vermiculite in a cool, frost-free location.

Propagate from the small corms that develop beside the large ones, or from seeds. Seeds sown in early spring may produce flowering-sized plants during the second year.

WIDOW'S-TEAR See *Achimenes*

Z

ZANTEDESCHIA, also called RICHARDIA

Z. aethiopica, Z. albo-maculata (spotted calla lily), *Z.* 'Apricot Sunrise' hybrids, *Z. elliottiana* (golden calla lily), *Z. rehmannii* (pink calla lily). (All called calla, calla lily)

Calla lilies blossom in spring and early summer, providing superb cut flowers; the smaller types make fine house plants. *Z. aethiopica* grows 2 to 4 feet tall and bears 6- to 8-inch white flowers; *Z. aethiopica minor* grows 18

SCARBOROUGH LILY
Vallota speciosa

WATSONIA
Watsonia rosea

146

inches tall and bears 4-inch white flowers; *Z. aethiopica* 'Crowborough' grows about 2½ feet tall and bears 6-inch white flowers. All are fragrant. Other good selections, 1½ to 2 feet tall with 4- to 6-inch flowers, are the spotted calla lily (white with purple throat), golden calla lily (yellow), pink calla lily (pink) and Apricot Sunrise Hybrids (pink, red or yellow).

HOW TO GROW. Calla lilies can remain in the ground through winter in Zones 8-10. They grow well in light shade, or in full sun with partial shade at midday. *Z. aethiopica* will blossom continuously if given sufficient food, moisture and 50° to 70° night temperatures; plant the rhizomes 1 to 2 feet apart; cover with 3 to 4 inches of soil and feed monthly with a dusting of 5-10-5 fertilizer. This species thrives even in muck covered by water. The other species and hybrids can be brought into blossom in about two months at any time provided they have had a three-month dormancy. Set the rhizomes a foot apart, and cover with 3 to 4 inches of soil. From Zone 7 north, plant calla lilies outdoors in spring, dig up in fall and store in dry peat moss, perlite or vermiculite at 40° to 50°. The hardier Crowborough variety can be left in the ground over the winter in Zones 5-7 if covered with a heavy winter mulch such as salt hay or wood chips.

As house plants, calla lilies need direct sunlight except at midday, when they must have bright indirect or curtain-filtered sunlight. They do best in night temperatures of 50° to 65° and day temperatures of 68° or higher. Plant the rhizomes in early fall, setting them 3 inches deep in the mixture recommended for *Scilla (page 138)*. Keep barely damp until the first shoot appears, then keep moist and feed monthly with a standard house-plant fertilizer. All except *Z. aethiopica* need summer dormancy; gradually withhold water until the leaves wither away. Start plants into growth again in the fall by moistening the soil.

Propagate by dividing the rhizomes in late summer or early fall; seedlings usually bloom during the second year.

ZEPHYRANTHES

Z. candida (autumn zephyr lily); *Z. citrina* (citron zephyr lily); *Z. grandiflora*, also called *Z. carinata* (rose-pink zephyr lily); *Z.* hybrids. (All called rain lily, fairy lily, flower of the west wind)

Zephyr lilies grow 6 to 8 inches tall and bear solitary upward-facing blossoms. They are delightful in rock gardens and naturalized in grass, and are easy to grow as house plants. Outstanding types include autumn zephyr lily with 2-inch white flowers, tinged pink inside, in late summer and fall; citron zephyr lily with fragrant 2-inch yellow flowers in midsummer; rose-pink zephyr lily with 4-inch pink flowers in late spring and early summer; and zephyr lily hybrids with flowers up to 5 inches across in white, pink, rose, apricot, salmon and yellow in summer and fall.

HOW TO GROW. In Zones 7-10 zephyr lilies can be planted in fall and left in the garden through many winters. From Zone 6 north, plant the bulbs in spring, dig in the fall and store over winter in dry peat moss, perlite or vermiculite at 50° to 60°. In all zones plant the bulbs 1 to 2 inches deep and 3 inches apart in full sun.

As house plants, zephyr lilies do best in at least four hours of direct sunlight a day, night temperatures of 40° to 45° and day temperatures of 68° or lower. Pot in the mixture recommended for *Scilla (page 138)*. Keep moist and feed monthly with a standard house-plant fertilizer. When the leaves wither, withhold water and food for about 10 weeks, then start the cycle again by moistening the soil. Propagate when dormant from the small bulbs that develop around the large ones.

LEFT: CALLA LILY
Zantedeschia aethiopica
RIGHT: PINK CALLA LILY
Z. rehmannii

ROSE-PINK ZEPHYR LILY
Zephyranthes grandiflora

For climate zones and frost dates, see maps, pages 148-149.

Appendix

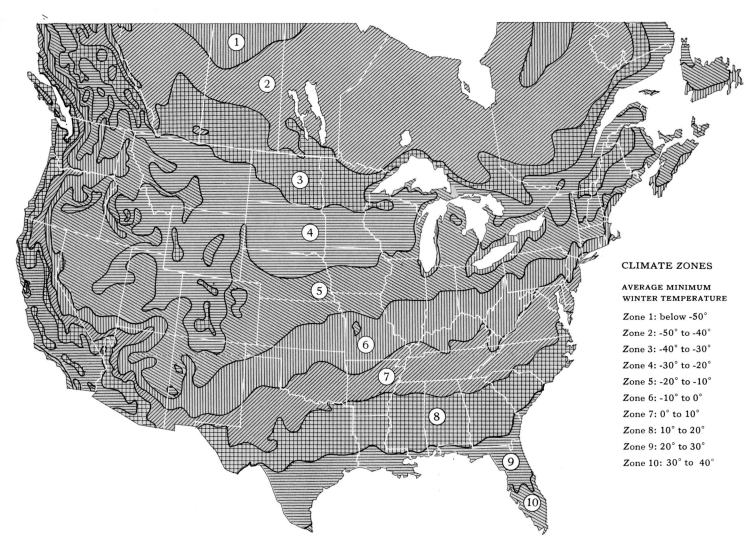

CLIMATE ZONES

AVERAGE MINIMUM
WINTER TEMPERATURE

Zone 1: below -50°
Zone 2: -50° to -40°
Zone 3: -40° to -30°
Zone 4: -30° to -20°
Zone 5: -20° to -10°
Zone 6: -10° to 0°
Zone 7: 0° to 10°
Zone 8: 10° to 20°
Zone 9: 20° to 30°
Zone 10: 30° to 40°

WHEN BULBS WILL BLOSSOM IN YOUR GARDEN

ZONE	EARLY SPRING BULB SEASON	SPRING BULB SEASON	EARLY SUMMER BULB SEASON	SUMMER AND FALL BULB SEASON
1	Late April to early June	Early June to mid-June	(Early summer bulbs rarely grown)	(Summer and fall bulbs rarely grown)
2	Mid-April to early June	Early June to mid-June	Mid-June to frost (mid-September)	Late July to frost (mid-September)
3	Early April to late May	Late May to mid-June	Mid-June to frost (mid-September)	Mid-July to frost (mid-September)
4	Late March to late May	Late May to mid-June	Mid-June to frost (late September)	Mid-July to frost (late September)
5	Mid-March to mid-May	Mid-May to mid-June	Mid-June to frost (late September)	Early July to frost (late September)
6	Early March to early May	Early May to early June	Early June to frost (early October)	Early July to frost (early October)
7	Late February to late April	Late April to late May	Late May to frost (mid-October)	Mid-June to frost (mid-October)
8	Mid-February to mid-April	Mid-April to mid-May	Mid-May to frost (late October)	Mid-June to frost (late October)
9	Late December to mid-February	January to March	(Early summer bulbs blossom all year)	Early June to mid-November
10	(Early spring bulbs not grown)	Late December to April	(Early summer bulbs blossom all year)	(Summer and fall bulbs blossom all year)

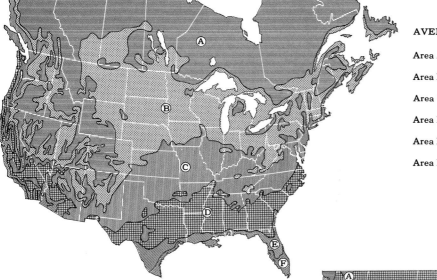

How climate affects bulb growing

The maps and table on these pages are designed to help you select bulbs that can grow in your garden, to alert you to the dates when some bulbs will need protection from frost, and to enable you to know when each season's bulbs will bloom.

In the encyclopedic entries in the preceding chapter, recommended growing areas are keyed by number to the zones on the climate map on the opposite page. A gardener in St. Louis, Missouri, for example, may be interested in planting acidantheras *(page 90)*. After determining from the climate map that he is located in Zone 6, he will know that he should plant acidanthera corms in spring after all danger of frost has passed. He will also know from the encyclopedic entry that because he is in Zone 6 he must dig up the corms

for winter storage before frost returns in fall.

To help him anticipate frost's departure and arrival in his own area, two additional maps are provided above; one shows the average dates of the last spring frost (in St. Louis, between March 30 and April 30), the other map shows the average dates of the first fall frost (in St. Louis, between September 30 and October 30).

From the last frost in spring until the first frost in fall, bulbs can provide continually blossoming flowers if species are chosen with an eye to their blooming schedules. Timetables to help you select bulbs for a display in every season—early spring, spring, early summer, and summer and fall—are on pages 52 through 61; the table at left lists the dates for those seasons in each zone.

A guide to pests and diseases

Bulbs are among the easiest plants to keep healthy if you buy bulbs of good quality, rejecting any that are spotted or spongy, and grow them in well-drained, fertile soil. But even under optimum conditions, pests and diseases sometimes strike. The chart below and at right describes the most common ones and the chemical and other defenses against them. All chemicals are potentially dangerous; follow the label directions closely.

PEST	DESCRIPTION	METHODS OF CONTROL
	GREEN PEACH APHIDS Green peach and other aphids are white to yellowish green insects about ⅛ inch long that settle on the undersides of leaves and on stems, buds and even stored bulbs. They suck the plant's juices, causing leaves to curl and flowers to become deformed. They also spread virus diseases and secrete honeydew, a sticky substance that attracts ants. More susceptible plants include dahlias, gladioluses, irises and lilies.	Knock aphids off the plants with a stream of water from a garden hose. Spray severely infested plants with malathion, rotenone or nicotine sulfate; do not neglect the undersides of leaves.
	GLADIOLUS THRIPS These sucking insects are 1⁄16 inch long with bristly wings. They are yellow when young, dark brown as adults. On the leaves they cause streaks that appear silver at first and then turn brown; they also streak and wither the edges of flowers, and they cause stored bulbs or corms (lower right in drawing) to become sticky, rough and brown. Thrips breed in winter at temperatures of 60° or more. Though their main target is gladioluses, thrips attack freesias, irises and lilies.	Spray with sevin, malathion, naled or diazinon, starting when plants are about 6 inches high. When bulbs are dug up for the winter, dry and spray them.
	JAPANESE BEETLES Metallic bronze in color and ½ inch long, Japanese beetles chew on foliage, stems and flowers, making sizable round or irregularly shaped holes in the leaves. They are most active on warm, sunny days, when they can be seen in clusters eating their way through one plant before they move on to eat the next one. Cannas and dahlias are two of their favorite flowers.	Pick off beetles by hand or knock them into a can of water covered with a film of oil or kerosene. Specially designed traps are sold in garden-supply stores. Spray heavy beetle infestations with carbaryl, malathion or methoxychlor.
	SLUGS Slugs resemble shell-less snails. Fat and legless, they grow ¾ inch to 5 inches long and may be gray, yellowish white, brown or black. They feed mostly at night, eating large, ragged holes in leaves near the ground, especially young shoots, and leaving a trail of silvery slime. Prime targets are dahlias and lilies.	Dust or spray the soil with metaldehyde or use metaldehyde pellets as a bait. Leave a bowl of beer or grape juice near the plants to lure and drown the slugs. Circle the inside edge of flower beds with strips of coarse sand, cinders or ground limestone, which block the slugs' passage.
	STEM AND BULB NEMATODES These microscopic, transparent, wormlike animals cause leaves to twist, split and blotch with yellow or brown; in severe cases foliage may not appear at all. Nematodes enter new shoots and go upward, then retreat to the bulb when the foliage withers, causing bulb tissue to turn brown. Affected plants include daffodils, dahlias, gladioluses, hyacinths, irises, lycorises, snowdrops, summer hyacinths, tigerflowers and tulips.	Destroy infested plants. Put new plants in a different location or fumigate the soil with DBCP or any other nematocide recommended by your garden-supply dealer or the local agricultural extension agent. Dip your garden tools in alcohol or formaldehyde to cleanse them and prevent spreading the infestation.

PEST	DESCRIPTION	METHODS OF CONTROL
NARCISSUS BULB FLY LARVAE	The fat, ½-inch-long, white or yellowish grublike larva of the narcissus bulb fly burrows into and eats the center of a bulb, reducing it to a soft, spongy brown mass. Usually one larva invades each bulb. Infested plants have yellow, twisted leaves and stop growing. The most susceptible plants are narcissuses and amaryllises, but other bulb fly targets are snowdrops, snowflakes, spider lilies, summer hyacinths and zephyr lilies.	Discard bulbs that feel soft or spongy. Dust or spray the soil at planting with chlordane; when the bulbs are in place, dust or spray them before covering with soil. Sprinkle naphthalene flakes around plants in late spring to prevent the flies from laying eggs.
WIREWORMS	Wireworms are long, smooth, segmented larvae yellowish brown in color and up to ¾ inch long; they develop from eggs laid in the soil by brown or black beetles known as click beetles. The larvae live entirely in the soil; they burrow into bulbs, hollowing out stems as they work their way up and causing the plant eventually to fall over. Principal targets are dahlias, gladioluses and tuberous begonias.	Spray or dust the soil with diazinon or chlordane and work it into the top 6 or 8 inches of earth before planting. Set the bulbs in place, spray or dust them as well; then cover them with soil. Spray growing plants with malathion.
BULB MITES	Tiny—less than ½₅ inch long—eight-legged creatures, bulb mites resemble little whitish spiders. They gather in colonies to feed on rotting bulbs, but they also tunnel into healthy bulbs, transmitting the organisms that produce the soft mushy condition known as bulb rots *(lower drawing)*. Bulb mites are most damaging to the bulbs of amaryllises, crocuses, freesias, gladioluses, hyacinths, lilies, daffodils and tulips.	Discard soft or mushy bulbs. Dust or spray healthy bulbs with naled, diazinon or dicofol. Store the bulbs in containers that have tight-fitting lids.
MOSAIC	Mosaic and other virus diseases, disseminated mainly by insects, especially aphids, turn leaves a mottled green and yellow or uniformly yellow, stunting the plants and often distorting both leaves and flowers. The "tulip breaking" mosaic has created the vivid multicolored blossoms of the Rembrandt tulips *(page 38)*. Mosaic also affects—adversely—calla lilies, cannas, crocuses, dahlias, gladioluses, hyacinths, irises, lilies, daffodils, squills and summer hyacinths.	Destroy infected plants. Although virus-infected plants cannot be cured chemically, the aphids that transmit the disease can be sprayed with malathion, rotenone or nicotine sulfate. Viruses that attack lilies also attack tulips, so do not plant them together; also, do not plant Rembrandt tulips near solid-colored and nonvirus-induced multicolored types.
BOTRYTIS BLIGHT	Botrytis blight produces small yellow, orange, brown or reddish brown spots on leaves, flowers and bulbs, especially during rainy, humid weather. Soon the spots grow together, causing affected parts to collapse and become slimy, often with a gray fuzzy covering of mold. Most susceptible bulbs are tulips, dahlias, gladioluses, hyacinths and tuberous begonias.	Do not plant any bulbs which have round brownish lesions. Remove any diseased plants and set new bulbs in another, well-drained and sunny location, spacing the bulbs generously to increase air circulation and reduce humidity. Spray plants with phaltan, zineb, thiram, captan, maneb or ferbam (do not use ferbam while the plants are flowering).
BULB ROTS	Bulb rots, produced by bacteria and fungi, bring about yellowish stunted shoots, with brown, mushy or dry, spongy bulbs; bacterial rot is usually accompanied by a sour odor. Rots are most destructive in badly drained soil in warm, wet weather, and become more advanced when bulbs are in storage, especially if the temperature is high or if air circulation is poor. Bulb rots affect amaryllises, calla lilies, daffodils, dahlias, gladioluses, hyacinths, spider lilies, tuberoses and tulips.	Destroy infected plants and bulbs and set new bulbs in well-drained soil in a higher sunny location. Space plants generously to provide good air circulation. Store bulbs in a dry, well-ventilated place at the temperature recommended *(Chapter 6)*; discard rotted ones at once. Treat bulbs with captan or phaltan before planting.

Characteristics of 149 bulbs

	FLOWER COLOR					BLOSSOM SIZE			BLOOMING SEASONS				PLANT HEIGHT			LIGHT		USES					
	White	Orange-yellow	Pink-red	Blue-purple	Multicolor	Under 1 inch	1 to 2 inches	Over 2 inches	Spring	Summer	Fall	Winter	Under 1 foot	1 to 3 feet	Over 3 feet	Sun	Partial shade	Beds and borders	Rock gardens	Naturalized plantings	Potted plants	Cut flowers	Notable fragrance
ACHIMENES 'MASTER INGRAM' (magic flower)			•				•		•	•	•		•				•				•		
ACIDANTHERA BICOLOR MURIELAE (acidanthera)	•						•	•		•	•			•		•		•				•	•
AGAPANTHUS AFRICANUS (agapanthus)	•			•			•	•		•				•	•	•		•				•	•
ALLIUM ALBOPILOSUM (giant allium)				•				•		•				•		•		•				•	
ALLIUM MOLY (golden garlic)		•					•	•		•	•		•			•			•	•			
ALSTROEMERIA AURANTIACA (Peruvian lily)		•					•			•				•		•		•				•	
AMARYLLIS BELLADONNA (belladonna lily)	•		•					•		•				•		•		•			•		•
ANEMONE BLANDA (Greek anemone)			•	•			•	•	•				•			•	•		•	•			
ANEMONE CORONARIA 'ST. BRIGID' (poppy-flowered anemone)	•		•	•			•	•	•				•			•	•	•				•	
ANTHERICUM LILIAGO (St.-Bernard's-lily)	•						•			•				•		•		•				•	
BABIANA STRICTA HYBRIDS (baboonroot)	•	•	•	•			•			•	•	•	•			•		•				•	
BEGONIA EVANSIANA (hardy begonia)			•		•			•		•	•		•				•	•			•		
BEGONIA TUBERHYBRIDA 'DOUBLE PICOTEE' (tuberous begonia)	•	•	•				•	•		•	•		•	•			•	•			•		
BELAMCANDA CHINENSIS (blackberry lily)			•				•			•				•		•	•	•		•			
BESSERA ELEGANS (coral drops)			•				•			•				•		•		•			•		
BLETILLA STRIATA (Chinese ground orchid)			•	•			•			•				•			•	•			•		
BRODIAEA LAXA (brodiaea)	•		•		•	•	•		•	•				•		•		•					
BULBOCODIUM VERNUM (spring meadow saffron)			•			•					•	•	•			•	•	•					
*CALADIUM HORTULANUM (fancy-leaved caladium)										•				•			•				•		
CALOCHORTUS VENUSTUS (Mariposa tulip)	•	•	•	•			•	•	•				•	•		•		•	•	•			
CAMASSIA QUAMASH (common camass)	•			•			•		•					•		•		•		•			
CANNA GENERALIS (canna)	•	•	•				•			•	•			•	•	•		•					
CHIONODOXA LUCILIAE (glory-of-the-snow)	•		•	•		•			•			•	•			•	•	•	•				
CHLIDANTHUS FRAGRANS (Peru chlidanthus)		•					•			•		•	•			•				•	•	•	•
CLIVIA MINIATA (Kafir lily)		•	•				•	•			•	•	•				•				•	•	•
COLCHICUM AUTUMNALE MINOR (colchicum)	•	•					•				•			•		•	•	•		•			
*COLOCASIA ANTIQUORUM (elephant's-ear)										•					•		•			•	•		
CONVALLARIA MAJALIS (lily of the valley)	•				•	•			•	•	•	•	•				•	•		•		•	•
CRINODONNA CORSII (crinodonna)			•					•		•				•		•		•			•		
CRINUM POWELLII (crinum)	•		•				•	•	•	•				•		•		•					•
CROCOSMIA CROCOSMIIFLORA (montbretia)		•	•				•			•	•			•		•		•				•	
CROCUS (spring-flowering crocus)		•					•		•			•	•			•	•	•	•	•			
CROCUS (autumn-flowering crocus)			•			•					•		•			•		•	•	•	•		
CYCLAMEN NEAPOLITANUM (Neapolitan cyclamen)	•		•				•				•	•	•				•	•	•				
CYPELLA HERBERTII (cypella)		•					•			•			•			•		•			•		
DAHLIA HYBRIDA (anemone-flowered dahlia)	•	•	•	•	•		•	•		•	•		•	•		•		•				•	
DAHLIA HYBRIDA (cactus-flowered dahlia)	•	•	•	•	•		•	•		•	•		•	•		•		•				•	
DAHLIA HYBRIDA (collarette dahlia)	•	•	•	•	•		•	•		•	•		•	•		•		•				•	
DAHLIA HYBRIDA (formal decorative dahlia)	•	•	•	•	•		•	•		•	•		•	•		•		•				•	
DAHLIA HYBRIDA (pompon dahlia)	•	•	•	•	•	•	•			•	•		•	•		•		•				•	
DAHLIA HYBRIDA (single dahlia)	•	•	•	•	•	•	•			•	•		•	•		•		•				•	
ERANTHIS HYEMALIS (winter aconite)		•				•					•	•	•			•	•	•	•	•			
EREMURUS 'SHELFORD HYBRIDS' (foxtail lily)	•	•	•		•		•	•		•				•	•	•		•		•		•	
ERYTHRONIUM ALBIDUM (white fawn lily)	•		•			•	•		•				•				•		•	•			
ERYTHRONIUM AMERICANUM (adder's-tongue)		•				•	•	•	•				•				•		•	•			
ERYTHRONIUM OREGONUM 'WHITE BEAUTY' (Oregon fawn lily)	•					•	•		•				•				•		•	•			
EUCHARIS GRANDIFLORA (Amazon lily)	•							•		•	•	•		•			•				•	•	•
EUCOMIS COMOSA (pineapple lily)	•							•		•				•		•		•			•	•	•
FREESIA (freesia)	•	•	•	•			•		•			•	•			•		•			•	•	•
FRITILLARIA IMPERIALIS (crown imperial)		•	•				•	•		•				•	•	•		•			•	•	

*This species is grown for its foliage.

152

	FLOWER COLOR					BLOSSOM SIZE			BLOOMING SEASONS				PLANT HEIGHT			LIGHT		USES					
	White	Orange-yellow	Pink-red	Blue-purple	Multicolor	Under 1 inch	1 to 2 inches	Over 2 inches	Spring	Summer	Fall	Winter	Under 1 foot	1 to 3 feet	Over 3 feet	Sun	Partial shade	Beds and borders	Rock gardens	Naturalized plantings	Potted plants	Cut flowers	Notable fragrance
FRITILLARIA MELEAGRIS (checkered fritillary)				●			●		●				●			●	●						
GALANTHUS NIVALIS (common snowdrop)	●				●		●				●	●	●			●	●		●	●			
GALTONIA CANDICANS (summer hyacinth)	●				●			●		●				●	●	●						●	●
GLADIOLUS BYZANTINUS (Byzantine gladiolus)			●			●	●	●	●	●		●		●		●		●				●	
GLADIOLUS 'CERULEAN' (gladiolus hybrid)				●		●	●	●	●	●		●		●		●		●				●	
GLORIOSA ROTHSCHILDIANA (glory lily)					●		●	●		●					●	●						●	●
HAEMANTHUS COCCINEUS (blood lily)			●				●	●			●		●			●					●		
HIPPEASTRUM 'APPLE BLOSSOM' (amaryllis)			●				●	●				●	●			●					●		
HYACINTHUS (hyacinth)	●	●	●	●			●		●			●	●			●				●	●	●	●
HYMENOCALLIS NARCISSIFLORA 'FESTALIS' (spider lily)	●						●	●		●			●			●	●				●	●	●
IPHEION UNIFLORUM (spring starflower)	●					●			●				●			●	●	●	●	●			
IRIS 'LEMON QUEEN' (Dutch iris)		●					●	●	●				●			●						●	
IRIS RETICULATA (netted iris)				●		●	●		●				●			●			●				●
IXIA HYBRIDS (African corn lily)	●	●	●			●	●		●				●			●						●	●
IXIOLIRION MONTANUM (ixiolirion)			●				●	●	●				●			●						●	
LACHENALIA ALOIDES LUTEA (Cape cowslip)		●					●				●	●	●			●	●				●		
LAPEIROUSIA LAXA (lapeirousia)			●				●		●	●			●			●	●				●	●	
LEUCOJUM AESTIVUM (summer snowflake)	●				●		●	●					●			●	●			●	●		●
LILIUM 'BUTTERCUP' (American hybrid lily)		●						●		●				●	●	●	●	●					
LILIUM CANDIDUM (Madonna lily)	●							●		●				●	●	●	●	●					
LILIUM 'CRIMSON BEAUTY' (Oriental hybrid lily)					●			●		●				●		●	●	●					●
LILIUM 'ENCHANTMENT' (Asiatic hybrid lily)		●						●		●	●			●		●	●	●		●			
LILIUM 'FIRST LOVE' (aurelian lily hybrid)					●			●		●				●		●	●	●					
LILIUM 'GREEN MAGIC' (aurelian lily hybrid)	●							●		●				●		●	●	●					
LILIUM 'HARLEQUIN' (Asiatic hybrid lily)	●		●	●				●		●				●		●	●	●				●	
LILIUM 'IMPERIAL GOLD' (Oriental hybrid lily)					●			●		●				●		●	●	●					
LILIUM LONGIFLORUM EXIMIUM (longiflorum lily)	●							●	●	●			●			●	●	●			●		
LILIUM MARTAGON 'ACHIEVEMENT' (martagon lily hybrid)	●							●		●				●		●	●	●					
LILIUM 'PAPRIKA' (Asiatic hybrid lily)			●					●		●		●		●		●	●	●					
LILIUM 'PINK PERFECTION' (aurelian lily hybrid)			●					●		●				●	●	●	●	●					
LILIUM SPECIOSUM 'RED CHAMPION' (Japanese lily)			●					●		●	●			●		●	●	●			●	●	
LILIUM 'SUNBURST' (aurelian lily hybrid)		●						●		●				●	●	●	●	●					
LILIUM TESTACEUM (candidum lily hybrid: nankeen lily)		●						●		●				●	●	●	●	●					
LYCORIS SQUAMIGERA (hardy amaryllis)			●					●		●	●			●		●				●			
MILLA BIFLORA (star lily)	●						●	●	●	●	●		●			●		●	●			●	
MOREA PAVONIA 'MAGNIFICA' (peacock iris)	●	●	●				●	●	●	●	●		●			●		●	●	●			
MUSCARI (grape hyacinth)	●	●		●	●		●	●	●			●				●	●	●	●	●	●	●	●
NARCISSUS 'ACTAEA' (poeticus daffodil)					●		●	●	●					●		●	●			●			
NARCISSUS 'ARANJUEZ' (large-cupped daffodil)		●					●	●	●					●		●	●			●			
NARCISSUS 'BEERSHEBA' (trumpet daffodil)	●						●	●	●					●		●	●			●			
NARCISSUS BULBOCODIUM (species daffodil)		●				●			●				●			●	●		●	●			
NARCISSUS 'CHEERFULNESS' (double daffodil)	●							●	●					●		●	●	●		●	●	●	●
NARCISSUS CYCLAMINEUS (species daffodil)		●					●	●	●				●			●	●		●	●			
NARCISSUS 'EDWARD BUXTON' (small-cupped daffodil)		●					●	●	●					●		●	●	●		●			
NARCISSUS 'ESTELLA DE MOL' (split-cup daffodil)					●		●	●	●					●		●	●	●		●			
NARCISSUS 'FEBRUARY GOLD' (cyclamineus daffodil)		●				●		●	●					●		●	●	●		●			
NARCISSUS 'FLOWER RECORD' (large-cupped daffodil)					●		●	●	●					●		●	●	●		●		●	
NARCISSUS JUNCIFOLIUS (species daffodil)		●				●			●		●		●			●	●		●			●	
NARCISSUS 'KING ALFRED' (trumpet daffodil)		●						●	●					●		●	●	●		●	●	●	
NARCISSUS 'LAURENS KOSTER' (tazetta daffodil)					●		●	●	●					●		●	●	●		●	●	●	●

153

	FLOWER COLOR					BLOSSOM SIZE			BLOOMING SEASONS				PLANT HEIGHT			LIGHT		USES					
	White	Orange-yellow	Pink-red	Blue-purple	Multicolor	Under 1 inch	1 to 2 inches	Over 2 inches	Spring	Summer	Fall	Winter	Under 1 foot	1 to 3 feet	Over 3 feet	Sun	Partial shade	Beds and borders	Rock gardens	Naturalized plantings	Potted plants	Cut flowers	Notable fragrance
NARCISSUS 'LIBERTY BELLS' (triandrus daffodil)		●					●		●				●			●	●	●		●		●	
NARCISSUS 'MRS. R. O. BACKHOUSE' (trumpet daffodil)			●				●	●	●				●			●	●	●		●		●	
NARCISSUS 'MUSIC HALL' (trumpet daffodil)			●				●	●	●				●			●	●	●		●	●	●	
NARCISSUS 'PEEPING TOM' (cyclamineus daffodil)		●					●		●				●			●	●	●		●		●	
NARCISSUS 'POLAR ICE' (small-cupped daffodil)	●						●		●				●			●	●	●		●		●	
NARCISSUS 'SCARLET LEADER' (large-cupped daffodil)				●			●		●				●			●	●	●					
NARCISSUS 'TREVITHIAN' (jonquilla daffodil)		●					●		●				●			●	●	●		●		●	
NARCISSUS TRIANDRUS ALBUS (species daffodil)	●						●		●			●		●			●	●		●		●	●
NARCISSUS 'VERGER' (small-cupped daffodil)			●				●		●				●				●			●		●	
NERINE SARNIENSIS (Guernsey lily)	●		●				●	●		●	●		●				●				●	●	
ORNITHOGALUM NUTANS (nodding star-of-Bethlehem)	●						●		●				●			●	●	●		●			●
OXALIS ADENOPHYLLA (Chilean oxalis)			●				●	●	●			●	●			●		●	●		●		
PANCRATIUM MARITIMUM (sea daffodil)	●							●		●			●			●		●					
PARADISEA LILIASTRUM (St.-Bruno's-lily)	●						●			●			●			●		●					
POLIANTHES TUBEROSA (tuberose)	●						●			●	●			●	●	●		●				●	●
PUSCHKINIA SCILLOIDES (striped squill)	●				●		●		●				●	●		●		●	●		●		
RANUNCULUS ASIATICUS (double-flowered Persian buttercup)	●	●	●				●	●	●				●			●		●			●		
RECHSTEINERIA CARDINALIS (cardinal flower)			●				●		●	●	●	●	●			●	●				●		
SCHIZOSTYLIS COCCINEA (crimson flag)			●					●			●		●			●					●	●	
SCILLA HISPANICA (Spanish bluebell)				●			●		●			●		●		●	●	●	●	●			
SCILLA SIBIRICA 'SPRING BEAUTY' (Siberian squill)				●			●		●				●			●	●	●	●	●			
SCILLA TUBERGENIANA (Tubergenian squill)	●				●		●					●	●			●	●	●	●	●	●		
SINNINGIA SPECIOSA (gloxinia)			●			●	●	●	●	●	●		●				●				●		
SMITHIANTHA HYBRID (temple bells)	●	●	●				●		●	●	●	●		●			●				●		
SPARAXIS TRICOLOR (harlequin flower)	●	●	●	●	●		●		●				●			●		●	●	●			
SPREKELIA FORMOSISSIMA (Aztec lily)			●				●	●	●				●			●		●			●		
STERNBERGIA LUTEA (sternbergia)		●					●				●	●	●			●		●	●	●			
TIGRIDIA PAVONIA (tigerflower)	●	●	●	●	●			●		●			●			●		●				●	
TRITONIA CROCATA (saffron tritonia)		●					●			●			●			●		●	●			●	
TROPAEOLUM POLYPHYLLUM (wreath nasturtium)		●					●			●			●				●	●	●				
TULBAGHIA FRAGRANS (fragrant tulbaghia)			●		●		●	●	●	●	●		●			●					●		●
TULIPA 'APRICOT BEAUTY' (Mendel tulip)		●					●		●				●	●		●		●			●	●	
TULIPA 'AUREOLA' (triumph tulip)			●				●	●	●				●	●		●		●					
TULIPA 'BRILLIANT STAR' (single early tulip)			●				●	●	●				●	●		●		●		●			
TULIPA 'CORDELL HULL' (Rembrandt tulip)				●			●	●	●				●	●		●		●					
TULIPA FOSTERIANA 'RED EMPEROR' (species tulip)			●				●	●	●				●	●		●		●					
TULIPA 'GOLDEN DUCHESS' (lily-flowered tulip)		●					●	●	●				●	●		●		●				●	●
TULIPA GREIGII 'ORIENTAL SPLENDOUR' (species tulip)				●			●	●	●				●	●		●		●	●				
TULIPA 'GUDOSHNIK' (Darwin hybrid tulip)		●					●	●	●					●		●		●				●	●
TULIPA KAUFMANNIANA (species tulip)				●			●	●				●	●			●		●	●				
TULIPA 'LA TULIPE NOIRE' (Darwin tulip)			●				●	●	●					●		●		●					
TULIPA 'NIZZA' (double late tulip)				●			●	●	●					●		●		●	●				
TULIPA 'PEACH BLOSSOM' (double early tulip)			●				●	●	●			●	●			●		●	●				
TULIPA 'PIERSON' (parrot tulip)			●				●	●					●			●		●					
TULIPA 'ROSY WINGS' (cottage tulip)				●			●	●	●					●		●		●	●			●	
VALLOTA SPECIOSA (Scarborough lily)	●		●				●			●	●		●			●		●			●	●	
WATSONIA ROSEA (watsonia)			●				●						●	●	●	●		●				●	
ZANTEDESCHIA (calla lily)	●	●	●				●	●	●	●	●	●		●	●	●		●			●	●	
ZEPHYRANTHES GRANDIFLORA (rose-pink zephyr lily)	●	●	●				●	●	●		●		●			●		●	●	●	●		

Picture credits

The sources for the illustrations that appear in this book are shown below. Credits for the pictures from left to right are separated by semicolons, from top to bottom by dashes. Cover—Malak, Ottawa. 4—Keith Martin courtesy James Underwood Crockett; Leonard Wolfe. 6—Malak, Ottawa. 10 through 13—Drawings by Richard Crist. 17 through 22—Drawings by Vincent Lewis. 24—Radio Times Hulton Picture Library. 28, 29—Frank Scherschel for LIFE courtesy The British Museum; Bibliothèque Nationale, Paris—Heinz Zinram for LIFE courtesy The British Museum; Bibliothèque Nationale, Paris; Bettmann Archive (2)—United Press International; © National Portrait Gallery; Agraci courtesy Musée du Louvre; Mary Evans Picture Library (2). 32, 33—Alinari courtesy Galleria Capitolina; Alinari courtesy Galleria Nazionali di Capodimonte; Bettmann Archive courtesy Kaiser Friederich Museum; Alinari courtesy Galleria Nazionali di Capodimonte—Photographie Bulloz; Culver Pictures; Samuel H. Kress Collection, National Gallery of Art, Washington, D.C.—Culver Pictures; Kress Study Collection, University of Notre Dame; Alinari courtesy Pinacoteca Vannucci. 37—Ara Güler courtesy Topkapi Museum, Istanbul. 38—Malak, Ottawa; Ara Güler courtesy Topkapi Museum, Istanbul—Malak, Ottawa; Museum National d'Histoire Naturelle—Sonja Bullaty; Bibliothèque Nationale, Paris—Hunt Botanical Library; Malak, Ottawa. 39—Malak, Ottawa. 40, 41—Bibliothèque Nationale, Paris. 42—Malak, Ottawa except top right John R. Freeman courtesy The British Museum, and second row center John Koopman courtesy Royal General Bulbs Growers Society in Hillegom. 43, 44—Malak, Ottawa. 47, 49, 51—Drawings by Vincent Lewis. 53—Gottlieb Hampfler. 54, 55—George de Gennaro; Malak, Ottawa (2). 56, 57—Dean Brown; Gottlieb Hampfler. 58, 59—Steven C. Wilson. 60, 61—Malak, Ottawa; Harry Smith; Enrico Ferorelli. 62, 63—Costa Manos from Magnum. 64—Malak, Ottawa. 68—Drawings by Vincent Lewis. 70, 71—Drawings by Richard Crist. 73, 76—Drawings by Vincent Lewis. 78—Manfred Kage. 83—Costa Manos from Magnum; drawings by Vincent Lewis. 84—Costa Manos from Magnum; drawings by Vincent Lewis. 85—Guy Burgess; drawings by Vincent Lewis. 88 through 147—Illustrations by Allianora Rosse except where otherwise indicated next to illustration. 148, 149—Maps by Adolph E. Brotman. 150, 151—Drawings by Davis Meltzer.

Acknowledgments

For their help in the preparation of this book, the editors wish to thank the following: Fred M. Abbey, The North American Lily Society, Inc., North Ferrisburg, Vt.; P. Boschman, Naarden, The Netherlands; Marie Brandstaetter, The Wayside Gardens Company, Mentor, Ohio; John E. Bryan, Director, Strybing Arboretum, San Francisco, Calif.; Centraal Bloembollen Comite, Hillegom, The Netherlands; Mrs. Edith Crockett, Librarian, Horticultural Society of New York, New York City; Mrs. Muriel C. Crossman, Librarian, Massachusetts Horticultural Society, Boston, Mass.; Miss Marie Giasi, Brooklyn Botanic Garden Library, Brooklyn, N.Y.; Miss Elizabeth Hall, Senior Librarian, Horticultural Society of New York, New York City; Heimlich's Greenhouse, Woburn, Mass.; Mrs. Hugh Hencken, Newton, Mass.; Dr. T. H. Hoog, Haarlem, The Netherlands; Jan de Graaff Nursery, Gresham, Ore.; Laboratory for Bulb Research, Lisse, The Netherlands; Charles A. Lewis, Director, Sterling Forest Gardens, Tuxedo, N.Y.; Mrs. Loretta McLaughlin, Braintree, Mass.; National Tulip Society, New York City; P. De Jager & Sons, Inc., South Hamilton, Mass.; Marc Reynolds, Edward Gottlieb & Associates, Ltd., New York City; Rijksmuseum, Amsterdam, The Netherlands; The Royal Dutch Association of Bulb Growers, Hillegom, The Netherlands; Gustave Springer, North American Director, Netherlands Flower Bulb Institute, Inc., New York City; George Wendler, Massachusetts Horticultural Society, Boston, Mass. The poem on page 35, "Hyacinths to Feed Thy Soul," is from *Best Loved Poems of the American People,* edited by Hazel Felleman, © 1936, reprinted by permission of the publishers, Doubleday & Company, Inc. Recipe for saffron cookies on page 81 is by Sidney Duerr, in *The Herb Grower Magazine,* Falls Village, Conn., © 1953, reprinted by permission of the editor, Gertrude B. Foster.

Bibliography

Baumgardt, John Philip, *Bulbs for Summer Bloom.* Hawthorn Books, Inc., 1970.

Blunt, Wilfrid, *Tulipomania.* Penguin Books, 1950.

Brooklyn Botanic Garden, *Handbook on Bulbs.* Brooklyn Botanic Garden, 1959.

Coats, Alice M., *The Plant Hunters.* McGraw-Hill Book Company, 1969.

Coats, Peter, *Flowers in History.* The Viking Press, 1970.

Cox, E. H. M., *Plant Hunting in China.* Collins, 1945.

de Graaff, Jan and Edward Hyams, *Lilies.* Funk & Wagnalls, 1968.

Everett, T. H., *American Gardener's Book of Bulbs.* Random House, 1954.

Feldmaier, Carl, *Lilies.* Arco Publishing Company, Inc., 1970.

Foley, Daniel J., *Garden Flowers in Color.* The Macmillan Company, 1943.

Hall, Sir A. Daniel, *The Book of the Tulip.* Frederick A. Stokes Company, 1928.

Lebar, T. R. H., *Dahlias for Everyone.* Blandford Press, 1957.

Miles, Bebe, *The Wonderful World of Bulbs.* D. Van Nostrand Company, Inc., 1959.

Randolph, L. F., *Garden Irises.* The American Iris Society, 1959.

Reynolds, Marc and William L. Meachem, *The Garden Bulbs of Spring.* Funk & Wagnalls, 1967.

Rockwell, F. F. and Esther C. Grayson, *The Complete Book of Bulbs.* The American Garden Guild and Doubleday & Company, Inc., 1953.

Rockwell, F. F., Grayson, Esther C. and Jan de Graaff, *The Complete Book of Lilies.* The American Garden Guild and Doubleday & Company, Inc., 1961.

Schauenberg, Paul, *The Bulb Book.* Frederick Warne & Company, Ltd., 1965.

Shurtleff, Malcolm C., *How to Control Plant Diseases in Home and Garden.* Iowa State University Press, 1966.

Sunset Books, *How to Grow Bulbs.* Lane Books, 1968.

Synge, Patrick M., *Collins Guide to Bulbs.* Collins, 1961.

Westcott, Cynthia, *The Gardener's Bug Book.* Doubleday & Company, Inc., 1946.

Index

Numerals in italics indicate an illustration of the subject mentioned.